A
Just and
Generous
Nation

A
Just and
Generous
Nation

ABRAHAM LINCOLN *and*
the FIGHT *for*
AMERICAN OPPORTUNITY

HAROLD HOLZER *and*
NORTON GARFINKLE

BASIC BOOKS

A Member of the Perseus Books Group

New York

Designed by Pauline Brown

Library of Congress Cataloging-in-Publication Data
Holzer, Harold.
    A just and generous nation : Abraham Lincoln and the fight for American
  opportunity / Harold Holzer and Norton Garfinkle.
        pages cm
    Includes bibliographical references and index.
    ISBN 978-0-465-02830-6 (hardcover) — ISBN 978-0-465-07396-2 (e-book)
    1. Lincoln, Abraham, 1809–1865—Political and social views.   2. United
  States—History—Civil War, 1861–1865—Causes.   3. United States—History—
  Civil War, 1861–1865—Economic aspects.   4. United States—History—Civil War,
  1861–1865—Social aspects.   5. Equality—Economic aspects—United States—
  History—19th century.   6. Economic development—United States—History—19th
  century.   7. Social mobility—United States—History—19th century.   8. United
  States—Politics and government—1861–1865.   I. Garfinkle, Norton   II. Title.
  E457.2.H753 2015
  973.7092—dc23

                                                            2015022842

10 9 8 7 6 5 4 3 2 1

To our wives,
Edith Holzer and Sally Minard,
for their individual and collective inspiration
throughout.

The prudent, penniless beginner in the world,
labors for wages awhile,
saves a surplus with which to buy tools or land,
for himself;
then labors on his own account another while,
and at length hires another
new beginner to help him.
This, say its advocates, is *free* labor—
the just and generous, and prosperous system,
which opens the way for all—gives hope to all,
and energy, and progress,
and improvement of condition to all.

—Abraham Lincoln,
speech in Milwaukee, September 30, 1859

This middle-class country had got
a middle-class President, at last.

—Eulogy to Abraham Lincoln
by Ralph Waldo Emerson, April 19, 1865

Contents

INTRODUCTION

T HE UNITED STATES HAS JUST CONCLUDED A FIVE-YEAR OBSERVANCE
of the sesquicentennial of the Civil War. As in the past, most new
books about the period have focused principally on matters military,
reexamining the familiar major battles or offering new biographies of
generals of the war. A few have explored new aspects of Lincoln's life
and presidency and the political conflicts immediately preceding and
during the war.

For all the merits of these recent volumes, too few have provided
satisfying answers to an essential question: why was the Civil War really fought? This subject still cries out for serious and informed exploration and analysis. The prevailing arguments—that the war occurred
to preserve the American Union for its own sake, to defend or destroy
slavery, or to expand or restrict federal authority—fall short because
they do not embrace the full vision for the future held by those engaged in the conflict. The most illuminating way to begin this essential
conversation is to focus on the commander in chief who chose war
rather than cede the democracy to those who would divide it rather
than recognize its legitimacy. That ever-compelling figure, of course,
is Abraham Lincoln.

True, Lincoln has already inspired thousands of books. Yet while
scores of new Lincoln volumes rolled off the presses during the period leading up to the bicentennial of his birth in 2009, and dozens
more have appeared to coincide with the sesquicentennial of the years

1

1860–1865, only a few have actually dealt with the causes of the conflict—the conflagration that consumed nearly every day of his presidency and cost 750,000 American lives. Few have explored Lincoln's motivations for fighting the war and maintaining the Union when the conflict expanded exponentially from a small struggle to an enormous war unprecedented in world history. The unanswered question remains more crucial to our own present and future than ever. Why would a basically peaceful man who might as easily have allowed the United States to divide in two, with no resulting loss of life or treasure, choose instead to lead a devastating American-versus-American war to maintain a fragile, still-experimental Union? This book offers a direct answer to that unresolved question with a new focus and a new emphasis.

For too long, historians have accepted without challenge the notion that Lincoln determined to preserve the Union primarily because nationhood held a powerfully symbolic, almost "mystical" importance to him from childhood on. Fueled by Weems's *Life of Washington* and similarly hagiographic stories of the American Revolution, the young Lincoln is said to have developed early a stubborn passion to cement the foundations of the Republic for all time. Another theory holds that Lincoln entered the presidency—and allowed the country to go to war with itself—to remove the stain of slavery that for more than fourscore years had blighted the original American commitment to "life, liberty, and the pursuit of happiness."

Elements of truth support both arguments, to be sure, but ignore the overwhelming evidence that Lincoln focused his entire political career, in peace and war alike, in pursuit of economic opportunity for the widest possible circle of hardworking Americans. To achieve this ambition he was willing to fight a war to maintain the perpetual existence of the one nation in the world that held the highest promise for people dedicated to this cause.

Lincoln's decision to resist Southern secession and fight a war to maintain the American Union was motivated primarily by his belief that the nation was founded on the idea that this country "proposed to give *all* a chance" and allow "the weak to grow stronger." The toxic combination of secession together with an unending commitment to unpaid human bondage by a new and separate Confederate nation, he calculated, would be fatal to the American Dream. It posed a direct threat to a self-sustaining middle-class society and to the promise of America leading the way to spreading the idea of opportunity and upward mobility throughout the world.

"I hold the value of life is to improve one's condition," Lincoln declared just three weeks before assuming the presidency, reiterating a lifetime of similarly expressed commitment to what historian Gabor Boritt brilliantly calls the uniquely American "right to rise." Seven slaveholding Southern states had already declared by their independence the converse: the right to establish a nation of their own based on the denial of opportunity. Lincoln believed that the American nation based on the credo of opportunity for all was worth fighting for. "Whatever is calculated to advance the condition of the honest, struggling laboring man, so far as my judgment will enable me to judge of a correct thing, I am for that thing," he said in 1861. In the face of unimaginable casualties and devastation, he remained for "that thing" for the rest of his life.

The origin, depth, and durability of Lincoln's commitment cry out for new exploration and interpretation, particularly now, as the ability to rise is being challenged in the United States by economic, social, and political conditions producing ever-increasing inequality.

We Americans believe we so fully understand Abraham Lincoln's contribution to our nation's beliefs about slavery and freedom that his role in shaping our uniquely American vision of a just and generous economic society has been largely neglected. In fact, Lincoln was unwavering in his commitment to preserve the American Dream of economic opportunity for future generations, a dream he lived by escaping the poverty of his childhood and one he advocated throughout his political life. It was this commitment that lay behind his determination to ensure that a government dedicated to providing economic opportunity for its citizens "shall not perish from the earth." Lincoln largely fought the Civil War over this principle, establishing a role for government in securing and guaranteeing economic opportunity for its citizens, a guarantee that has remained at the center of political debate and discord ever since, seldom so acrimoniously as today.

Lincoln was the first president to use the federal government as an agent to support Americans in their effort to achieve and sustain a middle-class life. Even as the Civil War commenced, Lincoln supported a program of direct government action to support his vision of America's middle-class society.

More than is often realized, the Civil War was fought not over the morality of slavery or the abstract sanctity of the American Union, but over what kind of economy the nation should have. It is difficult to grasp the degree to which the United States, on the eve of the Civil War, had truly evolved into what Lincoln called, quoting scripture, a "house divided": virtually two separate nations based on very different economic structures. More than anything else, the secession crisis and the Civil War became a clash over expanding the economic and social system of either section. The question became: which economy and society would define the future of America as it migrated westward, that of the North or that of the South?

The American economy in the North before the Civil War supported a largely middle-class society. With almost unlimited natural resources, most Americans in the Northern states and northwestern territories had the opportunity to secure a middle-class life. Unlike most European countries and the American economy of the South, there was no aristocratic economic tradition in the North. Farmers owned their own land, craftsmen operated independent businesses, and doctors, lawyers, and other professionals maintained their own practices. Wealth was not concentrated in a few hands, and economic opportunity for adult white men was widespread.

What Lincoln feared most was the spread of the Southern economic system. The fear was that the Southern slave-labor system would drive out free labor, first in the West, then later in the country as a whole. The fear was that the American Dream of unlimited economic opportunity—"a fair chance, in the race of life"—would no longer be available to future generations of Americans.

Lincoln believed the unique purpose of the United States was to clear the path for the individual to labor for himself and get ahead economically. He called it the "laudable pursuit" of economic advancement. Lincoln understood that this purpose was challenged by the

Politics as usual, nineteenth-century style: Lincoln supporters haul a log-cabin float through the streets of Manhattan during an 1860 campaign parade. This woodcut, *Grand Torchlight Procession of the Wide-Awake Clubs in the City of New York,* appeared in *Frank Leslie's Illustrated Newspaper* on October 11, 1860. FROM THE LINCOLN FOUNDATION COLLECTION, COURTESY OF THE ALLEN COUNTY PUBLIC LIBRARY AND INDIANA STATE MUSEUM AND HISTORIC SITES

slave-based, aristocratic economic and social system of the Southern states. It was this dichotomy that created a house divided: two separate societies based on very different economic and social structures. Lincoln saw saving the Union not simply as a political objective but as a moral imperative to secure for the America of the future the democratic society of the Northern states, what we have come to call the American "middle-class" society. This was the moral imperative that made him willing to fight the Civil War.

Lincoln was one of the first American leaders to fully grasp that economic opportunity to rise to the middle class was, in truth, the defining feature of America. More than any other president, Lincoln is the father of the American Dream that all Americans should have the opportunity through hard work to build a comfortable middle-class life. For Lincoln, liberty meant, above all, the right of individuals to enjoy the fruits of their own labor, which he saw as the best path to prosperity. Lincoln believed that the greatest evil of the Southern slave system—aside from the denial of liberty itself—was that it effectively blocked this economic pathway forever for white workers, who could not compete with slave labor, and for the slaves themselves, who could never hope to escape their bondage and eventually work for wages.

Slavery itself, Lincoln believed, was morally repugnant and a stain on the founders' vision that all men were created equal. But his commitment to economic opportunity was what spurred him on the path toward emancipation. It is crucial to remember that long before he was willing to entertain political or social rights for African Americans, including citizenship, voting rights, or racial equality, Lincoln insisted that African Americans were entitled to the same economic rights as all other Americans.

This book explores Abraham Lincoln's struggle to preserve, and ultimately redefine, the exceptionalism of the American experiment. Lincoln's vision evolved from his personal experiences. His perspective was that of a man born into abject poverty who worked his way up the social and economic ladders through sheer discipline, persistence, and force of will. It was a perspective he never lost. It shaped his core values. As he put it, "The prudent, penniless beginner in the world, labors for wages awhile, saves a surplus with which to buy tools or land for himself; then labors on his own account another while, and at length hires another new beginner to help him. This is the just, and generous, and prosperous system, which opens the way to all—gives hope to all, and consequent energy, and progress, and improvement of condition to all." This was, for Lincoln, the raison d'être of America and what made America a model to nations throughout the world.

This subject could not be presented at a more opportune time as we confront anew—often at a decibel level that seems only a single notch lower than another civil war—the basic question of what defines our American nation.

Americans today continue to pay lip service to the idea of a middle-class society. But there is no way to avoid the data that confirm the rising tide of income inequality in the United States as well as the rest of the world. Are we condemned to a new society with an ever-declining middle class? Or can we find our way back to public policies that nurture a reinvigorated middle-class society, a society that restores Lincoln's commitment to a nation that is not only "of the people" and "by the people" but also "for the people"? Understanding Lincoln's lifework challenges us to confront the ever-growing fragility of our present condition and the challenge of a new century to complete what Lincoln called, at Gettysburg, America's "unfinished work."

This book recalculates the foundations of Lincoln's political faith, examines the philosophical commitments that undergirded his actions in the secession crisis of 1860 and 1861, underscores the development of Lincoln's rhetoric into American nationalistic gospel, and describes the wildly varying efforts by his White House successors to align with, interpret, ignore, or co-opt his message. We seek to unravel the complete legacy of politics from Lincoln's time to ours to define its influence and assess the importance of Lincoln's enduring and ever-challenging call to action.

We have self-consciously let Lincoln speak for himself on the issues he was most concerned about. Rather than offering short phrases from Lincoln's speeches and writings, we present long quotations to provide our readers with the contextual framework that was critical to Lincoln's thoughts and arguments.

In writing this book, we have learned much from the many excellent scholarly studies of the role played by Lincoln in his lifetime. We were both fortunate to work over the years with David Herbert Donald, whose outstanding biography provides the frame of reference for any serious scholarly work on Lincoln. We have also brought to bear the work we have individually done in our previous studies of Lincoln's life and legacy. In this book, we have utilized some of the thoughts and some of the language of our previous individual works about specific aspects of Lincoln's life and legacy. We hope our readers will benefit from the way in which we have put Lincoln's actual words and our own earlier writings in the context of our new understanding of Lincoln's continuing role in the future life of our nation.

The question on the eve of the Civil War was whether the democratic system envisioned by the nation's founders would survive. Lincoln had long endured in a "house divided" between two ways of life. On the one side was a Northern middle-class society honoring labor and offering multiple opportunities for economic advancement by ordinary people, where government was assuming an increasingly constructive role in "clearing the path" for economic success. On the other side was a Southern aristocratic society rigidly divided between rich and poor, ensuring through law and oppression that labor—white and black—remained fixed in place, devalued and cheap, dedicated to an unfettered market, neglectful of the public sector, and offering few opportunities for ordinary people and none at all for a whole race of human beings.

For Lincoln, the choice, painful as it became, was never a hard one.

Until his dying day, fulfillment of the American Dream remained what Lincoln called at Gettysburg his "unfinished work"—and America's.

PART ONE

One

SIMPLE ANNALS
OF THE POOR

DREAMING THE AMERICAN DREAM

No one knows for sure if Abraham Lincoln ever heard of, much less read, Alexis de Tocqueville. But the ethos that animated Lincoln's entire political life was an unwavering belief in pursuing the so-called American Dream, a phrase frequently attributed to the nineteenth-century French writer. Tocqueville's book *Democracy in America,* based on his travels in the northern United States in the early 1830s, provided readers on both sides of the vast Atlantic Ocean the first real glimpse of what the American Dream was about. Tocqueville described the very milieu in which Lincoln labored, advanced, and succeeded against all human odds. The Frenchman's American journey concluded in 1832, the same year in which Lincoln first entered politics as a candidate for the Illinois legislature. Viewing the early-nineteenth-century northern American economy through Tocqueville's eyes is a good way to understand the unique society Lincoln entered in Illinois and embraced for himself.

"Amongst the novel objects that attracted my attention during my stay in the United States," Tocqueville wrote, "nothing struck me more forcibly than the general equality of conditions." No accepted aristocratic tradition existed in the northern states. In an underpopulated continent, wide opportunity remained for farmers to increase the size of their farms and for merchants and artisans of every kind to prosper with little competitive pressure on the prices they charged. In

11

this regard, the opportunities in the North were unique in the world. Tocqueville witnessed a land alive with individual enterprise, where virtually all citizens, some a bit poorer, some a bit richer, but very few of whom were "very rich" by European standards, strove tirelessly to better their condition.

Of course, the country was ideally suited for those seeking to improve their fortunes. It boasted virtually limitless land, a wealth of natural resources, a still small population, and a geographical location protected by ocean barriers that provided the security necessary for the peaceful flourishing of commerce.

Above all, Tocqueville, like Lincoln, was struck by the level of social mobility in the United States. Not only were differences in wealth between rich and poor much narrower than in Europe, but most of the wealthy persons he met had made, rather than inherited, their fortunes. Even the poor expected to be wealthy someday. "I never met in America," he noted, "with any citizen so poor as not to cast a glance of hope and envy on the enjoyments of the rich, or whose imagination did not possess itself by anticipation of those good things which fate still obstinately withheld from him."

Tocqueville believed that the fact that most Americans in the North were neither rich nor poor—they thought of themselves as "middle class"—lent American society enormous stability. He argued that, in combination with the opportunities for social mobility, the nation's middle-class nature provided a barrier against social upheaval and revolution. "Between these two extremes [wealth and poverty] of democratic communities stand an innumerable multitude of men almost alike, who, without being exactly either rich or poor, are possessed of sufficient property to desire the maintenance of order, yet not enough to excite envy. Such men are the natural enemies of violent commotions; their stillness keeps all beneath them and above them still, and secures the balance of the fabric of society."

Not that Lincoln could remotely consider himself—until astonishingly late in his life—as belonging to the middle class characteristic of the northern states. Lincoln started life in Kentucky, on the frontier of a slave state. Like many rural children, Lincoln was born, as he put it—perhaps the better to highlight his march to success—to parents descended from "undistinguished families." In a word, he was not only poor, but almost embarrassingly so. Isolated in rural poverty, he first saw the light of day on February 12, 1809, in a hut-size windowless, dirt-floored log cabin, in the depths of a cold prairie winter. It was no wonder that his cousin Dennis Hanks took one look at the newborn swathed in animal skins and predicted, "[H]e won't amount to much." As a child on the frontier of a southern state, Lincoln and his family needed to grow food and hunt and were constantly menaced by wild animals. His father was subjected to title claims that occasionally wrested their land from them. Mere survival, not upward mobility, was the family preoccupation.

Lincoln's early life was every bit as painfully hard as the myths have maintained: from early childhood, he worked the fields of his father's succession of hard-to-till farms, clearing land, planting seeds, harvesting crops, and famously chopping wood and building fences out of split wooden rails. Yet deprivation somehow made Lincoln strong and fired his ambition to escape from an upbringing we tend too often to romanticize. Until a stepmother came into his life, his home lacked even a wooden floor or a book.

Education, too, was meager—for Lincoln, no more than a year's worth of formal schooling in the entire course of his life. Lincoln's rise was even more remarkable because there was nothing in his early schooling, such as it was, "to excite ambition for education." What he was able to learn, he admitted, he "picked up from time to time under the pressure of necessity."

Like all but the wealthiest families of the day, Abraham's father, Thomas Lincoln, expected his spouse and children to contribute their own labor to the family farming enterprise. Every hand was needed for the task. Gender roles were, of course, strictly prescribed in these remote rural environs. Lincoln's mother and sister cleaned, cooked, and sewed, and Abe was ordered into the fields when he was still young, though old enough to resent the backbreaking tasks to which he was assigned. Small, independent farmers like Thomas Lincoln usually tried to sire large families, not because feeding additional mouths was routinely easy, but in the hope of producing enough strong sons to create a dependable labor force to help work in the fields and ultimately

Young Lincoln as the legendary young fireside reader:
The Boyhood of Lincoln—An Evening in the Log Hut,
a widely reproduced chromo by L. Prang & Co., Boston, after the influential 1868 painting by Eastman
Johnson. LIBRARY OF CONGRESS

inherit the property. In this ambition, as in so many others, Thomas
proved unsuccessful. Neighbors whispered that he became sterile at
one point. There is no way to know whether that rumor was true, but
Abraham turned out to be Thomas Lincoln's only male offspring, at
least the only one to live to working age (a baby brother died in early in-
fancy). Lincoln's mother, Nancy, had no other documented pregnancy.

As the sole male child, Abraham had no choice but to work hard
alongside his father. The fact that he grew large and extremely strong
for his age made his contributions even more essential. He learned early
that the work could be not only grueling but dispiriting. At one point
during his youth, Abe helped plant pumpkin seeds on a precarious

hillside, then watched helplessly one day as a violent downpour flooded
the field and sent the seedlings down the hillside to their destruction.
It is no wonder Lincoln later frustratingly likened his childhood to
Thomas Gray's "Elegy Written in a Country Churchyard." As he later
put it, "It is a great folly to make anything out of my early life. It can all
be condensed into a single sentence, and that sentence you will find in
Gray's Elegy: 'The short and simple annals of the poor.'"

In fact, the full passage from the elegy—rarely quoted in the Lincoln literature—evokes the kind of resentment over the low esteem in
which some contemporaries held their impoverished neighbors. These
people were the planters and harvesters, but many condemned them
to a destiny of hard labor with no chance for improvement or escape.
They were born to toil, not to aspire. As the poem advises:

> *Let not ambition mock their useful toil,*
> *Their homely joys, and destiny obscure;*
> *Nor grandeur hear with a disdainful smile,*
> *The short and simple annals of the poor.*

But even if Thomas Gray embraced this fixed-destiny idea for the
"obscure," Lincoln did not. Obscurity was not for him. After all, that
same elegy boasts a subsequent passage that suggests even the "simple
poor" could enjoy the heady possibility of fame through achievement.
In fashioning his own version of his life for public consumption, Lincoln liked to emphasize the grinding poverty from which he sprang,
not the grinding ambition that led him to escape it. But in the later
stanza from Gray's elegy—which he likely knew—even the poor might
enjoy

> *Th' applause of list'ning senates to command,*
> *The threats of pain and ruin to despise.*
> *To scatter plenty o'er a smiling land,*
> *And read their hist'ry in a nation's eyes.*

Thus, the young Lincoln understood early the path toward making history before "a nation's eyes" and knew it required hard work,

learning, and the striving for respect to secure the admiration of one's peers and the right to advance in society without recourse to violence and lawlessness. It also called for "gratitude to our fathers," as he later put it—if not to his own unsympathetic father, then to the national fathers who had created an America where a "penniless beginner," as Lincoln described himself, could "toil up from poverty."

Of course, Lincoln's own father, at best barely one step ahead of abject poverty himself, had no sympathy for such dreams, or those who harbored them, particularly his only son. Tensions thickened as Abe grew more adept at felling trees and splitting rails, even if the skill and speed at which he worked did not make him love the job. Here is where the epic confrontation between father and son really swung into high gear: Thomas wanted Abe to devote his time exclusively to his farm obligations, while Abe, encouraged by a sympathetic new stepmother who brought the family's first books into their home, wanted more time to read and learn. To the son, farmwork meant subsistence, no more. Books opened doors to a world of opportunities beyond. To the father, books were a luxury, and his boy needed to tend to his farm obligations first and foremost, even if Thomas had to take a strap to beat some sense into him. The tension and probable domestic violence—routine as it may have been in the early nineteenth century—destroyed whatever love the son may have had for his father. Eventually, though, it helped propel young Lincoln into political sympathy with the Whigs, a party founded by a supposedly probusiness elite, but equally devoted to lifting men like Lincoln out of the grinding poverty to which they had been born and helping them toward a limitless future that depended primarily on hard work and skill.

An additional tension between father and son complicated young Lincoln's fraught evolution from laborer to learner. Thomas Lincoln staked his earliest claim to lands in Kentucky, where slavery was legal, even though he apparently opposed the institution vehemently. This sensibility had little to do with enlightened racial attitudes or sympathy with enslaved blacks, a number of whom the Lincoln family would have seen marching, perhaps in chains, when they lived later along the Cumberland Gap trail. For the pathway through the Appalachian Mountains, once famously explored by Daniel Boone, was later used not only by poor white settlers heading into the western territories to work the land themselves but also by wealthy slave owners transporting their black slaves to labor in plantations in the southwestern territories. Thomas was no apostle of black freedom for its own moral sake—although his local Baptist church did drum home an antislavery message. Rather, Thomas thought the slave system unfair because it advantaged rich men who could afford to own people to do their work for them and made life exponentially harder for poor whites who could not afford to buy, much less maintain, slave laborers. Proof of Thomas's overall ambivalence came when, fully empowered by local laws and mores, he "rented" his strapping son out to local farmers to perform day labor—keeping all the money the minor earned for himself. At least one historian has claimed that the experience of performing his own service as a "slave" to his father may have converted Abe into something of an abolitionist. This is, perhaps, a bit of an exaggeration, but the experience surely reinforced Abe's rebellion against being relegated to fixed labor in any circumstance, and for any "master," as a permanent way of life.

Lincoln rejected his father's life on the frontier for another reason: it was a world in which violence—whether from predatory beasts or his fellow frontiersman—was a constant threat. The violence Lincoln encountered in the remote forests where he and his parents lived required a perpetual vigil against bears, panthers, and other "wild animals still in the woods." Lincoln also experienced a kind of preparatory introduction to human violence when he accompanied a group of young men on a wooden flatboat loaded with cargo all the way to New Orleans. He made two such voyages down the Mississippi. On one of them, he saw a slave auction, which reportedly hardened his attitudes against the horrors of the institution. On another, he actually had to battle for his own life against people of color. "[O]ne night," he later reported in the third person, his group was "attacked by seven negroes with intent to kill and rob them. They were hurt some in the melee, but succeeded in driving the negroes from the boat." Lincoln bore a knife scar on his thumb for the rest of his life.

To his credit, Lincoln did not use the episode as an excuse to hate or fear African Americans, as might many of his white contemporaries after similar experiences. Perhaps his subsequent exposure to the degradation and constant threat of violence attending slavery itself helped him to understand the anger that so easily arose both among people constantly subjected to the yoke, chain, and whip and among those who used cruelty and physical intimidation to keep them in a servile condition.

Years later, Lincoln described his personal reaction after observing a particularly harrowing sight:

> A gentleman had purchased twelve negroes in diferent [sic] parts of Kentucky and was taking them to a farm in the South. They were chained six and six together. A small iron clevis was around the left wrist of each, and this fastened to the main chain by a shorter one at a convenient distance from, the others; so that the negroes were strung together precisely like so many fish upon a trot-line. In this condition they were being separated forever from the scenes of their childhood, their friends, their fathers and mothers, and brothers and sisters, and many of them, from their wives and children, and going into perpetual slavery where the lash of the master is proverbially more ruthless and unrelenting. . . .

That young Lincoln rejected this violent frontier world and his stagnant economic condition—for himself and for his generation, both politically and philosophically—comes as no surprise. What remains astounding is that, opportunity notwithstanding, he did not strike out on his own for a full year after he reached the age of legal emancipation, twenty-one.

Lincoln left home at the age of twenty-two, after helping his family move one final time, from the wilderness of southern Indiana to yet another hardscrabble farm in central Illinois. It is difficult to imagine that he had even a faint hint of what lay before him. The pro-Lincoln *Chicago Tribune* surely hit the mark exactly when, in a post-1860 election biographical sketch, it portrayed him as "toiling under the weight of poverty with a view of better days." The comment precisely crystallized his rapidly evolving theory of American economic

Lincoln the Rail-splitter, by Norman Rockwell, who hoped this painting would "inspire the youth of this land to appreciate this man who believed so much in the value of education." Lincoln, who also believed in the value of banking, might also have appreciated that Rockwell's 1965 work was commissioned by the Bank of Spokane. COURTESY OF THE BUTLER INSTITUTE OF AMERICAN ART, YOUNGSTOWN, OH

possibility—that even in the midst of grueling poverty he had a chance to survive, perhaps even thrive.

In a very real way, Lincoln learned the value of economic opportunity by observing—and suffering through—his father's frustratingly unsuccessful struggle to improve his own family's economic circumstances. Thomas Lincoln was so unlearned that he could only "bunglingly sign his own name," as his son remembered somewhat disparagingly. In reality, Thomas Lincoln was nowhere near as lazy or shiftless as some early Lincoln admirers maintained in an effort to make Abraham Lincoln's energy, ambition, and rise seem all the more miraculous.

Thomas may have been unlucky in pursuit of secure land titles. But it was an age in which owning and operating even a small farm meant the difference not only between stagnation and opportunity, but between survival and starvation. Unfortunately, in an age of westward expansion, competing claims for land often ensnared barely literate men like Thomas Lincoln into futile battles over legal title to their property. Whenever and wherever he established new family farms, he at least labored hard to build cabins, clear land, plant seeds, and harvest crops. And he tried building an ancillary income stream by doing carpentry. If the surviving attributable examples of his labors are any indication, he became surprisingly accomplished in this field, so highly skilled that he could summon the professional ability to build his first wife's coffin, while he insisted his son at least observe and probably aid in the task. This may seem to us to be an example of bad parenting, but it was also evidence of a dispassionate commitment to do what had to be done to survive the ordeals of both life and death.

Abraham Lincoln finally left the family farm in 1830 and moved to New Salem, in the free state of Illinois. He bought a local grocery store, which sold liquor, among other items, a source of political embarrassment for him later. The enterprise eventually "winked out," and Lincoln found himself owing so much money to his creditors that he began jokingly referring to his obligations as the "national debt." This early attempt to lift himself out of poverty through commerce proved even less fruitful than his earlier attempt to move produce on the rivers. New Salem itself was something of a commercial house of cards. It was a mill town whose sole energy source was really no more than a stream, enough to power the local mill perhaps, but not even sufficiently deep to welcome ships that might dock there, trade goods, and expand the local economic base. Though it might have gained some benefit from the kind of "internal improvement" or, in modern terms, "infrastructure project" that Lincoln favored, New Salem eventually became a town Lincoln yearned to escape as urgently as he had thirsted to flee from the family farm. New Salem was as firmly locked into its narrow conditions as were farmers and slaves on the prairie. Lincoln eventually wanted out.

Military life was one outlet for ambitious young men, but Lincoln had no hope of ever securing a recommendation to West Point, even if he contemplated such an opportunity. He did enjoy his experience as a military volunteer in Illinois's brief war against the Indian chief Black Hawk in 1832. Lincoln joined up principally because all the young men in his village did so, but surely not far from his mind was the knowledge that his own grandfather, also named Abraham, had been killed by an Indian attack in Virginia years before. Had not his future father, then still a child, killed the Indian who shot the first Abraham Lincoln, Thomas would almost certainly have been the next victim— and the future president would never have been born.

Lincoln later said that his "surprise" election as captain by his fellow militiamen constituted his biggest honor to date. As late as 1860, he insisted that he had not "since had any success in life which gave him so much satisfaction." Many young men gain unforgettable life experiences in the maelstrom of war, but one reason Lincoln so enjoyed his military service—he even reenlisted as a private when his original term of service (and status as captain) lapsed—is that it required no real test against the enemy. Lincoln's war was entirely free of violence.

After his service ended in July 1832, Lincoln returned to New Salem and wisely chose to become a lawyer. The law offered a life of rationality. Finally, he could define and pursue his destiny based on talent and energy, not by the accidents of birth and blood or the physical endowments of brute strength and a fast temper. He had chosen a profession where success depended instead on rational thinking, orderly presentation of intelligent argument, and quick wit. The law provided not only a reliable source of income and an open path for career development, but also an opportunity for public service and a political platform. Perhaps most appealing of all, he could use the law to help establish order in his own life in a still chaotic frontier society. As Lincoln had come to understand, order and structure were needed to facilitate personal opportunity and upward mobility. At one and the same time, Lincoln made a personal career decision and an ideological commitment to the "rule of law" as one of the most important pillars of a democratic society.

From the first, Lincoln sought a degree of order and equity through his new law practice: he seldom refused paying clients, even if he found their economic claims dubious and political views obnoxious. Lawyer Lincoln routinely handled corporate cases, divorces, bankruptcies, land-title disputes, and debt collection as well the defense of people accused of violent crimes.

Some of the clues to Lincoln's thinking about politics and government became apparent in the way in which attorney Lincoln argued some of the legal cases he took on before his return to politics in 1854. Many were routine, but the occasional case reflected Lincoln's belief that all clients (including, once, a slave owner seeking to recover his "runaways") deserved the best available legal representation. Other cases gave Lincoln the opportunity to propound his belief that government-sponsored infrastructure improvements were crucial to the economic development of the nation and would prove beneficial to its citizens, however poor or wealthy.

Lincoln probably took great pleasure in winning perhaps the most famous and influential decision of his legal career in the 1857 "*Effie Afton* Case" (officially *Hurd vs. Rock Island Bridge Co.*). The owners of the steamboat *Effie Afton* had sued the railroad company that had erected a bridge across the Mississippi River between Illinois and Iowa. Because the ship had crashed into the bridge, the company claimed the span was an unnatural impediment and that the railroad was responsible for its losses. This case gave Lincoln the opportunity to argue that the proliferation of railroads—the great economic development of the decade—was positive and irreversible. In the future, ships would have to make way for trains and bridges, not vice versa. The case presented a challenge to Lincoln's nimble legal mind: he cleverly demanded proof that the captain had shown reasonable judgment in navigating and piloting his vessel. Absent such proof, the trial ended with a hung jury that absolved Lincoln's bridge-owning client from liability. The presiding judge dismissed the case. The decision created important case law for Illinois, establishing a precedent that accepted the inevitability of vast improvements to the nation's infrastructure.

Lincoln's work as a lawyer convinced him that governments could play a positive role in supporting economic opportunity for all citizens. And his entry into politics allowed him to take an active part in these efforts. He first won election to the state legislature in 1834 and promptly became a leading advocate for state investments in the roads and canals that not only provided jobs and other economic benefits but also, in the long term, created pathways for people like himself to move out of the remote frontier into the limitless world of urbanized society.

As if practicing what he preached, Lincoln in April 1837 packed up his meager belongings and moved to Springfield, Illinois, a flourishing city filled with opportunity unlike any in which he had ever lived. In 1839 the city would, with legislator Lincoln's support, become the new capital of Illinois. By some macabre twist of fate, Lincoln was twenty-eight years old on the day he moved and had precisely twenty-eight years, to the day, left in his life. Now Lincoln rebranded himself as a rising star in Springfield in both politics and the law.

Interestingly—and, as it turned out, fleetingly—Lincoln at this early point in his career in the Illinois General Assembly promoted the idea of extending the right to vote to females. He was, though, still far from endorsing the idea of granting the suffrage to one and all (he made no mention of free people of color). Being born female in the first half of the nineteenth century, especially female and poor, relegated one to yet another kind of American slavery. By the time Lincoln reached national fame, however, and despite having served in Congress during the first well-publicized women's rights convention at Seneca Falls, New York, the cause had faded from his political consciousness. Just as the more enlightened founding fathers had called for a gradual end to slavery, only to retreat from that position in the wake of opposition from wealthy southern aristocrats such as Jefferson, the male leaders of the next century retreated from their brief flirtation with women's rights. The founding mothers encountered continuing opposition to their calls for equal rights for women. For another half century, serious-minded progressive women were often mockingly depicted in caricatures as promiscuous antifamily advocates.

As a young politician, Lincoln's central idea was to combine ingenuity and ambition with proposals for government support for positive infrastructure programs. Innovation remained key. New Salem's pathetic little Sangamon River appeared to be forever doomed to the status of a mere stream. Lincoln developed and sought a patent for a clever if impractical device to raise vessels up in its shallow waters. Lincoln may have gone on to politics and the law, but he still believed that his invention could improve the aspirations of river villages like New Salem to become thriving ports by investing in what would later be called infrastructure improvements. It is no surprise that Lincoln became the first—and only—president to hold a federal patent, even if *Scientific American* said of his device, on the eve of Lincoln's 1861 inauguration, "[W]e hope the author of it will have a better success in presiding as Chief Magistrate over the people of the entire Union than he has had as an inventor."

* * *

Lincoln entered politics as a Whig, and more particularly as a follower of the revered political lion Henry Clay. Clay, who served as a congressman, senator, secretary of state, and Speaker of the House, was a nationally renowned politician who ran unsuccessfully for president five times. He was the nation's leading proponent of a strong Union and a strengthened federal government. By the mid-1820s, Clay had devised a comprehensive political program under the nicely marketable label of the "American System." And Lincoln embraced it enthusiastically—even though, it should be noted, it also included the idea of freeing, and then colonizing, African American slaves.

Clay's American System featured three major components: a national bank, to provide the nation with a sound currency and stable financial system; high tariffs, to encourage the growth of domestic manufacturing; and federal spending, financed by the tariff to create roads, bridges, canals, and other transportation infrastructure to aid in the development of the domestic economy. When Lincoln ran unsuccessfully for a seat in the Illinois General Assembly in 1832, he said, "My politics are short and sweet, like the old woman's dance. I am in favor of a national bank. I am in favor of the internal improvement system and a high protective tariff." Behind what seemed like a quip lurked a deft summary of the three key economic issues that divided the nation, and the political parties, in the decades leading up to the

Civil War, before the issue of slavery overwhelmed them all. Lincoln's "old woman's dance" was in fact astutely choreographed; it was a reiteration of Clay's entire program.

Importantly, Lincoln understood that Clay saw his American System as something that would aid the common people by promoting economic development. Clay always claimed a concern for ordinary citizens. And he certainly believed in America as a land of opportunity. As Lincoln surely knew, Clay was responsible for putting the term "self-made man" into political circulation.

When Lincoln embraced Clay's economic "system," he did so not out of a sense of nationalism but because, in very practical terms, he thought Clay's program would aid ordinary working people, people like himself, those striving to become, and remain, middle class. The whole nation had witnessed the vast benefits that accrued to the citizens of New York from the construction of the nearly four-hundred-mile Erie Canal between 1817 and 1825. The engineering marvel opened up the Great Lakes to the Atlantic Ocean and helped transform New York City into the most important seaport in the entire country. As an inhabitant of a still undeveloped frontier state—a land bereft of decent roads and dependably navigable rivers, to say nothing of canals and railroads—Lincoln wanted something of the same for Illinois. Lincoln supported state funding for economic development throughout his career in the legislature. Even though the state government boasted few resources at its disposal, Lincoln's major undertaking when he entered the Illinois state assembly was to push through an ambitious package of "internal improvements," partially state-financed roads, bridges, canals, and railroads. Lincoln's program nearly bankrupted Illinois, but its high fiscal and political cost never changed his view that government should engage proactively to build, expand, and provide opportunities for working people to improve their economic status.

Early on, Lincoln saw a need for positive federal government action: to provide infrastructure that would allow the expansion of internal commerce, to guarantee a sound currency to enable economic transactions, and to protect homegrown manufacturing from the threat of (mostly British) manufactured goods from abroad. The government's job was to clear the path for its citizens to get ahead. By the standards of his

time—when the federal government's size and budget were minimal—
Lincoln was in favor of an activist federal government, on the grounds
that a primary purpose of the United States was to support the economic opportunities of its citizens.

Even at this still early stage of his political career, Lincoln found
a way to address the question of building and maintaining the nation's
infrastructure practically as well as philosophically. He acknowledged
that there was a need to recognize that certain internal improvements
funded by the federal government would be more beneficial to some
states, while others would benefit other states. Somehow, the competition, even then, often pitted southern interests against northern—
especially when politicians began proposing plans for a transcontinental railroad. Yet Lincoln shunned the human tendency to characterize
one's own self-interest as "good" and others' self-interest as "evil." As
Lincoln saw matters, "The true rule, in determining to embrace, or
reject any thing, is not whether it have *any* evil in it; but whether it
have more of evil, than of good. There are few things *wholly* evil, or
wholly good. Almost every thing, especially of governmental policy, is
an inseparable compound of the two; so that our best judgment of the
preponderance between them is continually demanded."

In his first and only term in the US Congress, Lincoln forcefully presented the view that the federal government should play its
proper role in financing infrastructure. The freshman congressman
argued on the floor of the US House of Representatives on June 20,
1848, "[T]he question of internal improvements . . . can no longer be
avoided . . . and the friends of the policy must now battle." Lincoln
declared there was an important role for both the federal government
and the state government. Facing the threat of a public-works veto
from conservative president Democrat James Knox Polk, he proposed
a compromise: "Let the nation take hold of the larger works, and the
states the smaller ones."

If the drive for economic advancement and material progress represented one great thrust of America's early national life, then the
other great thrust aimed toward increasing political democracy. In
the years leading up to Lincoln's entry into politics, most states had
expanded their suffrage to include not just property owners but all free

Congressman-elect Abraham Lincoln, ca. 1846. This is his first photograph, taken by Nicholas H. Shepherd in Springfield, Illinois, after Lincoln won his House seat on the pro–internal improvements Whig ticket. NATIONAL PORTRAIT GALLERY/LIBRARY OF CONGRESS PHOTOGRAPH

white males. The expansion of voting rights in the decades since the founding had given a new more raucous and populist cast to national politics. No one better epitomized this new populism than President Andrew Jackson. On the occasion of his inauguration in 1829, he famously opened the doors of the White House to one and all. Farmers stood on the fine chairs in their muddy boots and cut souvenir slices from the carpets and drapery. Damage to the presidential residence by the end of the affair amounted to thousands of dollars. But the point had been made. "The people" were now in charge.

Many historians have seen in Jackson a kind of founding father of the modern Democratic Party. But on economic policy, the positions of Jackson's party bore a closer resemblance to those of today's Republicans than to those of today's Democrats. The Jacksonian Democratic Party was, in our present-day terms, "anti–big government," viewing with deep suspicion economic development, urbanization, and virtually all the other developments that the Whigs hailed as "progress." Jackson's economic policy approach was of a piece with his skepticism about what we would call today the "public sector."

Jackson's attack on the activist American System—proposed by Clay and supported by Lincoln—was manifested in his campaign against the Second Bank of the United States, which forced its liquidation by 1838. Jackson's suspicion of the bank carried with it an element of sectionalism. He thought the bank disproportionately benefited northern financial interests. The bank had suffered its share of problems, but on the whole it lent a vital stability to the nation's financial system. Jackson's destruction of the bank would condemn the nation to currency instability and a terrible cycle of booms and busts for decades to come. Jackson also demonstrated his opposition to internal improvements by vetoing bills to provide federal aid for the construction of roads. Jackson may have been elected as a military hero, but the president was a plantation owner from North Carolina, and as such he came almost naturally to oppose the key elements of Clay's American System.

The most explosive issue facing American politicians North and South in the Jacksonian era proved to be the tariff. Tariffs were the financial centerpiece of Clay's American System. As Speaker of the House of Representatives, he had engineered passage of a major tariff bill in 1824—the first true protective tariff in American history. From the start, much of the South opposed tariffs because they were designed to protect manufacturing, largely a northern enterprise. At the same time, in the southern view, tariffs threatened the southern economy, which was critically dependent on export trade with Great Britain. Britain was by far the United States' largest trading partner, and the most important American export was southern cotton to British factories.

It should come as no surprise that the southern politicians found political arguments to support their sectional economic interests, opposing not only high tariffs but also federal government expenditures for internal improvements. Southern politicians questioned the constitutionality of such ambitious federal action. In the south, the idea of public investment in infrastructure remained largely an alien notion. Southerners argued that these activist government programs unduly benefited Northern financial and industrial interests. At the time, southern legislatures were firmly controlled by slave owners, who had little economic interest in public improvements, saw no need to provide an active economy for a free labor force, and had a substantial ability to surround themselves with luxury within the private preserves of their plantations. The southern political mind increasingly viewed both tariffs and internal improvements as northern ideas that would not benefit its section in the least. Pursuing social mobility through internal improvements provided no positive benefit, in the view of slave owners who dominated southern economic and political society.

Views in the North were practically the opposite. In the decades before the Civil War, the notion of material progress and the dream of social mobility took fire in the northern mind. The opportunity of "ordinary people" to acquire land or work as independent artisans encouraged the growing sense of equality of all citizens. For the first time, voting rights existed for all adult male citizens, not just for all property holders. Northern and western states from New York to Illinois actively pursued internal improvements and built up their public infrastructure to support the dream of equality and the reality of opportunity.

America was increasingly dividing into two distinct sectional societies. The North was expanding its internal economy, while the South clung to its highly profitable slave-based agricultural economy, heavily reliant on cotton exports to Great Britain.

Two different economies, with different, and in many respects opposed, sets of interests now coexisted anxiously under one flag. And with the two economies came two different cultures and worldviews, North and South, one dependent, to be sure, on the output of slaves. The growing sectional divide—the growing crisis between North and South—initially played out as a struggle over economic policy. Only later did it also become an explicit conflict over the morality of slavery.

During the three decades before the Civil War, politicians dedicated to the Union struggled to keep the division over slavery from tearing the nation apart. What ultimately forced the issue was the nation's continued westward expansion. Would the new states added to the Union have an economy based on slave labor or free labor? The repeal of the Missouri Compromise that accompanied passage of the Kansas-Nebraska Act in 1854 forced the issue of slavery in the territories to the center of the national stage. The Kansas-Nebraska Act specified that each territory could choose between the northern and southern economic systems through a political solution dubbed "popular sovereignty." In each territory, this encouraged an explosive political battle between supporters of each system, bringing the long-seething conflict to the heart of national life.

It was during this tumultuous period that the new Republican Party was founded. It was an uncoordinated combination of Whigs and antislavery former Democrats, but what unified them was an economic vision. Lincoln was the best and most philosophical, though by no means the only, exponent of its outlook. Its watchword was the concept of *free labor*. This becomes especially clear against the background of its alternative: the aristocratic economic life as it was known in the slave-owning South. The vision, especially in Lincoln's eyes, was aimed primarily at improving the lot of ordinary citizens, of building and sustaining a middle-class country.

When his hero Henry Clay died in 1852, Lincoln delivered a eulogy in his Springfield, Illinois, hometown, parts of which were less a description of Clay than a thinly veiled self-portrait of Lincoln. The heart of the eulogy featured a description of the very core of Lincoln's political and economic philosophy, which he artfully attributed to Clay: "Mr. Clay's predominant sentiment, from first to last, was a deep devotion to the cause of human liberty—a strong sympathy with the oppressed everywhere, and an ardent wish for their elevation. With him, this was a primary and all controlling passion. . . . He desired the prosperity of his countrymen partly because they were his countrymen, but chiefly to show to the world that free men could be prosperous."

Significantly, for Lincoln and the new Republican Party, the doctrine of "free labor" implied an active role for government in fulfilling this mission. It was the slave-owning South, rather than the Republican North, that adhered to the doctrine of pure "free-market" economics. It was the slave-owning South that sought to diminish the size and powers of the federal government. It was the slave owners of the South, secure in their vast personal wealth, who saw little point to investments in the public sector to build a national infrastructure. It was the South that was sharply divided between the few rich and the many poor, a region with minimal social mobility and no ethic of social responsibility. It was the open society of the North that provided the economic opportunity for all free men to build a middle-class life. That society, Lincoln believed, came closest to fulfilling the American Dream, and as such should expand and endure.

Two

RIGHT MAKES MIGHT

LINCOLN THE CANDIDATE

LINCOLN CAME LATE TO THE FIGHT OVER EXTENDING SLAVERY INTO America's western territories. He was only twelve years old and living in isolation on the prairie when the conflict between northern and southern members of Congress led to the Missouri Compromise of 1820–1821, which was intended to settle the issue for all time.

When the controversy resurfaced thirty years later with the passage of the Kansas-Nebraska Act in 1854, Lincoln was ready to do battle against slavery on economic as well as moral terms. By then he had begun to interpret his own escape from poverty as a cautionary argument against keeping people in a hopelessly fixed condition for life.

The Missouri Compromise between proslavery Southern states and antislavery Northern states specified that western territories below the Mason-Dixon line—interpreted at 36°30' latitude—would remain open to slavery, while those above would remain free, with slavery barred. When Lincoln served in Congress from 1847 to 1849, he did not focus much on the future of slavery in the territories beyond his support of the ill-fated Wilmot Proviso, prohibiting slavery from all western lands acquired in the Mexican-American War (the measure failed repeatedly). For all intents and purposes, the issue had been settled by law, leaving white Americans free to pursue their ambitions and dreams in the territories north of the Mason-Dixon line.

Then in 1850 Whig Party leader Henry Clay, Lincoln's "beau ideal of a statesman," persuaded Congress to pass the Compromise of

1850—with considerable help from an increasingly influential young Democratic senator from Illinois: Stephen A. Douglas. Lincoln was by then back home in Illinois, out of office, and soured on politics. This new compromise barred the slave trade in Washington, DC, admitted California as a free state, introduced the nation's first fugitive slave law, and ushered in the idea of "popular sovereignty" by giving New Mexico and Utah the right to leave to its white voters the question of whether to organize as slave or free states. Four years later Senator Douglas, who had shepherded Clay's Compromise of 1850 through Congress, was extending the use of "popular sovereignty" by persuading Congress to pass the Kansas-Nebraska Act of 1854. Douglas hoped his plan for giving white western settlers the right to vote slavery up or down in new states would calm the ongoing conflict between the North and South.

Lincoln's personal history made him different from most politicians of this period and perhaps more attuned to America's unique promise to its citizens. Somehow, he had escaped a life of physical labor, hunger, and hardship and taught himself to be an attorney. Understandably, Lincoln became a lawyer with a pronounced sympathy for clients whose pursuit of upward mobility was frustrated by powerful interests or archaic precedents. When he turned to politics as a man of the people, he naturally began to interpret his own escape from poverty as a cautionary argument against keeping people, white or black, in a fixed condition for life.

It was Douglas's Kansas-Nebraska Act that spurred Lincoln to reenter politics and defend the economic system he saw as crucial to the American way of life. By 1854 Lincoln was prepared to argue that the battle over the economic structure of the western territories amounted to an unavoidable conflict over the future of the United States. Lincoln saw no value in the Douglas plan for the West, even if Douglas meant it to spur economic expansion to the Pacific. It was in response to Douglas's Kansas-Nebraska Act that former congressman Abraham Lincoln was "aroused," as he put it, to return to politics and argue against popular sovereignty.

Lincoln's experience as a lawyer in civil cases had taught him that there was no requirement that litigants bring opposing viewpoints together with a compromise solution. When compromise failed and Lincoln found himself trying a case in a court of law, he was willing to go all out to make an overarching argument based on first principles. Looking at the Kansas-Nebraska Act, what was at stake was the basic right of American citizens to life, liberty, and the pursuit of happiness.

Lincoln and his contemporaries lived in a nonstop political environment. Voters found politics the major public entertainment, and participation in the political process was almost universal. The voters—some barely literate—avidly craved public oratory and came out to hear candidates speak for hours at a time. Community response to political speech making was reminiscent of the level of interest in old-time preaching at revival meetings or modern enthusiasm for sporting events and rock concerts. Elections of some kind occurred throughout the calendar year. Voters followed politics continuously and took their families to political events as eagerly as they might go to the community church or the annual county fair. Famous political figures enjoyed a built-in audience. Their speeches were not just all talk. They were frequently accompanied by fireworks, music, torch-lit processions, and still more speeches.

The future president thrived in this culture. Even Douglas, his lifelong rival, acknowledged that Lincoln was "full of wit, facts, dates—and the best stump speaker, with his droll ways and dry jokes." Lincoln was wise not only in the ways of enthralling crowds, but also in creating words that could be reprinted in newspapers, the only medium of the time that provided regular information to party loyalists and other voters. For many voters, especially those locked into rural isolation far from the scenes of rallies and lyceums, newspapers were their primary access to the ideas and arguments of aspiring politicians.

Lincoln initiated his reentry into Illinois politics with a speech in Peoria on October 16, 1854. Showcasing a leaner new oratorical style, he fashioned the address in the form of a lawyer's argument and made the case against Douglas's Kansas-Nebraska Act largely on economic terms. As he put it, "The whole nation is interested that the best use shall be made of these territories. We want them for homes of free white people. This they cannot be, to any considerable extent, if slavery shall be planted within them. Slave States are places for poor white people to remove FROM, not to remove TO. New free States are the places for poor people to go to and better their condition. For this use, the nation needs these territories."

Lincoln's emphasis on slavery's economic consequences was quite different from the argument of the abolitionists of his time, who insisted on immediate action to end slavery and begin the process of establishing racial equality. As Lincoln argued in Peoria, slavery might remain legal in the South, but that did not mean it should or could be introduced in the western territories. What set Lincoln apart from many of his Northern contemporaries was his refusal to affix sole blame for slavery on white Southerners. Had their climates been reversed, he often volunteered, Northerners might well have embraced and defended slavery with equal vigor.

> When southern people tell us they are no more responsible for the origin of slavery, than we; I acknowledge the fact. When it is said that the institution exists; and that it is very difficult to get rid of it, in any satisfactory way, I can understand and appreciate the saying. I surely will not blame them for not doing what I should not know how to do myself. . . . When they remind us of their constitutional rights, I acknowledge them, not grudgingly, but fully and fairly; and I would give them any legislation for the reclaiming of their fugitives, which should not, in its stringency, be more likely to carry a free man into slavery, than our ordinary criminal laws are to hang an innocent one.
>
> But all this; to my judgment, furnishes no more excuse for permitting slavery to go into our own free territory, than it would for reviving the African slave trade by law.

While Lincoln was adamantly opposed to the extension of slavery to the western territories, he made it clear he was not joining the abolitionists in demanding racial equality in the South or in the North. "Let it not be said I am contending for the establishment of political and social equality between the whites and blacks," he said. Indeed, Lincoln did not even support the elimination of the Black Laws that banned free people of color from living in many Northern states, including his own Illinois. Rather, he took the position that the fight against slavery should center on expanding the Northern economic system in the West for the benefit of future generations of aspiring white Americans. Even this was a radical notion in the halls of Congress in 1854.

Lincoln couched his opposition to the spread of slavery with a cautious mix of constitutional interpretation and muted moral indignation. But behind his argument—though it remained unstated—was a shrewd political calculus. If slavery was banned forever from the West, then every new state admitted to the Union in the future would be a free state, with each of them sending antislavery congressmen and senators to Washington. As often as Lincoln assured Southern interests that he would never interfere with slavery where it existed, the slow but sure arrival of an ever-growing western antislavery bloc meant that at some point in the future, there might be sufficient votes on Capitol Hill for Congress to initiate the death knell of slavery with an achievable constitutional amendment to prohibit slavery everywhere. Lincoln understood this potential future tipping point. And it helps explain his seemingly restrained and limited public antislavery sentiments: time was on his side, as long as slavery did not spread.

Southern proslavery elements comprehended this from the start, too, which is why they remained so fearful of Lincoln's political rise. Presenting himself as a common man who rose because of American guarantees of freedom and economic opportunity, Lincoln was the one populist who might actually place slavery "in the course of ultimate extinction." The absolute prohibition of slavery from the western territories was his way to achieve the ultimate goal of ensuring that the United States would continue to provide equality and economic opportunity for its white citizens.

It was not that Lincoln ignored morality and was solely interested in the economic impact of the extension of the Southern slave system on white Americans in the Northern states and western territories. Lincoln clearly believed that slavery was fundamentally immoral because it deprived slaves of the just economic rewards they earned from their labor. At Peoria on October 16, 1854, an impassioned Lincoln decried "the spread of slavery . . . because of the monstrous injustice of slavery itself." He was not averse to criticizing the slave system or its adherents, for slavery violated the founding fathers' belief in the individual right to freely engage in the pursuit of happiness: "I hate it because it deprives our republican example of its just influence in the world—enables the enemies of free institutions, with plausibility, to taunt us as hypocrites—causes the real friends of freedom to doubt our sincerity, and especially because it forces so many really good men among ourselves into an open war with the very fundamental principles of civil liberty—criticizing the Declaration of Independence, and insisting that there is no right principle of action but *self-interest.*"

The Peoria speech—with its extraordinary emphasis on America's responsibility to inspire the expansion of democracy worldwide—signaled Lincoln's reentry into politics as a major figure in the emerging Republican Party of Illinois. Between 1854 and 1858, he traveled the state to rally support for himself and his views with a continuing emphasis on the largely economic argument presented in his Peoria speech. In 1858 Lincoln captured the Republican nomination to oppose Democrat Stephen Douglas for the US Senate seat from Illinois. In an immediately controversial, and justly famous, speech accepting the Republican designation, Lincoln threw down the gauntlet not only to Douglas but also to the slave states and all supporters of compromise:

> Under the operation of the policy of compromise, the agitation has not only *not ceased*, but has *constantly augmented*.
>
> In *my* opinion it *will* not cease, until a *crisis* shall have been reached, and passed.
>
> "A house divided against itself cannot stand."
>
> I believe this government cannot endure, permanently half *slave* and half *free*.
>
> I do not expect the Union to be *dissolved*—I do not expect the house to *fall*—but I *do* expect it will cease to be divided.
>
> It will become *all* one thing or *all* the other.
>
> Either the *opponents* of slavery, will arrest the further spread of it, and place it where the public mind shall rest in the belief that it is in the course of ultimate extinction; or its *advocates* will push it forward, till it shall become alike lawful in *all* the States, *old* as well as *new*—*North* as well as *South*.

Lincoln on April 25, 1858, the year of his legendary
senatorial campaign debates with Stephen A. Douglas, as photographed by Samuel Alschuler in Quincy,
Illinois. Alschuler thought Lincoln's coat unsuitable
for a rising political leader and lent his subject his own
velvet-trimmed jacket to pose. LIBRARY OF CONGRESS

As Lincoln put it, "Have we no tendency to the latter condition?"
Here he referred to the Southern effort to extend slavery based on the
Supreme Court decision in the *Dred Scott* case in 1857, which gave
slaveholders the "right" to take their human property everywhere in
the United States without restriction. That decision forbade Congress
and local legislatures from banning slavery in the western territories.
Lincoln was reminding his audience that unless its geographic spread
was restricted, the Southern economic, social, and political system was
threatening to expand nationwide immediately. Here he was speaking
not just for a faction of the Republican Party, but for the large body of
outraged Republicans who believed that Douglas and his compatriots
in Congress were engaged in a "conspiracy" to make slavery "perpetual,
national and universal."

Throughout the summer and fall of 1858, in their widely publicized debates across Illinois, Lincoln and Douglas clashed repeatedly
over popular sovereignty, the *Dred Scott* decision, the extension of slavery, the dire warnings in Lincoln's "house divided" speech, and one

Lincoln-Douglas debate at Charleston, Illinois—at which Lincoln insisted he believed in equal opportunity, but not yet in equality of the races. Douglas, an unrepentant race-baiter, can be seen at Lincoln's right. The scene was envisioned by artist Robert Marshall Root, who was born ten years after the event. ABRAHAM LINCOLN PRESIDENTIAL LIBRARY AND MUSEUM—ALPLM

issue that the Democrats repeatedly denounced and the Republicans consistently deflected: equal rights for blacks.

For Lincoln and the vast majority of his fellow Republicans, the extension of slavery remained an issue that principally concerned white people in the North. Black slavery was tolerable, if hateful, where it had long existed, below the Mason-Dixon line and east of the Mississippi River. There the Constitution protected it. But when it expanded into the new territories, it threatened to limit opportunity for free white labor in a growing nation. Knowing they could not appeal to mainstream white voters by inviting sympathy for oppressed blacks at a time when even freedmen generally lacked the right to vote, Republicans like Lincoln often expressed their opposition to slavery by stressing that it poisoned white citizens' opportunities to succeed in life. As Lincoln warned his audience of Northern white voters, the "greedy chase to make profit of the negro" could "'cancel and tear to pieces' even the white man's charter of freedom." Slavery's effect on the enslaved was never his primary public consideration, although to his credit Lincoln did insist, throughout his debates with Douglas, that blacks were inalienably entitled to the pursuit of happiness.

He reiterated this position during the Lincoln-Douglas debates: "I have no purpose to introduce political and social equality between the white and black races." This sentiment placed him squarely within prevailing white sensibilities of the day, however regressive they sound in the twenty-first century. What elevated Lincoln above the prejudices of most of his contemporaries was this insistence: "But in the right to eat the bread, without leave of anybody else, which his own hand earns, *he is my equal and the equal of Judge Douglas, and the equal of every living man.*"

Lincoln further argued that there should be a moral core to American economic democracy—that every person, black or white, deserved to benefit from the fruits of his labor. Slavery was morally wrong, both repugnant to the ideals of the Declaration of Independence and alien to the founders' concept of natural rights, which included the right to economic opportunity. Even though slavery's existence in the United States was acknowledged in the Constitution, the expectation that it would, in the long run, cease to exist had been acknowledged by the framers with the abolition of the slave trade. Lincoln argued both that slavery was immoral and that preventing any extension of slavery to the western territories was necessary to reaffirm the commitment to a national future free of slavery and open to economic opportunity for white Americans. This was politically astute. It gave Lincoln an argument against slavery that did not explicitly run counter to the majority opinion of Northern whites that African Americans were inferior and therefore not entitled to all the same rights as white Americans.

The wildly popular Lincoln-Douglas debates established Lincoln as a significant figure in the leadership of the Republican Party and familiarized people with the party's platform. The disappointing result was still a promising one for the fledgling Republican Party. Lincoln and Republican candidates statewide won a bit more of the popular vote. But Senate elections were then decided by state legislatures, Douglas kept his Senate seat in Illinois, and Lincoln himself was catapulted onto the national stage.

Lincoln's ambition was not deflected by his failure to win the Senate seat in 1858. Wisely, he decided to take advantage of the publicity-generating debate of ideas with Douglas. He understood that his best hope of keeping his name alive was to continue as if nothing had really been decided by the Senate election, especially since Lincoln's party had won the popular vote.

Douglas unknowingly facilitated Lincoln's rebuttal efforts with an inflammatory article in *Harper's New Monthly Magazine* in September 1859. In one sense, Douglas's piece presented a response to the "house divided" arguments "advocated and defended by the distinguished Republican standard bearer" in the Lincoln-Douglas debates. Douglas continued to insist that it revealed Lincoln as inviting civil war over slavery. The article also gave Lincoln the opportunity to claim an increasingly important place in the political hierarchy. Lincoln was able to claim that Douglas had put Lincoln's argument that "this government 'cannot endure permanently half slave and half free'" on a par with the argument of the leading Republican aspirant to the presidency, Senator William H. Seward of New York, who foresaw "an 'irrepressible conflict' between the principles of free and slave labor." Now, Lincoln could boast that Douglas believed that Seward and Lincoln were equally important when he described them as equally guilty of seeing "no truce in the sectional strife," because they refused to accept the Union as the founders had created it: "divided into free and slave States."

The publicly combative Lincoln-Douglas relationship flared up again when, hungry for the Democratic nomination for president in 1860, the senator marched into Ohio in September 1859 to deliver speeches on behalf of local candidates. Douglas continued advocating popular sovereignty in speeches throughout Ohio. Worried Ohio Republicans asked Lincoln to provide a counterweight. Not surprisingly, Lincoln packed his bags and headed to the Buckeye State, acting as if he was resuming his debates with Douglas. He spoke in Columbus on September 16 and then went on to Dayton and Cincinnati. On October 9, in Cincinnati, Douglas replied: "Did you ever hear a Republican that dissented from Lincoln's warnings of a house divided?" Lincoln replied on October 17: "We want, and must have, a national policy, as to slavery, which deals with it as being a wrong." The battle was never drawn more sharply. Douglas persisted in attempting to portray Lincoln as a radical threat to national unity, while Lincoln was painting his Democratic rival as a reactionary threat to national moral principles and economic opportunity for all.

An exhausted Lincoln returned to Springfield on October 15. The night before his arrival home, voters in Ohio and many other states across the country went to the polls in contests for governor and other statewide offices. Republicans triumphed not only in Ohio, but also in Pennsylvania, Indiana, Iowa, and Minnesota. Lincoln was welcomed home from his successful campaign in Ohio by several hundred cheering Republicans and a brass band serenading him from the street. To his ardent supporters, Lincoln had not only saved the day for the advocates of the Free Soil position—those who believed in the moral and economic superiority of the free labor system—but also emerged as an important regional, perhaps national, spokesman for the Republican Party and its point of view.

Among the pile of letters waiting for Lincoln at home was a telegram with an invitation to deliver yet another speech, this time in New York. Lincoln at once understood that it offered an opportunity to advance his ambitions to office at the national level. After all, his latest regional efforts in support of the Republican Party had been a success. He had boldly followed the leading national Democratic presidential candidate to Ohio to continue the Lincoln-Douglas debate over the major issue that divided not only them but the rest of the country: the extension of slavery. Ohio had gone Republican in 1859 by seventeen thousand votes. It was reasonable to believe the tide was turning on the issue and that Lincoln himself could claim some responsibility for it.

An ambitious, ingenious politician who hungered for a return to elective office, Lincoln knew that the biggest prize of all, the presidency of the United States, would be decided only a year down the road. He sensed that Senator Douglas would likely become the Democratic candidate for the White House in 1860. Now, amid the excitement of Lincoln's return from his successful speaking tour in Ohio, it suddenly seemed possible that the Republican candidate for president might actually beat Douglas in 1860. Improbable as it seemed just a few hours before the election results had filtered in from across the country in 1859, Lincoln now had substantial reason to imagine himself that candidate. And here was an invitation to introduce himself where he was least known: in New York, the heart of the vote-rich East.

The invitation to speak in New York suggested the date of November 29, 1859. But Lincoln, ever the savvy politician, asked for a later date, closer to the Republican National Convention, scheduled for May 1860. The negotiations proved successful, and the date for his New York address was rescheduled to February 27, 1860.

Lincoln was a deliberate politician. He was totally committed to his continuing effort to achieve high office as a way to prove to himself, as well as to others, that he was worthy of high regard. Losing an election or failing to secure a nomination only spurred him to continue his efforts in the next election. But personal ambition was not his only motivation. Lincoln was determined to make a difference, to leave a lasting legacy to future generations of Americans. The issue on which he believed he could influence both politics and history was economic opportunity for all, and slavery was the stubborn impediment to his long-standing belief in that cause. The person who knew Lincoln best, his law partner, William H. Herndon, captured these two facets of Lincoln's life in a private letter written in 1866. "I love Mr. Lincoln dearly, almost worship him," Herndon wrote. "He's the purest politician I ever saw, and the justest man."

On a purely political level, Lincoln recognized that his speech in New York might propel him into contention for the Republican nomination for the presidency of the United States. He focused on writing the speech as if preparing an argument in a court of law before a jury of his peers.

Lincoln's first task was to define the issue of the impending election on his own terms. He had already said in the Lincoln-Douglas debates all there was to say about the moral, economic, and philosophical issues underlying the debate over the extension of slavery to the territories. For this speech in New York, he decided to confront the claim of Douglas and other Democrats, North and South, that the framers of the Constitution had not taken a position on the morality of slavery and had expressly said the federal government should take no actions to regulate its future. Douglas had made this the central point of his recent article in *Harper's New Monthly Magazine*.

Superb advocate that he was, Lincoln proceeded to direct all his talents to making a case for his position. First, he thoroughly researched the question of what each of the signers of the Constitution really said and did on the slavery question, both before and after the constitutional convention. The more Lincoln researched, the more framers he determined to have been opposed to the extension of slavery. Washington, for one, had said that slavery could indeed be controlled by "legislative authority" and had expressed his personal conviction, "There is no man living who wishes more sincerely than I do to see a plan adopted for the abolition of it." By his estimation— flawed and oversimplified though it may have been—Lincoln calculated that of the thirty-nine signers of the Constitution who expressed any opinion on the subject, twenty-three had clearly indicated that they believed the federal government had the power to regulate slavery.

With no researchers to assist him, no professional scholars to unearth documents, and no private secretary to take dictation, Lincoln sought his own access to history. Never in his life did Lincoln labor over an address so strenuously, over such an extended period of time, and in the face of major ongoing political and business distractions that competed for his precious time.

Working to develop arguments that would connect his newly assembled facts into a coherent narrative, Lincoln hit upon a novel device. The best way to present the fruits of his research was to make the facts themselves the core of his speech. Douglas might try to convince the public that the federal government had no right to control slavery in the federal territories, "[B]ut he has no right," Lincoln wrote in his draft, "to mislead others, who have less access to history, and less leisure to study it, into the false belief that the founders believed any such thing."

Six days before his scheduled speech in New York, the *Chicago Tribune*, the most influential newspaper in Illinois, endorsed Lincoln for president. He was no longer just a potential candidate for the nomination; he was now his state's favorite son.

Almost as if to welcome him to the city, Horace Greeley's newspaper, the *New York Tribune,* provided a two-column life story of the speaker together with an announcement of his scheduled speech at Cooper Union. Never particularly impressed by Lincoln—they had served together briefly in Congress more than a decade earlier—Greeley was suddenly viewing the visiting orator not just as a spokesman for free labor, but as a living example of its promise. The seeds of a legend—the self-made rail splitter—were taking shape. The biographical sketch praised Lincoln for "hard work and plenty of it, the rugged experiences of aspiring poverty . . . the education born of the log-cabin." He had evolved into the remarkable Republican whose party had outpolled Stephen Douglas's Democrats in the senatorial race in Illinois less than two years ago. "Such is Abraham Lincoln, emphatically a man of the people," trumpeted the *Tribune,* "a champion of Free Labor, of diversified and prosperous industry, and of that policy which leads through peaceful progress to universal intelligence, virtue and freedom."

Lincoln's mission at Cooper Union, now that he had been endorsed at home as a presidential candidate, was to defeat two formidable potential opponents at the same time: Senator William H. Seward of New York, the prevailing favorite for the Republican presidential nomination, and Senator Stephen A. Douglas of Illinois, the presumptive Democratic opponent in the general election. Lincoln surely understood too that the Cooper Union address would be his last major political speech both before and after the Republican nominating convention in May. If he were to win the nomination, Lincoln knew that the prevailing political culture dictated that he should remain silent until after the national election.

When Lincoln began to speak at Cooper Union in New York on February 27, 1860, the stakes could not have been higher. But Lincoln rose to the challenge, pointedly reminding the audience that the real issue remained the extension of slavery. Almost immediately, he quoted the words Douglas had used to support his argument for compromise on slavery: *"Our fathers, when they framed the Government under which we live, understood this question just as well, and even better, than we do now."* The orator then surprised his audience, declaring, "I fully endorse this." He was perfectly willing for the great divisive issue of the day to be left to the founders. Lincoln was prepared to describe their true views. Douglas had introduced them as expert witnesses. Lincoln, in rebuttal, proceeded to recite their history on slavery extension from the days of the early Republic.

As an initially dubious, eventually mesmerized crowd listened with increased attentiveness, Lincoln drew from his vast arsenal of historical data, legalistic argumentation, and rhetorical flourish to offer three distinct speeches in one: an appeal to history, a criticism of the South, and a rallying cry aimed at his natural constituency—Northern Republicans.

In the speech's first section, Lincoln invoked the memory of the founding fathers, harnessing their implicit endorsement for his antislavery position by offering a staggering quantity of historical data about the views of the majority of the founders in support of the power of the federal government to restrict the spread of slavery. Implicitly, he invited personal endorsements of Lincoln himself for his ability to master the nuances of the historical investigation.

Lincoln cited the words of George Washington, Thomas Jefferson, Alexander Hamilton, and Benjamin Franklin and reported on the views of the less memorable founding fathers as well. In a brilliant display of lawyerly technique and witty argumentation, Lincoln demonstrated that Douglas and the Democrats were tampering with the lessons of "our fathers." The orator reminded his audience again and again that the founding fathers understood the slavery issue better than Douglas and other American Democratic politicians in 1860. Lincoln said the founders supported the elimination of the slave trade, thus preventing any new importing of slaves into the United States. And he reminded his fellow Republicans that preventing the extension of slavery to the western territories would provide new economic opportunities for white people who chose to settle in the territories.

In Lincoln's widely reported speech accepting the Senate nomination two years earlier, the message "a house divided against itself cannot stand" had been biblical: slavery was doomed according to the word of God as revealed in the books of Matthew and Mark. Now at Cooper Union, he was documenting that slavery was doomed by the

Lincoln as he looked the day of his career-transforming "right makes might" Cooper Union address in New York City, February 27, 1860, photographed just hours before by Mathew B. Brady at his Broadway gallery. LIBRARY OF CONGRESS

word of the secular gods of the American Dream, the founding fathers, the architects of what he had once dubbed America's civil religion.

In the second part of his speech, while ostensibly asking Southerners for patience, peace, and understanding, he seasoned his conciliatory words with an implicit warning: if disaffection led to disunion, it would be the fault of a hostile South, not a tolerant North (especially if the country was led by moderates like Lincoln).

Then in the third part, Lincoln turned his attention to his fellow Republicans and, in a majestic coda, urged them never to abandon the very principles that were unnerving Southerners in the first place. Lincoln brought his argument back from scholarly historical fact to emotional fervor, making the positive case for his antislavery position. Lincoln said, "Neither let us be slandered from our duty by false accusations against us, nor frightened from it by menaces of destruction to the Government. . . . LET US HAVE FAITH THAT

RIGHT MAKES MIGHT, AND IN THAT FAITH, LET US, TO THE END, DARE TO DO OUR DUTY AS WE UNDERSTAND IT."

The Cooper Union address was at one and the same time calm and impassioned, argumentative and scholarly, moderate in tone but accompanied by a forceful statement of moral purpose, and a clear vision of justice animated by the confident expectation that it would prevail. Lincoln used the occasion to present himself, as his future secretary John G. Nicolay would put it, as "yielding and accommodating in non-essentials" and "inflexibly firm in a principle or position deliberately taken."

The editor of the *New York Times,* Henry J. Raymond, a Seward loyalist, was convinced that the "pre-eminent ability" Lincoln displayed at Cooper Union "compelled" easterners to acknowledge him as not only a leader among westerners, but a national figure as well. Greeley's *Tribune* agreed that "the speech of Abraham Lincoln . . . was one of the happiest and most convincing political arguments ever made in the city." And William Cullen Bryant's antislavery *New York Evening Post* headlined its recap "The Framers of the Constitution in Favor of Slavery Prohibition; The Republican Party Vindicated; Great Speech of Hon. Abraham Lincoln."

Lincoln emerged from New York a legitimate alternative to Seward for the Republican presidential nomination. Overnight, he achieved his goal of challenging both Republican Seward and Democrat Douglas for the ultimate prize. What was more, overnight reports of his Cooper Union triumph in the New York dailies inspired a series of invitations to speak in other northeastern states. On his way to see his son Robert at Phillips Exeter Academy in New Hampshire, Lincoln stopped to make eleven more speeches, in Connecticut, Rhode Island, and New Hampshire. Recycling the core of his Cooper Union address, Lincoln unfailingly reassured his audiences that their cause would prevail by invoking the rallying cry he had introduced in New York: "Let us have faith that right makes might."

"Right makes might" summed up his new presidential-year argument against the extension of slavery. Lincoln was cannily suggesting that the peculiar institution would thus peacefully fade away. He was now preaching a more optimistic approach than the fatalistic inevitability of a national conflagration implicit in the "house divided" speech. Arguably, there was no real space between the two visions. But the rallying cry "Right makes might" struck a more positive note, summoning the original intent of the founding fathers to justify placing slavery once more "in the course of ultimate extinction" by curbing its spread and reaffirming economic opportunity as the core value of American democracy, a society committed to the rejection of the Southern idea that people should remain in fixed positions in life.

Lincoln made this view more explicit in some of his subsequent orations on his post–Cooper Union speaking tour in New England. The "'equality of man' principle which actuated our forefathers" was "right," he declared at Hartford, and "slavery, being directly opposed to this," was "wrong." And in New Haven, site of a controversial labor strike at a shoe factory, he added, "What is the true condition of the laborer? I take it that it is best for all to leave each man free to acquire property as fast as he can. Some will get wealthy. I don't believe in a law to prevent a man from getting rich; it would do more harm than good." And then he offered his most direct synthesis of his economic beliefs: "I want every man to have a chance—and I believe a black man is entitled to it—in which he *can* better his condition—when he may look forward and hope to be a hired laborer this year and the next, work for himself afterward, and finally to hire men to work for him! That is the true system."

Within hours of his return from the East, Lincoln learned that his Cooper Union speech would be printed in pamphlet form by his hometown newspaper. And the Springfield daily was not alone. Lincoln's speech was also printed in pamphlet form by the *New York Tribune* and the *Chicago Tribune* and was quoted widely by other Republican-oriented newspapers. More important, Republican politicians everywhere began speaking with one voice, identifying antislavery with the founders, attacking the *Dred Scott* decision, and drawing a dividing line on slavery extension. Lincoln was not the only Republican candidate who defined the issues this way, but he was frequently credited with having said it best. As the *New York Tribune* reported, "Mr. Lincoln's is probably the most systematic and complete defense yet made of the Republican position with regard to slavery."

Lincoln exhibited exceptional tactical skills during his campaign for the presidential nomination. He knew the view that slavery should be abolished immediately was held by only a minority of Americans. He believed that calling for immediate abolition would keep him from being nominated for the presidency, preclude him from taking action as president to put slavery "in the course of ultimate extinction," and prevent him from undertaking federal government initiatives based on his economic philosophy. While he continued to say that slavery was immoral and eventually needed to die out, he did not call for its immediate abolition. Lincoln said the federal government had the power to ban the extension of slavery to the western territories. But he accepted the constitutional provision that prevented the federal government from interfering with slavery in the existing slave states.

After adopting a platform that called for free labor and free land, immigrant rights, internal improvements, and no extension of slavery, the delegates to the Republican National Convention commenced their voting for a presidential nominee in Chicago on May 18, 1860. The convention, conveniently located in Lincoln's home state of Illinois, was packed with wildly cheering Lincoln enthusiasts who had used counterfeit tickets to elbow out Seward men from the galleries. The first ballot gave Seward 170½ votes, Lincoln 102, Pennsylvania senator Simon Cameron 50½, Senator Salmon P. Chase of Ohio 49, and elder statesman Edward Bates of Missouri 48. The surprise came in both Seward's failure to get close to the 233 votes needed for the nomination and Lincoln's strong second-place showing. Lincoln had won the unanimous support of the western delegations of Illinois and Indiana. Equally important, New Hampshire and Connecticut, states where Lincoln had spoken only a few months earlier, gave more votes to Lincoln than to Seward. On the second ballot, Seward gained only 11 votes, while Lincoln gained 79 from New Hampshire, Rhode Island, Ohio, and Pennsylvania. The second ballot ended in a virtual tie between Seward, with 184½ votes, and Lincoln, with 181. The trend seemed irreversible. The convention proceeded immediately to a third ballot. When Lincoln handily won the nomination on this final delegate count, the "wildest enthusiasm" erupted inside the Wigwam convention center.

Almost from the moment he became the Republican candidate, Lincoln decided to follow the accepted tradition to make no further speeches. He would not "write, or speak anything upon doctrinal points." He even assigned to an aide the task of sending form letters in response to all requests for his political opinions, emphasizing that his "positions were well known when he was nominated." Lincoln had worked hard in the Lincoln-Douglas debates and in his Cooper Union address to make the case against the extension of slavery. He did not want to open the door to new interpretations of new words that were not as carefully crafted as his original speeches.

Instead, Lincoln built his 1860 campaign for the presidency on his well-known uncompromising rejection of any expansion of the Southern economic, social, and political system. Silence spoke louder than words: he offered no new assurances to the Southern states and no hope of compromise on these crucial issues. That silence was deafening, especially to Southerners who feared—rightly so—that his election to the presidency would threaten their way of life.

Lincoln was already on record as viewing slavery as "a moral, political and social wrong" that "ought to be treated as a wrong . . . with the fixed idea that it must and will come to the end." That much about him voters already knew. They knew that he had not embraced immediate abolition, knowing, if nothing else, that such a position would have isolated him from mainstream white American voters and rendered him unelectable.

Unalterably opposed to the extension of slavery, Lincoln remained willing to "tolerate" it where it already existed, believing that containment would place it "in the course of ultimate extinction." Lincoln was not alone in sincerely believing that slavery could be destroyed simply by hemming it in where it already existed and isolating the slave states with a border composed both of free states and oceans that no longer bore newly kidnapped slaves from Africa.

Until the catharsis of rebellion made immediate abolition of slavery possible, Lincoln confessed that he thought slavery might exist in some form in Southern states, and without serious challenge, perhaps into the next century. Lincoln would say so himself as late as 1862, three months *after* issuing his Preliminary Emancipation Proclamation. He acknowledged slavery might not completely disappear from America until 1900.

Ultimately, Lincoln and other adherents of the "ultimate extinction" philosophy believed, newly admitted free western states would join the already antislavery North to create a "supermajority" in Congress capable of passing constitutional remedies to eradicate slavery. This is precisely what did happen in 1865, of course, though it took the bloody Civil War and the Emancipation Proclamation issued by the commander in chief finally to set the stage for national abolition through a constitutional amendment.

Lincoln's well-known commitment to prevent the expansion of slavery to the territories proved enough to alarm Southerners. When a worried visitor from New England nonetheless urged him, the very day before the election, to "reassure the men honestly alarmed" over the consequences of his victory, Lincoln hotly explained: "This is the same old trick by which the South breaks down every Northern victory. Even if I were personally willing to barter away the moral principle involved in this contest, for the commercial gain of a new submission to the South, I would go to Washington without the countenance of the men who supported me and were my friends before the election; I would be as powerless as a block of buckeye wood."

As for "those who will not read, or heed, what I have already publicly said," Lincoln insisted, they "would not read, or heed, a repetition of it. He went on to say: "What is it I could say that would quiet alarm? Is it that no interference by the government, with slaves or slavery within the states, is intended? I have said this so often already, that a repetition of it is but mockery, bearing an appearance of weakness, and cowardice."

As the 1860 campaign reached its climax, Lincoln rejected anxious last-minute appeals, from supporters and opponents alike, that he simply assure the South that, if elected, he had no intention of interfering with slavery where it existed. A less astute politician might have regarded such reassurances as pabulum: easy to concoct, easier to swallow. But Lincoln not only maintained his eloquent silence; he spoke out to defend his silence, contending that any policy reiterations would be superfluous, a sign of indecisiveness that could cripple him as president-elect—and as president.

Lincoln relied on his belief that right really could make might. He also relied on the prospects for a successful battle for political success against expansion of the Southern slave-based economic system. To achieve this goal would mean gaining public support for his belief that the future of the nation hinged on acceptance of his animating idea that economic opportunity required a level playing field and an equal chance in the race of life—for all.

Three

CHAIN OF STEEL

DEFENDER OF THE UNION

ABRAHAM LINCOLN WON ELECTION AS PRESIDENT OF THE UNITED States by carrying every Northern state except New Jersey. No candidate—not even Thomas Jefferson in his divisive 1800 race against John Adams—had ever before taken the presidency with such an exclusively regional vote. Lincoln failed to carry a single Southern state—and his name did not even appear on the ballot in ten of them. But even in those Dixie states where voters could vote Republican if they so chose, Lincoln fared disastrously. In Virginia the Lincoln ticket received just 1,929 votes out of 167,223 statewide—barely 1 percent. The result was even more pronounced in his native Kentucky, where only 1,364 out of 146,216 voters, *less* than 1 percent, cast their ballots for the Republican candidate. Lincoln could find some solace in the fact that both of these Upper South states, along with Missouri, at least went for the moderate John Bell rather than the conservative Southern choice, Democrat John C. Breckinridge. As the ominously divided vote confirmed, and just as Southern foes had warned, Lincoln's victory was entirely sectional. The total result gave Lincoln a decisive 54 percent in the North and West, but only 2 percent in the South—the most asymmetrical plurality in American election history. The Northern Democratic candidate, Stephen Douglas, finished in second place in the popular vote, but won almost no electoral votes.

Lincoln's election triggered the secession crisis. One by one, the seven states of the Lower South began to move toward separation from

The *Lincoln Quick-Step*—an 1860 campaign sheet-
music cover by Thomas Sinclair of Philadelphia—
highlighted the Lincolnian virtue of hard work. Note
the scenes (*top and bottom*) of a young Lincoln splitting rails and piloting a flatboat and (*left and right*)
the tools of those humble trades. FROM THE LINCOLN
FINANCIAL FOUNDATION COLLECTION, COURTESY OF
THE ALLEN COUNTY PUBLIC LIBRARY AND INDIANA
STATE MUSEUM AND HISTORIC SITES

the Union. In Washington prominent senators proposed new compromise legislation designed to persuade the Southern states to stay in the
Union by assuring them that the institution of slavery would remain
untouched by the new administration—and all future administrations.

Lacking anything but symbolic power, and with sixteen long weeks
remaining before his inauguration, Lincoln believed he could do nothing official to avert the crisis as long as the lame-duck James Buchanan
administration remained in office. The new president-elect calculated

Lincoln and Douglas in a Presidential Footrace—an 1860 campaign cartoon by J. Sage & Son of Buffalo—shows the long-limbed Republican
candidate proudly toting a rail splitter's maul as he outdistances his
short-legged rival toward the White House. Douglas is saddled with
a bag marked "MC," a reminder of the Missouri Compromise that his
controversial Kansas-Nebraska Act effectively repealed, opening the
American Northwest to slavery. Outraged by that 1854 legislation, Lincoln had come roaring back into politics. LIBRARY OF CONGRESS

that any public comment on his part during this period might prove
fatally dangerous. He was worried that inflammatory statements might
even jeopardize the Electoral College balloting that would make the
November 6 presidential election results official in February.

For generations after 1800, Americans had regarded these sessions
as mere formalities, a kind of postelection coronation devoid of sus-
pense, with each of the 303 "delegates" firmly pledged in advance to
support the ticket on which he had run. But nothing about this interregnum was going according to tradition. Never before had a president-
elect been subjected to so much pressure to pronounce himself on
doctrinal issues before his inauguration. Never before had an entire

section of the country threatened to abandon the United States altogether in response to an election.

Not even the electoral vote could be regarded as pro forma. What if Southern messengers withdrew their votes and threw the required quorum into jeopardy? What if the "fire-eaters" disrupted the meeting of electors—or, worse, prevented the votes from being counted or the vote from taking place at all?

For better or worse, Lincoln concluded that whatever he might say would unavoidably alarm at least part of the country in such a way that he might not be able to govern when he took office. Soothing words of reassurance on the constitutional rights of slaveholders might inflame Northern Republicans who had just voted for him with the expectation that he would limit the spread of slavery. Defiant pronouncements on the sanctity of the Union would probably arouse Southern Democrats who had not voted for him and for whom anything less than substantial conciliation amounted to coercion. To Lincoln, saying nothing was preferable to saying too much.

Lincoln likely believed, too, that expending political capital too early in the national arena might render him less effective when he took over the government in March. Historians who have suggested that he misjudged the growing crisis by exaggerating Union sentiment in the South have both overestimated his legal and political ability to allay the growing panic and underestimated Lincoln's logic-driven conviction that the best time to confront the secession crisis directly was after his inauguration.

But that is not to suggest that Lincoln was unaware of the severity of the secession crisis. Indeed, as his private statements during the so-called secession winter make clear, it was very much on his mind, if not his chief concern. "I feel constrained, for the present, at least, to make no declaration for the public," he said on November 10, 1860, in defense of his silence. Convinced that any such "declaration" might undo the perilous balance under which he had just been voted into office, he refused to modify the policy of restraint that had won him the election in the first place. Still fearful that he might embolden his foes by appearing weak or worried, and recognizing that the all-important Electoral College would not cast its votes for president for another three months and must not be impeded or threatened, Lincoln further justified his position this way: "I could say nothing which I have not already said, and which is in print, and open for the inspection of all. To press a repetition of this upon those who *have* listened, is useless; to press it upon those who have *refused* to listen, and still refuse, would be wanting in self-respect." Lincoln's views had been fully expressed in the recently published Lincoln-Douglas debates, the Cooper Union address, and the Republican Party platform. Popular sovereignty was dead. Under no circumstances would his new government allow slavery to spread into the West.

There was little danger Lincoln could forget, even for a moment, the pressures that continued mounting for an official preinaugural statement. "Every newspaper he opened was filled with clear indications of an impending national catastrophe," journalist Henry Villard observed from Springfield, Illinois. "Every mail brought him written, and every hour verbal, entreaties to abandon his paralyzed silence, repress untimely feelings of delicacy, and pour the oil of conciliatory conservative assurances upon the turbulent waves of Southern excitement."

But still Lincoln would not speak, believing that while he yet enjoyed no power to govern, he did possess significant potential for sparking further discontent through anything he might now declare. Lincoln believed he had as much to fear from dissatisfaction among his Northern allies as from secession-minded Southern fire-eaters. As if to punctuate that danger, black abolitionist leader Frederick Douglass, speaking in Boston on December 3, declared with impolitic frankness: "I want the slaveholders to be made uncomfortable. . . . I rejoice in every uprising in the South." How could Lincoln reply to such a provocative statement without either offending abolitionists with his condemnation or frightening pro-Union Southerners with a positive comment?

In fact, Lincoln did not remain entirely silent during those tense weeks, however. Convinced as he was of the validity of this position, Lincoln knew disaster would follow if wavering border Southern states came to regard him as pro–equal rights. In one private letter to Henry J. Raymond, the influential pro-Republican editor of the *New York*

Times, he did separate himself from the "radical" abolitionist view in support of racial equality. Speaking in the third person, he wrote, "Mr. Lincoln is not pledged to the ultimate extinctinction [*sic*] of slavery." He went on to say that he "does not hold the black man to be the equal of the white, unqualifiedly . . . and never did stigmatize their white people as immoral & unchristian." Lincoln fully expected the *New York Times* to present his views to the public without attribution.

Judged by modern attitudes on race, of course, this was not Lincoln's finest moment. But it was true to his long-expressed belief that the Constitution did not permit direct action to abolish slavery where it existed in the Southern and border states and with certainty did not provide the president or the Congress with the federal power to mandate civil or legal equality for African Americans.

Lincoln's public silence was tested yet again when he received the news that Congress, which convened in December, might appropriate to itself a legislative compromise to avert secession. This unsettled Lincoln. The president-in-waiting wanted nothing less than for a lame-duck House and Senate to enact policy that would bind the new administration, especially if it permitted slavery to expand westward in violation of the 1860 Republican platform and if that policy arrogated powers Lincoln believed he was elected to exercise, and certainly not if it left future decisions on slavery to local constituencies, in total disregard of his determined opposition to popular sovereignty.

Keeping the western territories open to limitless opportunity for free white labor—and free of slaves—had been Lincoln's holy grail since 1854, the year Douglas had engineered passage of the Kansas-Nebraska Act. In Lincoln's mind, his position on the Free Soil issue had gotten him elected in November and bound him to that policy for the future. Now, to his dismay, before he began his presidency, he sensed congressional Republicans might entertain softening the party's opposition to slavery extension in return for guarantees against secession.

Lincoln could easily have decided to accept a congressional compromise that might keep the country intact, to support a revival of the old Missouri Compromise line that would allow slavery to migrate into the Southwest. Or he could draw his own line in the sand and oppose compromise entirely.

For Lincoln, drawing a line in the sand was the only choice he was willing to make. But even so, he remained unwilling to do so publicly. Privately, Lincoln decided to engage in unprecedented activity to prevent, even sabotage, any compromise solutions that would allow for the expansion of slavery. His letter to Henry Raymond was only the first of many such efforts. Making his feelings known only in private letters to loyal senators and congressmen, the president-elect insisted that Republicans hold fast to party principles and do nothing that might open the popular-sovereignty debate afresh. He especially did not want to give Southerners the hope that they might use their legislative power to extend slavery to territory west of the Mississippi or even by acquiring new territory in Cuba or elsewhere in the Caribbean.

When William H. Seward, Lincoln's first choice to lead his cabinet as secretary of state, began to make noises from Washington about bending to the compromisers, Lincoln fired off a confidential letter that made his unwavering position clearer than ever (even if it still remained only privately expressed). Lincoln was preoccupied with the early stages of composing his Inaugural Address, but he knew an existential threat when he faced one. He realized at once how crucial it was to assume leadership of the national party even in absentia, even without formal office, and even with private, not public, communication. So he wrote to Seward to clear up once and for all the issue of whether he was prepared to accept the expansion of slavery in return for peace and union. He was, he wrote, "inflexible," explaining, "I am for no compromise which *assists* or *permits* the extension of the institution on soil owned by the nation. And any trick by which the nation is to acquire territory, and then allow some local authority to spread slavery over it, is as obnoxious as any other. I take it that to effect some such result as this, and to put us again on the high-road to a slave empire is the object of all these proposed compromises. I am against it."

Thus, Lincoln began injecting himself quietly but forcefully into the debate on Capitol Hill to ensure that there would be no additional compromise on the issue of extending slavery to the western territories. As self-conscious as he had been about assuming control of the secession crisis, Lincoln had in fact done just that. No previous president-elect ever made such a show of power and influence before his swearing in. The politically astute Lincoln still delivered no public speeches and issued no state papers on the compromise issue; to do so, he believed, would only exacerbate matters by angering both antislavery men and border-state conservatives. Instead, he made his views clear in many more remarkably tough private letters to key allies on Capitol Hill, which he probably knew would be widely shared with other Republicans.

In a letter to his friend Senator Lyman Trumbull of Illinois, Lincoln left little doubt where he stood. "Let there be no compromise on the question of *extending* slavery," came the pointed instructions. "If there be, all our labor is lost, and, ere long, must be done again. The dangerous ground—that into which some of our friends have a hankering to run—is Pop[ular]. Sov[reignty]. Have none of it. Stand firm. The tug has to come, & better now, than any time hereafter." The very next day, Lincoln employed the same emphatic phrase in a similar message to Illinois congressman William Kellogg, who had joined the new House committee seeking "the remedy for the present difficulties." Reiterated Lincoln: "The tug has to come & better now than later."

The president made the same line-in-the-sand point to Republican congressman Elihu Washburne, insisting that he would not bend on the crucial issue of slavery expansion. What was more, as the head of the Republican Party, he expected support from others. His self-assurance on manifest display, Lincoln reiterated on December 13: "Prevent, as far as possible, any of our friends from demoralizing themselves, and our cause, by entertaining propositions for compromise of any sort, on '*slavery extention.*' There is no possible compromise upon it, but which puts us under again, and leaves all our work to do over again." For good measure, the president-elect reminded New York State Republican boss Thurlow Weed: "My opinion is that no state can, in any way lawfully, get out of the Union, without the consent of the others; and that it is the duty of the President, and other government functionaries to run the machine as it is." No doubt he expected that Weed and his ally Henry Raymond, editor of the *New York Times,* would make this view known and that Raymond would endorse it in his newspaper. Publication of such an editorial in the *New York Times* would be perceived as the official view of the upcoming administration.

In the middle of December, that "machine" finally stopped functioning. The long-feared South Carolina secession convention opened in Charleston on December 17. Three days later, in an atmosphere of defiant celebration, delegates to the convention chose the course of secession, formally adopting an ordinance to take South Carolina out of the Union and "resume a separate, equal rank among nations." Over the next nineteen days, while Lincoln watched from Springfield and Congress debated compromises that no longer seemed to matter, six more Southern states held referenda and elected delegates to secession conventions of their own: Mississippi, Florida, Alabama, Georgia, Louisiana, and Texas. The momentum unleashed in South Carolina became impossible to contain. Secession fever had grown incurable.

Although congressional maneuvering continued through the month in Washington, by late December meaningful compromise solutions appeared doomed. Lincoln had achieved his objectives. "Compromise has gone up the spout," one newspaper reported on December 28, the day before a crucial vote. "The compromisers go about the street like mourners." Any new constitutional amendment required approval of two-thirds of the House and Senate, and it seemed highly unlikely that enough Northern Republicans would support a compromise package to send it on to the states.

In the end, Congress failed fully to heed Lincoln's admonitions. Despite the warnings and clear signs that secession could not be averted, legislative leaders kept busy exploring compromises. Seeking refuge in a last-minute proposal advanced by an ad hoc "Peace Convention" that brought to Washington a collection of fossil politicians from many (but not all) the states, the House and Senate offered a token to the Southern states in the form of a proposed new amendment to the Constitution. It merely banned future congressional action to end slavery where it existed. Lincoln would later dutifully send it to the states, so the amendment proposal represented something of a political victory for the president-elect, one he could point to later as proof of his efforts to tolerate reasonable conciliation as long as it did not include the expansion of slavery. Although the amendment had no chance of ratification, it represented a sincere effort to forestall the crisis by codifying Lincoln's oft-repeated vow not to interfere with slavery where it already existed.

While the debates continued into January, Lincoln took up his pen to write a deeply felt private manifesto of principle that he shared with absolutely no one. It confirms Lincoln's steadfast determination to preserve the permanence of the Union as the basis for extending the promise of economic opportunity. He had thought much about this question during the secession crisis, pondering concepts that went well beyond the planks of the Republican platform he so often cited. The result was an appeal not just to reason but also to emotion, a heartfelt justification for resisting any compromise that reneged on the original promise of the American Dream.

Lincoln began his statement by referring to the nation's outstanding economic growth since its founding: "Without the *Constitution* and the *Union*, we could not have attained the result; but even these, are not the primary cause of our great prosperity. There is something back of these, entwining itself more closely about the human heart. That something, is the principle of 'Liberty to all'—the principle that clears the *path* for all—gives *hope* to all—and, by consequence, *enterprize*, and *industry* to all." Lincoln was determined to sustain the survival of a government that "clears the path for all" to take advantage of the opportunities offered by the Northern economic system.

Lincoln's private musings, political statements, and political maneuvering make it clear that the incoming chief magistrate remained morally and politically committed to the democratic middle-class society of the Northern states. He was viscerally opposed to the aristocratic alternative in the Southern states and thus rejected the rationale for the political compromises advanced between the sections during the decade preceding the Civil War. Lincoln was determined that the new states to be admitted to the Union would have a political, social, and economic structure consistent with that of the Northern states rather than the Southern states. It was this determination that formed the basis for his willingness to engage in the Civil War. It was this determination that poet Ralph Waldo Emerson commemorated when he said in his eulogy to Abraham Lincoln in 1865: "This middle-class country had got a middle-class President, at last."

This determination would also serve Lincoln well as he faced an unprecedented challenge on the eve of his inauguration. Lincoln had spent the months between his election in November 1860 and his inauguration in March 1861 ensuring that his supporters would block congressional efforts at compromise. Throughout the secession winter, Lincoln had remained steadfast in his commitment to prevent any extension of slavery. The states of the Lower South were equally uncompromising. When Lincoln boarded the train that would take him out of Springfield toward Washington on February 11, 1861, one crisis had passed, while another loomed even larger. Virtually the entire Deep South—South Carolina, Mississippi, Florida, Alabama, Georgia, Louisiana, and Texas—had seceded from the Union. While Lincoln's election had itself been the trigger, his silence added to the determination of Southern leaders to protect their way of life at all costs. Even before Lincoln departed for his inauguration, they had formed a separate government and chosen its president: former US senator from Mississippi Jefferson Davis.

As he headed east, Lincoln began to accept the idea that armed conflict might be required to protect political democracy, economic opportunity, and what he perceived as the national destiny. Southern secession based on what Lincoln believed to be an unjust defense of human slavery and the right to continue it forever was threatening the existing national order, majority rule, and the sanctity of the law.

Still only president-elect, with no formal power to enforce national authority but on the move at last, Lincoln now began responding to the secession crisis in the way he knew best: through oratory. Compelled for the first time since 1860 to speak in public as his journey took him eastward, and then southward toward Washington, with more than a hundred scheduled stops along the way, secession was uppermost on his mind, but he pointedly refrained from acknowledging it directly. Instead, he insisted on "adherence to the Union and the Constitution." Lincoln used the occasions not to pronounce new policy (this must be withheld, by custom, until his Inaugural Address), but to employ humor, assurance, and a purposefully benign confidence in the future.

Lincoln knew the challenge of the "seceding" states was insurmountable as long as he refused conciliation that accepted the expansion of slavery. In a new kind of speech for him—short and almost elegiac, the harbinger of his future rhetorical style—he told his Springfield neighbors before boarding the train that he had "a task before me greater than that which rested upon Washington," an astounding claim in an age in which no living politician dared compare himself to the pater patriae. Going a step further, Lincoln now called not only on the loyal citizens of the country but on God to sustain him. "Trusting in Him, who can go with me, and remain with you and be every where for good," he said at his parting, "let us confidently hope all will yet be well."

Lincoln never approached this level of sublimity during his subsequent preinaugural comments, nor did he ever use his many speaking opportunities to hammer away at specific policy demands. But in several speeches, he made manifest his ongoing, unbreakable commitment to the rule of law and majority rule as the essential features of American democracy.

Perhaps the most impressive of Lincoln's preinaugural speeches came when he appeared before the New Jersey state legislature on February 21. Here he harked back nostalgically to the American past, once again identifying himself with the enlightened "fathers" who had struggled to unite the disparate colonies into a cohesive country four score years earlier:

> [A]way back in my childhood, the earliest days of my being able to read, I got hold of a small book, such a one as few of the younger members have ever seen, "Weems' Life of Washington." I remember all the accounts there given of the battle fields and struggles for the liberties of the country, and none fixed themselves upon my imagination so deeply as the struggle here at Trenton, New-Jersey. The crossing of the river; the contest with the Hessians; the great hardships endured at that time, all fixed themselves on my memory more than any single revolutionary event; and you all know, for you have all been boys, how these early impressions last longer than

any others. I recollect thinking then, boy even though I was, that there must have been something more than common that those men struggled for. I am exceedingly anxious that that thing which they struggled for; that something even more than National Independence; that something that held out a great promise to all the people of the world to all time to come; I am exceedingly anxious that this Union, the Constitution, and the liberties of the people shall be perpetuated in accordance with the original idea for which that struggle was made, and I shall be most happy indeed if I shall be an humble instrument in the hands of the Almighty, and of this, his almost chosen people, for perpetuating the object of that great struggle.

Against this backdrop, Lincoln had taken his pen to do what he did better than any politician of his day: express himself convincingly in a public speech. There is no doubt that Lincoln drafted his Inaugural Address—all of it—alone. Lincoln planned to use this message to reintroduce himself by reminding the public that he remained "bound by duty, as well as by inclination," to the principles of the Republican platform, put forth at the convention in Chicago; by opposition to the spread of slavery; and by a commitment to a government that would "clear the path for all."

Lincoln had intended to begin his Inaugural Address with an oblique but unmistakable reiteration of the Republican Party plank that specifically forbade the extension of slavery: "Having been so elected upon the Chicago Platform, and while I would repeat nothing in it, of aspersion or epithet or question of motive against any man or party, I hold myself bound by duty, as well as impelled by inclination to follow, within the executive sphere, the principles therein declared. By no other course could I meet the reasonable expectations of the country."

But after consulting in Washington with the compromise-minded Seward, he deleted this paragraph entirely. Instead, Lincoln went further than he had ever gone to attempt to placate his slaveholding critics. As president he would continue to enforce the much-hated

Fugitive Slave Act (an announcement abolitionist leader Frederick Douglass greeted with alarm and disgust). He remained committed against interfering with slavery where it existed. He would not even force Republican federal appointees on overwhelmingly Democratic constituencies. But he would not tolerate the dissolution of the Union.

And he would not sugar-coat—one of his favorite phrases—his unyielding opposition to the spread of slavery, even if he found a less threatening way of expressing it. Redeploying a sentiment he had recently shared in a letter to his old Whig congressional colleague from Georgia, Alexander H. Stephens—now the vice president of the new Confederate States of America—Lincoln insisted: "One section of our country believes slavery is *right,* and ought to be extended, while the other believes it is *wrong,* and ought not to be extended. This is the only substantial dispute. . . . Why should there not be a patient confidence in the ultimate justice of the people? Is there any better, or equal hope, in the world?"

Lincoln opted for a tried-and-true lawyer's brief against secession. Regardless of the "disruption" of secession, Lincoln insisted, both universal law and the Constitution must be regarded as "perpetual." It was unthinkable that some of the states could destroy a Union that all of the states had created. And since "no State, upon its own mere motion, can lawfully get out of the Union," Lincoln argued, "I therefore consider that the Union is unbroken; and, to the extent of my ability, I shall take care that the laws of the Union be faithfully executed in all the States." Plainly spoken, this meant that as president, he would use all the power at his disposal to ensure that federal military presence in the South would be maintained, import duties would be collected, the mail would be delivered, and where necessary, federal property would be not only held but reclaimed.

Lincoln presented a direct defense of his unwillingness to compromise on slavery expansion—"to shift the ground upon which I had been elected"—arguing that such a "surrender would not be merely the ruin of a man, or a party; but, as a precedent, would be the ruin of government itself."

On March 4, 1861, Lincoln delivered his Inaugural Address before a vast crowd from the portico of the Capitol. "Fellow citizens of the United States!" he began. He gave pronounced emphasis to the word *united* to an eruption of "loud cheers." Lincoln was unyielding. "Physically speaking," he declared in a loud voice that was said to reach the outer fringes of the vast crowd, "we cannot separate." The Union was older than the Constitution: it was "perpetual" and could not be dissolved. In any case, "the laws of the Union" would be "faithfully executed in all the states." And he left little doubt that slaves would never inhabit America's new territories.

Lincoln intended a stern warning against disunion, asserting that war would be the South's fault, not his. "In *your* hands, my dissatisfied fellow countrymen, and not in *mine,* is the momentous issue of civil war. The government will not assail *you.* . . . You can have no conflict, without being yourselves the aggressors. *You* have no oath registered in Heaven to destroy the government, while *I* shall have the most solemn one to 'preserve, protect and defend' it. *You* can forbear the *assault* upon it; *I* can *not* shrink from the *defense* of it. With *you,* and not with *me,* is the solemn question of 'Shall it be peace, or a sword?'"

At the urging of Seward and others invited to vet the speech in advance, Lincoln had agreed to give the appearance of moderation. At Seward's suggestion, Lincoln modified the wording of the challenge—but only slightly. He took out the provocative antiphony "unless you *first* assail *it*" after "The government will not assail *you,*" but he retained the most provocative phrase: "You can have no conflict, without being yourselves the aggressors." While retaining the charge that Southern intransigence could be blamed for the onset of war, he added a new concluding paragraph that ended with a beautifully crafted plea he likely knew would be expressed in vain: "We are not enemies, but friends. We must not be enemies. Though passion may have strained, it must not break our bonds of affection. The mystic chords of memory, stretching from every battle-field, and patriot grave, to every living heart and hearthstone, all over this broad land, will yet swell the chorus of the Union, when again touched, as surely they will be, by the better angels of our nature."

And then a visibly trembling Chief Justice Roger Taney—the man who had done more than anyone living to demean the worth of the black man through the *Dred Scott* decision—administered to Lincoln the oath of office. As the new president swore on the Bible to uphold the Constitution, the roar of a canon salute erupted from the nearby plaza. The volley, far more than Lincoln's final, eloquent attempt to soothe the enemies of freedom, proved a portent of things to come.

Lincoln was hardly surprised when South Carolina fired on the Federal troops in Fort Sumter six weeks later. He all but invited the aggression by openly communicating his determination to resupply, though not to rearm, the garrison. What is not fully recognized is the power of Lincoln's immediate reaction to the firing, in deeds as well as words. The new, untested commander in chief responded within hours, suspending habeas corpus privileges in Maryland so troops could pass through the slaveholding state en route to the defense of Washington, ordering a naval blockade of Southern ports, and calling for seventy-five thousand volunteers to "maintain the honor, the integrity, and the existence of our National Union." Southern reaction followed quickly: four more states seceded from the Union: Virginia, Arkansas, Tennessee, and North Carolina.

Lincoln made no effort to win immediate congressional approval—much less appropriations—to pay for his initiatives. The public reason seemed simple enough: Congress was out of session and out of town. Enemies of the administration predictably bristled at its exercise of executive power in the wake of Fort Sumter. The *New Orleans Daily Picayune* denounced Lincoln as a "military dictator . . . grasping at the power of a despot." And the hostile *New York Evening Day-Book* likened his threat to "save the Union" with "the bayonet" as no less inhumane than French emperor Louis Napoleon's repressive actions against his own people.

The new president might have avoided charges of despotism simply by calling Congress back to Washington immediately. Railroad and steamboat technology had made the capital far more accessible than it had been in the days when congressional sessions were preceded by weeks of travel. Instead, Lincoln gambled that once he had ordered resources into the fray, none would be recalled, not even by a Congress populated by dubious Northern and border-state Democrats.

Lincoln largely avoided a negative reaction from Congress and the harsh judgment of history by again deploying the most effective weapon in his personal arsenal: words. For at least two weeks in June, during which time he saw few visitors so he could focus on writing his formal appeal for support from Congress, he crafted a lengthy, deceptively simple, yet ingenious message for the Special Session. His final text combined lawyerly logic, populist language, and evangelical zeal to accomplish his daunting but essential goals.

Lincoln argued that secession was plainly illegal and unacceptable and, moreover, a sophistry: treason masquerading as states' rights. Americans had chosen their president, and even those who had voted for others had the obligation to unite around the new government. In turn, the government would fight to "maintain its own existence."

Using the stirring language that we associate with his best speeches, Lincoln presented a compelling case for suppressing the rebellion. In one particularly sublime passage, he foresaw the approaching war as presenting "to the whole family of man, the question, whether . . . a government of the people, by the same people—can, or cannot, maintain its territorial integrity, against its own domestic foes." The war would be a fight to sustain the one country in the world that was the model of democracy for the future. In one of the strongest statements of American exceptionalism ever made, Lincoln said: "This is essentially a People's contest. On the side of the Union, it is a struggle for maintaining in the world, that form, and substance of government, whose leading object is, to elevate the condition of men—to lift artificial weights from all shoulders—to clear the paths of laudable pursuit for all—to afford all, an unfettered start, and a fair chance, in the race of life."

Lincoln's political and economic philosophy guided his response to the Southern secession movement. He refused to acknowledge the legitimacy of secession because to do so would accept the principle that the unique American middle-class nation, "conceived in liberty" and "dedicated to the proposition that all men are created equal," could be destroyed by a willful aristocratic minority of slaveholders.

Here we find the basis for Lincoln's refusal to accept any further extension of the Southern economic system by limiting it to the existing Southern states. Now he was willing to commit American lives to limit its expansion, to put slavery "in the course of ultimate

extinction." Lincoln was not an abolitionist advocating the immediate end to the institution. What he was determined to maintain and
spread was the Northern political, social, and economic system that
ensured that all men "should have an equal chance," and that meant
arresting the spread of slavery in the hope of placing it in the course
of ultimate extinction.

Lincoln believed that the founders of American society had defined its essence in the famous words of the Declaration of Independence: "We hold these truths to be self-evident, that all men are
created equal, that they are endowed by their Creator with certain
unalienable Rights, that among these are Life, Liberty and the pursuit of Happiness.—That to secure these rights, Governments are in-
stituted among Men, deriving their just powers from the consent of
the governed."

Lincoln was at one and the same time an economic realist, a pragmatic politician, and a moral philosopher committed to the rule of
law. As early as the Lincoln-Douglas debates in 1858, Lincoln had a
clearly defined position on slavery that he defended on all three levels.
As to the morality of slavery, he held that the institution was evil and
that a nation dedicated to the proposition that "all men are created
equal" could not permanently continue "half slave and half free." As
to economic realism, he understood that a nation dedicated to building a middle-class society could not permanently harbor a substantial
slave-based economy. As to pragmatic politics, he said that while the
Constitution barred the president and Congress from taking immediate action to abolish slavery in the existing Southern states, there was
no barrier to banning the extension of slavery to the western territories.

With the clarity of distance, England's great philosopher John Stuart Mill wrote in 1862 in *Contest in America,* "The day when slavery
can no longer extend itself, is the day of its doom. The slave-owners
know this, and it is the cause of their fury." What animated Mill and
the majority of nonaristocrats in Britain was Lincoln's concept that preserving the Union was essential to prove that a nation based on democracy, equality, and opportunity could protect itself from dissolution.

Lincoln believed his approach was not only moral, legal, and practical but also consistent with his personal commitment to sustain and

implement the principles of American exceptionalism enunciated in the Declaration of Independence. He was determined that the one nation in the world founded on the principle that all men are created equal and endowed by their creator with the rights to life, liberty, and the pursuit of happiness would endure in perpetuity. He was willing to take any and all actions to preserve the Union—to ensure that the American experiment in an enduring middle-class economy and society would not fail. The America of the future, he believed, should be based on equality and opportunity, just as it already existed for citizens of the Northern states. In essence, this is why Lincoln was willing to fight a war to "save the Union"—to establish once and for all that America would continue to be a model of middle-class democracy.

Abraham Lincoln was willing to raise his sword in 1861 because he believed that it was worth fighting a "civil war" to establish once and for all that the United States of America would continue to serve as the model of democracy for the future—that this just and generous nation of the people, by the people, for the people, shall not perish from the earth. For Lincoln, this was a commitment to sustain the American Dream of economic opportunity for future generations.

Four

SAVING THE UNION

LINCOLN THE LEADER

AFTER SOUTH CAROLINA TROOPS FIRED ON FORT SUMTER, NORTHERN volunteers rallied to Lincoln's calls to suppress the rebellion. Lincoln committed himself to his role as commander in chief of a nation at war. He understood the need to rally both the troops and the civilian population to support a just war for a just cause. He described the nation as the last best hope of mankind because it was the only nation in the world committed to promoting economic opportunity for all its citizens. At its core, there was a philosophical logic to Lincoln's vision of an active government in the service of the people. The founding principle of the nation was liberty. The purpose of liberty was to enable individuals to improve their condition. The role of government therefore was to serve that central purpose by, as Lincoln liked to put it, "clearing the path" for Americans to achieve economic success. "Clearing the path" for Lincoln did not mean government "getting out of the way." It was a frontier metaphor, suggestive of the hard work of clearing forest for a farm or a road, pulling stumps out of the ground with teams of oxen. "The legitimate object of government," he wrote in a note around 1854, "is to do for a community of people, whatever they need to have done, but can not do, at all, or can not, so well do, for themselves in their separate, and individual capacities."

In one sense, the political and economic issues that dominated Lincoln's age were quite different from those that characterize divisions in our era. In another sense, they were eerily similar. Many of the debates of the 1830s and 1840s focused on whether there should be "more" or "less" government, meaning the federal government. Lincoln—despite, or rather because of, his ardent belief in individual and community economic opportunity—identified himself firmly on the side of those who favored "more."

Like political philosophers from the time of Thomas Hobbes and John Locke, Lincoln saw the first purpose of government as providing for physical security and the common defense. But he also believed that government should take positive action to promote the common good. "There are many such things—some of them exist independently of the injustice of the world. Making and maintaining roads, bridges, and the like; providing for the helpless young and afflicted; common schools; and disposing of deceased men's property are instances." He saw "charities, pauperism, orphanage" as government responsibilities. By the standards of his time, when the federal government was minimal, and even state governments often had few resources at their disposal, Lincoln was in favor of activist government, on the grounds that the government should play its proper role in assisting the effort of all Americans to improve their economic condition.

It was this active role of government that Lincoln alluded to in the most famous phrase from his Gettysburg Address. The essence of the United States was not merely government "of the people" and "by the people," but also government "for the people"—government in an active role clearing the path for its citizens to advance economically. It was a belief he had already put into practice as an Illinois state assemblyman, when he had promoted the construction of roads and canals and education for its citizens.

Lincoln went to war in 1861 to ensure that the middle-class society of the North rather than the aristocratic society of the South would define the future of the nation. Now that he was president and now that the country was in the throes of that war, he had to make good on his commitment. Ten days before taking the oath of office, President-elect Abraham Lincoln had spoken to an audience in Independence Hall in Philadelphia, in the shadow of the Liberty Bell, where Thomas Jefferson had first presented the Declaration of

Independence to the Continental Congress in 1776: "I have never had a feeling politically that did not spring from the sentiments embodied in the Declaration of Independence," Lincoln said that day, "that which gave promise that in due time the weights should be lifted from the shoulders of all men, and that *all* should have an equal chance. . . . Now, my friends, can this country be saved upon that basis? . . . If it can't be saved upon that principle . . . if this country cannot be saved without giving up that principle . . . I would rather be assassinated on this spot than to surrender it."

Just days before his inauguration, Lincoln was still emphasizing the economic basis for limiting slavery: that each person—white or black—was entitled to the fruits of his labor. A war to "Save the Union" would be a just war—because success in the war would ensure the survival of the upwardly mobile society envisioned by the Declaration of Independence and because the future American society would continue to be the example to the world that liberty, freedom, and economic opportunity were inseparable.

In his Inaugural Address and in his Special Message to Congress in 1861, Lincoln barely mentioned slavery while extolling the message of equality and freedom in the Declaration of Independence.

The Congress that convened on July 5, 1861, to hear Lincoln's Special Message was controlled by members of his party. After the members from the rebellious Southern states left Washington, Republicans assumed large majorities in both houses—32 out of 48 members of the Senate and 106 out of 176 members of the House of Representatives. It was not surprising that this one-sided Congress supported the president's call to support his effort to maintain the Union. Nor was it surprising, given Lincoln's rousing words about the government's role, that Congress proceeded to pass legislation consistent with Lincoln's vision of an activist government working to improve the economic life of all Americans.

As president—with the support of the Republican Congress—Lincoln signed into law measures decisively strengthening the role of the federal government in American economic life.

Lincoln signed the National Banking Act, which not only revived the national bank that President Jackson had killed in 1833, but also gave the country its first unified currency and created a national system of chartered national banks, replacing a system in which states and state banks created their own money. The 1862 Homestead Act provided 160 acres of inexpensive land to settlers willing to migrate west. Lincoln favored high protective tariffs to encourage the development of domestic manufacturing. He chartered the first transcontinental railroad, which would link the country from East to West Coasts, the greatest "internal improvement" up to that time. He signed the Morrill Act in 1862, which provided states with grants of land to establish colleges, designed to provide useful education to help "clear the path" for ordinary people to achieve the American economic dream. And these colleges became the basis of the nation's state university system. All these programs were embodiments of what Lincoln believed to be government's legitimate and vital role in building and expanding America's middle-class economy and society. In the process, he created what distinguished historian Leonard P. Curry has called "a blueprint for modern America."

On issue after issue, Lincoln was not only a philosopher, but also a pragmatic politician—and a cautious one at that. As a result, his path to guaranteeing equal treatment and widening paths to economic opportunity was not always clear. Yet Lincoln consistently proved willing to adjust initiatives that did not, at first, go far enough.

To help pay for the war, Lincoln signed the first federal income tax bill on August 5, 1861, levying a flat 3 percent tax on annual incomes above eight hundred dollars. After midwestern farmers howled that the new levy imposed disproportionate hardships on their region, Congress and the president on July 1, 1862, changed the law by passing the first graduated income tax law: 3 percent on incomes between six hundred and ten thousand dollars and 5 percent on incomes above that amount. Over time, Lincoln had learned the efficacy and inherent fairness of the graduated income tax system. Though the courts declared the entire system unconstitutional in 1872, it later served as the model for the graduated income tax system reintroduced in the twentieth century.

In another case of an imperfect initiative later improved, the first conscription law offered wealthy Northerners the opportunity to buy a substitute enlistee for three hundred dollars, leading to charges that Lincoln's was a "rich man's war," meant to be fought by the poor. The ill-conceived buyout clause (Lincoln actually purchased his own substitute when the law was introduced) soon vanished—another lesson in the need for economic equality that Lincoln learned late, but well, as president.

Lincoln was also overcautious in introducing the idea of black enlistment in 1863. Initially, he approved a plan to pay African American soldiers lower salaries than white troops. And while white soldiers would continue to receive a bonus for buying uniforms, black soldiers would be charged extra for theirs. The glaring disparity brought a furious Frederick Douglass—who was expected to encourage black recruitment—storming to the White House to demand equal pay at once. "You must give colored soldiers the same pay that you give white soldiers," Douglass bluntly demanded at his historic White House meeting with the president.

"Mr. Lincoln listened with earnest attention and with very apparent sympathy," Douglass remembered. But the president did not yield. "First he spoke of the opposition generally to employing negroes as soldiers at all, of the prejudice against the race, and of the advantage to colored people that would result from their being employed as soldiers in defense of their country." Unequal pay, he frankly admitted, was a necessary "concession to prejudice." But if the "experiment" succeeded, Lincoln said, "I assure you, Mr. Douglass, that in the end they shall have the same pay as white soldiers." The experiment did succeed, and Lincoln kept his promise, another case of a revolutionary policy introduced slowly, letting economic equity catch up with, and alter, the result.

Cautious he may have been, but Lincoln proved remarkably consistent in his efforts to introduce controversial new policies slowly and having them evolve over time. In much the same way, the man who came to office vowing to leave slavery alone where it existed eventually formulated a compensated emancipation plan and, when that failed, substituted the Emancipation Proclamation. And when that order, too, proved limited, Lincoln fought for a constitutional amendment banning slavery everywhere.

The progressive ferment unleashed by Lincoln's federal government programs for the people also led to a surprising first step in the creation of America's national and state park systems. California senator John Conness, with the help of the Lincoln administration's General Land Office, drafted legislation to authorize the federal government to give a large tract of land in the Yosemite Valley to the state of California—to create a natural park for the recreational enjoyment of all Americans. The legislation was passed by a large majority of votes in the Senate and in the House of Representatives. Lincoln signed the law on June 30, 1864. This initiative was followed eight years later in the Grant administration by the creation of the first US national park—the 2 million acre Yellowstone National Park. Four decades later, Lincoln's ardent admirer President Theodore Roosevelt encouraged Congress to create new national parks throughout the United States to enable Americans to enjoy natural beauty as part of their collective heritage. With this initiative, as with so many others, Lincoln's vision and his specific policies provided the foundation stones for future presidents to build on as they implemented new progressive policies to improve the lives of all Americans.

The basis of Lincoln's political philosophy, one he put into practice through these policies, was a vision of an economic society in which all citizens had an equal chance. It was a vision that he wanted to make a reality, especially after the South had seceded and the war had begun; in doing so, he would be living up to the reasons he had given for fighting the war in the first place: to ensure that the unique American middle-class nation "conceived in liberty" and "dedicated to the proposition that all men are created equal" would endure. It was a vision based on his understanding of the pre–Civil War middle-class economy in the Northern states. He did not anticipate that the Industrial Revolution that began to take hold in Great Britain in the decades before 1860 would radically change the middle-class society of the North during and after the Civil War.

Lincoln's vision of the American middle-class society was remarkably specific. He took pains to describe it in detail in his first Annual Message to Congress on December 3, 1861. It is a remarkable address, long overshadowed by both his July Special Message and his more famous Annual Message the following year. But it is instructive that Lincoln used his *first* such report to Congress—the equivalent of today's State of the Union messages—to share his rationale for fighting to save the Union. Never before had he delivered such a frankly economic justification for his commitment to preserving the Union. First, Lincoln offered a new and finely honed version of his long-standing belief that labor was superior in standing to capital:

> It is not needed, nor fitting here, that a general argument should be made in favor of popular institutions; but there is one point, with its connexions, not so hackneyed as most others, to which I ask a brief attention. It is the effort to place *capital* on an equal footing with, if not above *labor*, in the structure of government. It is assumed that labor is available only in connexion with capital; that nobody labors unless somebody else, owning capital, somehow by the use of it, induces him to labor. This assumed, it is next considered whether it is best that capital shall *hire* laborers, and thus induce them to work by their own consent, or *buy* them, and drive them to it without their consent. Having proceeded so far, it is naturally concluded that all laborers are either *hired* laborers, or what we call slaves. And further, it is assumed that whoever is once a hired laborer, is fixed in that condition for life.
>
> Now, there is no such relation between capital and labor as assumed; nor is there any such thing as a free man being fixed for life in the condition of a hired laborer. Both these assumptions are false, and all inferences from them are groundless.
>
> Labor is prior to, and independent of, capital. Capital is only the fruit of labor, and could never have existed if labor had not first existed. Labor is the superior of capital, and deserves much the higher consideration. Capital has its rights, which are as worthy of protection as any other rights. Nor is it denied that there is, and probably always will be, a relation between labor and capital, producing mutual benefits. The error is in assuming that the whole labor of the community exists within that relation.

It was clear from these bold statements that Lincoln meant to sharply contrast the opportunities guaranteed by the Northern middle-class society with the insurmountable barriers that blocked social and economic advancement in the Southern slave-based society. As Lincoln put it:

> Again: as has already been said, there is not, of necessity, any such thing as the free hired laborer being fixed to that condition for life. Many independent men everywhere in these States, a few years back in their lives, were hired laborers. The prudent, penniless beginner in the world, labors for wages awhile, saves a surplus with which to buy tools or land for himself; then labors on his own account another while, and at length hires another new beginner to help him. This is the just, and generous, and prosperous system, which opens the way to all—gives hope to all, and consequent energy, and progress, and improvement of condition to all. No men living are more worthy to be trusted than those who toil up from poverty—none less inclined to take, or touch, aught which they have not honestly earned. Let them beware of surrendering a political power which they already possess, and which, if surrendered, will surely be used to close the door of advancement against such as they, and to fix new disabilities and burdens upon them, till all of liberty shall be lost.

Lincoln's famous peroration reminded Congress that its members were obliged to continue supporting the war not just to put down a surprisingly strong rebellion, but to ensure the triumph of freedom and opportunity for future generations: "The struggle of today is not altogether for today—it is for a vast future also. With a reliance on Providence, all the more firm and earnest, let us proceed in the great task which events have devolved upon us."

Lincoln returned to this argument the following year in his second and most famous Annual Message to Congress. In that message he described the commitment to save the Union in almost biblical terms, though the arguments were the same as they had been in 1861.

> Fellow-citizens, *we* cannot escape history. We of this Congress and this administration, will be remembered in spite of our-selves. No personal significance, or insignificance, can spare one or another of us. The fiery trial through which we pass, will light us down, in honor or dishonor, to the latest genera-tion. We *say* we are for the Union. The world will not forget that we say this. We know how to save the Union. The world knows we do know how to save it. We—even *we here*—hold the power, and bear the responsibility. In *giving* freedom to the *slave*, we *assure* freedom to the *free*—honorable alike in what we give, and what we preserve. We shall nobly save, or meanly lose, the last best, hope of earth.

In 1863 Lincoln introduced the idea of a "new birth of freedom" in the United States. In doing so, he placed greater emphasis on the immorality of the Southern slave system in contrast to the free labor system of the North. Now he was urgently committed to the immedi-ate and permanent abolition of slavery throughout the United States. This was not a new cause; instead, it was an expanded commitment to the belief that liberty, freedom, and economic opportunity were insep-arable. Lincoln, our most philosophic president, called all Americans to battle for this universalist ideal for the American nation as well as for all nations of the world. Eighty years later, another president in the midst of World War II echoed and expanded these sentiments in describing the commitments of Americans to support the right of all people everywhere in the world to enjoy freedom of speech, freedom of religion, freedom from want, and freedom from fear.

In order to achieve his "new birth of freedom" by saving the Union and abolishing slavery, Lincoln understood that he first needed to win the war. Lincoln accepted his expanded responsibility as commander in chief, which meant both defeating the rebels on the battlefield and providing the economic tools of war on the home front.

Before 1861 the federal government was limited in size and scope. The budget of the executive branch of the government reflected a small number of employees engaged in a minimalist level of activity. Even the military and foreign service offices were small in size and activity. The annual federal budget before 1861 was funded almost exclusively by tariff revenues from imported goods. There was only a tiny federal army. When Lincoln arrived in Washington on February 23, 1861, there were few, if any, federal soldiers in the nation's capital. Lincoln was a largely unprotected president until the first contingent of New York militia arrived in Washington in April 1861. They were originally scheduled to remain for only ninety days.

The new tasks Lincoln, his cabinet, and his generals faced were unprecedented, and they would never be able to carry them out by relying on a federal government and military at their existing sizes. It quickly became clear that the war demanded an increase in US federal government activities—both military and civilian. The first and foremost task was creating from scratch a large and disciplined army. Securing funds to enable the federal government to conduct the war was even more important.

Expanding the size of the government and the army could have easily ignited a backlash from the Northern public. Fortunately, however, Lincoln brought to the presidency a brilliant record in managing "public sentiment," honed by decades of experience influencing individual judges, juries, and both small and large audiences of potential voters. He was a skillful political practitioner—wise in the ways of gaining widespread support from voters in political campaigns. He was the most effective national politician in using the newspapers to get his messages to the public. He also drew on his ability to manage individual and small-group sentiment to build a cabinet capable of managing a rapidly growing federal government and winning the war. He successfully persuaded his most ardent political rivals in the contest for the 1860 Republican presidential nomination—William Seward, Salmon Chase, and Edward Bates—to join his cabinet, along with other talented men such as Edwin Stanton and Gideon Welles.

Nor did Lincoln shy away from taking the steps needed to fund a larger government. He had spent his political life as a devoted advocate of the Whig Party's Hamiltonian tradition of active federal management of the financial affairs of the nation. He did not hesitate to act directly to provide the national government with the money needed to pay for the war. Lincoln and his secretary of the treasury, Salmon P. Chase, secured approval of legislation on February 25, 1862, that authorized the issuance of national notes convertible into government bonds redeemable in five to twenty years. Lincoln's administration could now print federal money (greenbacks) and issue federal bonds. Lincoln also persuaded Congress to pass legislation to create the nation's first income tax. These financial programs provided the federal government with an ongoing source of funds to pay the Union's soldiers and sailors and provide them with food, supplies, and weapons. As Lincoln explained in his Annual Message to Congress of 1862: "In no other way could the payment of the troops, and the satisfaction of other just demands, be so economically, or so well provided for."

When Lincoln took office as president on March 4, 1861, he also assumed the role of chief executive officer of the American economy. The increasing prosperity of the North, during the war and most particularly between 1863 and 1865, was one of the most significant factors leading to eventual Union victory. By 1864 the gross national product of the Union states was $4,019,000,000—larger than the combined GNP of the North and South in 1860. Lincoln's National Banking Act of 1863 provided the financial underpinning of the federal government's conduct of the war. In June 1863 there were only 66 national banks. By 1864–1865 the number had increased to 1,294. The new national banks were required to purchase and concurrently deposit US bonds with the Treasury before issuing notes to customers, a policy that provided ready cash to the government to conduct the war.

Federal government expenditures rose from $475,000,000 in 1862 to $1,298,000,000 in 1864, the last full year of the war. Nearly all of the federal debt was financed internally. Personal bank savings, which were already substantial in 1860, increased year by year during the war. The savings banks invested their deposits in government notes and bonds. Individuals purchased government bonds directly. Government receipts increased so substantially that they covered the rapidly rising costs of government.

Year	Government Expenditure	Government Borrowing	Government Tax Receipts	Total Government Receipts
1862	475,000,000	423,000,000	52,000,000	475,000,000
1865	1,298,000,000	976,000,000	322,000,000	1,298,000,000

The war brought a substantial increase in federal government activities, civilian as well as military. First, there was a major increase in direct expenditures to pay the soldiers and sailors and the civil personnel directly engaged in the war. In addition, Lincoln and his advisers raised and spent unprecedented amounts of money to pay for munitions and supplies and ships to conduct the war. For the first time in the life of the Republic, federal government expenditures provided a substantial stimulus to the private economy. Lincoln's wartime economic policies had a profound impact on the growth of the American economy. The Northern economy went through a period of difficult readjustment in 1861 and 1862. But by 1863 federal wartime expenditure to supply and support the Northern armies had created what can only be described as booming economic growth throughout the Northern states.

Between 1863 and 1865 the American economy in the North grew from a preindustrial society to a rapidly growing industrial society that by the end of the century would rival Great Britain as the leading industrial economy in the World. The speed of the growing industrial revolution in the Northern states proved breathtaking, and the region had Lincoln's wartime economic policies to thank for it. An incipient prewar movement toward industrialization was strongly accelerated by federal government expenditures for the war. In his Thanksgiving Day Proclamation of 1863, Lincoln marked this spectacular growth, reporting that population and wealth had grown substantially despite battlefield losses of men and treasure. He said that the prospects for future growth were increasingly positive.

In his Message to Congress in December 1863, Lincoln reported: "It is easy to see that under the sharp discipline of civil war the nation is beginning a new life." He urged Congress to recognize that foreign immigration was growing despite the war and proposed legislation to encourage even more immigration to build the economy. A year later he reported that the economy had experienced great growth of railroad tracks and railroad cars to provision Union armies as well as the Northern civilian population. He also reported on a substantial increase in telegraph lines to provide instant communication between the battlefield and the home front. Most important, Lincoln said, "We do not approach exhaustion in the most important branch of national resources—that of living men. . . . [W]e have *more* men *now* than we had when the war *began*." Lincoln went on to say, "Material resources are now more complete and abundant than ever. The national resources, then, are unexhausted, and, as we believe, inexhaustible."

Lincoln was right to celebrate the striking increase in immigration and the role immigrants played in the growth of the American economy in the North—and in winning the war for the Union. The total number of new immigrants, which was fewer than 100,000 per year in 1861 and 1862, increased to 176,000 in 1863, 193,000 in 1864, and 248,000 in 1865. Most of the immigrants came from Great Britain, Ireland, and Germany; most were young men between the ages of fifteen and forty; and most were readily available to work as laborers in the expanding manufacturing sector of the economy. Notably, one out of ten immigrants in 1864 enlisted in the army or navy as soon as they arrived. The *American Railroad Journal* reported that despite the efforts of foreign countries to discourage emigration, the movement to the United States of able-bodied male workers continued to grow because wages in the US Northern states were three to four times greater than in Europe. The promise of upward mobility, so critical in Lincoln's thinking, here provided the same opportunity to rise for a new generation of able-bodied immigrants.

It was not only foreign-born immigrants that benefited from the economic boom. When Lincoln took office in 1861, half the people in the United States lived on farms, and three quarters of the population lived and worked in rural areas. During the war, economic growth increased rapidly in urban areas—most notably in Chicago and other northwestern cities that were benefiting from their new railroad connections to the rest of the nation. The supply of farm labor was reduced when men left the nation's farms to enlist in the Northern army, but that did not slow agricultural production. Instead, it fostered innovation to meet the increased need for agricultural machinery on farms. Inventors had long since devoted countless hours to creating agricultural labor-saving machinery. Now they were being produced and used on increasingly productive farms. And the government's Homestead Act made land available to farmers and immigrants to expand agriculture. By the end of 1864, Lincoln could boast that 1.5 million acres of public land had been sold under the Homestead Act.

Lincoln was not a passive bystander in supporting and monitoring the economic growth of the nation. Establishing the new federal Department of Agriculture was one more of the president's aggressive efforts to spur the domestic economy, even in wartime. In his first Annual Message in 1861, while acknowledging that the nation's farmers were by disposition "independent," Lincoln had bemoaned the absence of an agency to represent agricultural interests at the federal level. Here was yet another example of astonishing personal and political growth for the once isolated young farm laborer who perhaps remained haunted by his father's chronic difficulties with both faulty land titles and imperfectly planted crops in the era before federal assistance and advice were even a dream. "Agriculture," as he lamented in December 1861, "confessedly the largest interest of the nation, has, not a department, nor a bureau, but a clerkship only, assigned to it in the Government." Though he considered it "fortunate that this great interest is so independent in its nature as to not have demanded and extorted more from the government," he believed there would be "general advantage" to elevating federal attention to the agrarian sector from which he himself had risen.

Five months later, legislation was on Lincoln's desk for his signature to establish a new government department focused on agriculture. It was not yet cabinet level—that would not come for another generation—but the president took immense pride in its rapid progress. The department created an extensive mailing list of farmers nationwide—"our most valuable citizens"—and made available to them expert advice on the latest cultivation techniques. The department began an agricultural library and would soon be ready to distribute "seeds, cereals, plants, and cuttings," a kind of direct federal aid to the farm community. By late 1864 Lincoln would proudly describe the young agency as "peculiarly the people's Department, in which they feel more directly concerned than in any other."

In its first monthly report in July 1863, the Department of Agriculture said, "No nation has ever developed such agricultural resources as the United States. . . . The amount of capital it has invested in lands and farming implements is nearly seven billions of dollars." The Department of Agriculture reported that the increase in wartime demand for agricultural products was the primary factor in the doubling of the output of American farms from $707 million in 1862 to $1.4 billion in 1864.

Lincoln served with great skill as a principal architect of the expanded American economy during the Civil War. The Northern economy grew rapidly in each year of the war, stimulated by increasing government expenditures and supported by government receipts from taxes and borrowing. Lincoln's military and economic programs played a substantial role in stimulating the civilian economy. As government expenditures increased year by year, the economy first grew substantially and then exponentially. The result was the great boom of 1863–1865, and ordinary Americans reaped the benefits. It is no surprise that the substantial increase in federal government expenditures resulted in raising the national income in the Northern states to more than $4 billion by 1865.

The federal government's stimulus programs under Lincoln provided the basis for the great thrust forward of the new Industrial Revolution in the Northern states both during and after the end of the Civil War. Lincoln's domestic policies provided the first clear example of the positive role that could be played by the federal government to encourage the economic growth of the nation.

Of course, these successes came at a staggering human cost. Historians now believe that 750,000 Union and Confederate soldiers lost their lives in the Civil War—greater than all American wars combined through the Vietnam era. What sustained Lincoln throughout the conflict, notwithstanding the horrifying military casualties, was the belief that the Union cause was just. In his Inaugural Address on March 4, 1861, Lincoln had insisted, "Intelligence, patriotism, Christianity, and a firm reliance on Him, who has never yet forsaken this favored land, are still competent to adjust, in the best way, all our present difficulties."

Once the seven states of the lower South seceded and created the Confederate States of America, Lincoln had understood that there was little likelihood of preserving the Union and sustaining the democratic society envisioned by the Declaration of Independence without war. He was clear-eyed and practical about what needed to be done. Rather than ceding control of the South to the Confederacy, he insisted on maintaining a federal presence where he could, announcing that federal control over military and civilian facilities in the seceded states would not be relinquished. He fought the Civil War to retain or reclaim them. And he labored to build a future domestic economy based on free land and government-supported education, railroad expansion, and agricultural improvement. Lincoln never doubted that the Union would be preserved. As he declared in August 1863: "Let us diligently apply the means, never doubting that a just God, in his own good time, will give us the rightful result."

Five

WHOLLY EVIL OR
WHOLLY GOOD

NOT QUITE AN ABOLITIONIST

ABRAHAM LINCOLN ENTHUSIASTICALLY COMMITTED HIMSELF TO the ideal of free labor, criticized the abhorrent aspects of mob rule, and championed the boundless opportunities embedded in his generous interpretation of the American Dream. But he did not embrace outright abolitionism as a means of enlarging the pool of dreamers to include African Americans—at least not until the final years of his presidency. Whether his attitude stemmed from a natural resistance to radicalism, a politically calculated desire to remain in the mainstream, or an initial resistance to racial equality has remained a matter of historical debate ever since. Perhaps the answer lies with some or all of the above.

One thing, however, is certain. Lincoln hated slavery, not only because it subjected one race to unspeakable cruelty, but also because it placed slaves in a fixed condition for life, unable to advance, denied any right to upward mobility. Slavery made a mockery of the American Dream and the right it promised to all Americans: the ability to work oneself into the middle class. "I am naturally anti-slavery," he told Kentucky governor Thomas Bramlette and a Frankfort journalist when the two men visited the White House in 1864. "If slavery is not wrong, nothing is wrong. I can not remember when I did not so think, and so feel."

Lincoln's early opposition to slavery was based on his settled conviction that every person—black or white—was entitled to receive full payment for his labor. As a young man, Lincoln was offended by the notion that any man should labor without pay. As a freshman US congressman in 1849, Lincoln recoiled when a black waiter—just a few dollars shy of buying his own freedom after years of paying his master off—was violently seized by the police right in Lincoln's own boardinghouse, after the owner of the slave cruelly decided to sell him south. Lincoln and his fellow lawmakers were forced to face the violence of slavery even in the capital of the United States. But Lincoln did not sit idly by; instead, he joined in an effort to overturn the seizure legislatively and, when that failed, helped to raise the funds to buy the waiter's freedom. A longtime apostle of free *white* labor, Lincoln thus extended his advocacy to a (nearly) free *black* laborer. He was genuinely incensed that a man who had so faithfully paid the increments to secure his own freedom could be sold as a piece of property before the final installment could be raised, allowing his master to keep the waiter's contributions and reap a further windfall by selling him to another owner. This surely aroused Lincoln's sense of fairness. As he later expressed it, "Fair play is a jewell."

Lincoln's embrace of antislavery was a matter of personal belief and a commitment to fairness, and it became a singular political focus as soon as he reentered politics in 1854. Lincoln had based his return on opposing Senator Stephen Douglas's newly enacted Kansas-Nebraska Act, which authorized white citizens of each of the new territories to vote to welcome slavery if a majority wished it. Lincoln insisted from 1854 onward that the extension of slavery should be outlawed in all US territories, knowing full well that it would place the institution "in the course of ultimate extinction." Speaking in Chicago shortly after he became a candidate for the US Senate in 1858, Lincoln declared to a burst of applause: "I have always hated slavery, I think as much as any Abolitionist," and used the phrase *ultimate extinction* no fewer than seven times.

At his final debate with Stephen Douglas in 1858, Lincoln presented a clear and eloquent statement on human rights, explaining why, though he was still opposed to immediate abolition, he remained committed to free labor for blacks as well as whites:

That is the issue that will continue in this country when these poor tongues of Judge Douglas and myself shall be silent. It is the eternal struggle between these two principles—right and wrong—throughout the world. They are the two principles that have stood face to face from the beginning of time; and will ever continue to struggle. The one is the common right of humanity and the other the divine right of kings. It is the same principle in whatever shape it develops itself. It is the same spirit that says, "You work and toil and earn bread, and I'll eat it." No matter in what shape it comes, whether from the mouth of a king who seeks to bestride the people of his own nation and live by the fruit of their labor, or from one race of men as an apology for enslaving another race, it is the same tyrannical principle.

That was indeed the issue. There is a clear difference, Lincoln explained, between those who believe in the "common right of humanity" and the "divine right of kings," a disparity that had been in place "from the beginning of time." Lincoln put himself firmly on the side of humanity and asserted that slavery must be placed "in the course of ultimate extinction," while the Democrats continued "to avow a policy looking to its perpetuation." Lincoln was clearly against slavery as both immoral and as an impediment to extending economic opportunity. Even so, Lincoln said there should be "no war, no violence" in order to achieve freedom—no convulsive act of outright abolition. His solution at that time was to end slavery through attrition by preventing any and all extension of slavery into the new American territories west of the Mississippi River.

While Lincoln always believed that slavery was immoral, immediate abolition was not in his lexicon until 1863, after the country had been consumed by the war and violence he had once hoped to avoid. Before that, however, Lincoln conceded that since slavery was protected in the Constitution, abolition implicitly required upheaval, maybe even revolution. And to young Abraham Lincoln, finding his way in the political landscape, the adherents of immediate abolition seemed to encourage violence as a means to an end: violence in pursuit of a virtuous outcome, perhaps, but nonetheless anathema to a politician who believed sincerely in the Constitution and the law. The abolitionist movement that seemed to encourage lawlessness and incite agitation, however horrifically violent the system of brutality it sought to overturn, was not for Lincoln.

Lincoln's rejection of the abolitionist movement did not mean that he was not vocal about bringing an end to slavery. In his earliest days in political life, the future president was clear and direct in saying that "the institution of slavery" was "founded on both injustice and bad policy." Even this minimalist statement placed Lincoln in the liberal wing of the Illinois Whig Party. But distancing himself from the vocal abolitionist movement ensured that he would remain a viable political force. From that time forward, Lincoln pursued a political career devoted to arresting the spread of slavery into the western territories. This was for Lincoln not a compromise but a solution based on a balanced combination of his opposition to slavery as immoral and his effort to find a peaceful solution that would put slavery "in the course of ultimate extinction." If slavery were banned from the western territories, they would eventually become free states, electing antislave representatives to Congress, and creating a supermajority in favor of putting an end to slavery in the United States.

Lincoln changed little in a quarter of a century of thinking about the impact of Southern slavery on economic and political opportunity for the Northern white population. He was also consistent in his concern about the potential for unlawful behavior by extremist proponents and opponents of slavery. One of his early demonstrations of hand-wringing over these thorny issues came in his speech before the Springfield Young Men's Lyceum in 1838, when he was a few days short of his twenty-ninth birthday.

Lincoln's speech reveals the limits to his ongoing struggle with what he clearly regarded at the time as twin evils, each likely to foment violence: support of slavery and support of immediate abolition. He expressed equal disdain for the "increasing disregard for law which pervades the country; the growing disposition to substitute the wild and furious passions, in lieu of the sober judgement of Courts; and the worse than savage mobs, for the executive ministers of justice." Lincoln went on to remind his listeners: "Accounts of outrages committed by mobs, form the every-day news of the times. They have pervaded the country, from New England to Louisiana. . . . [N]either are they confined to the slaveholding, or the nonslaveholding States. Alike, they spring up among the pleasure hunting masters of Southern slaves, and the order loving citizens of the land of steady habits. Whatever, then, their cause may be, it is common to the whole country."

Lincoln chose not "to recount the horrors of all of them." It would be "useless" to do so. But he went on to mention a few anyway. He was particularly horrified, he said, that "negroes, suspected of conspiring to raise an insurrection," had recently been "caught up and hanged" in Mississippi, together with "white men, supposed to be leagued with the negroes . . . till, dead men were seen literally dangling from the boughs of trees upon every road side." But even atrocities like this had not yet converted Lincoln to abolitionism. He was not yet willing to support the idea of "positive violence" for a good cause against "negative violence" for a bad cause.

Lincoln entitled his Lyceum speech "The Perpetuation of Our Political Institutions." Psychobiographers have found in Lincoln's yearning for a new generation of accomplished successors to the nation's founders a conscious and significant emergence on his part from the shadow of the fathers of the country—and perhaps from his own father as well. Lincoln certainly did make clear in his speech that he worried often that chances for fame and immortalization had ebbed. "The field is harvested," he fretted aloud. And in the void, he warned, a tyrant yet might emerge to lull the people into danger.

But the Lyceum speech was above all a call to reject violence, the "mobocratic spirit," as Lincoln put it, "which all must admit, is now abroad in the land." Lincoln did not mean to suggest that Illinois alone was experiencing an outbreak of rage. Violence was spreading everywhere. And Lincoln refused to deny that many of the acts had been perpetrated by proponents of slavery. As he reminded his audience:

Those happening in the State of Mississippi, and at St. Louis, are, perhaps, the most dangerous in example, and revolting to humanity. . . . Turn, then, to that horror-striking scene at St. Louis. . . . A mulatto man, by the name of McIntosh, was seized in the street, dragged to the suburbs of the city, chained to a tree, and actually burned to death; and all within a single hour from the time he had been a freeman, attending to his own business, and at peace with the world. Such are the effects of mob law; and such are the scenes, becoming more and more frequent in this land so lately famed for love of law and order; and the stories of which, have even now grown too familiar, to attract anything more, than an idle remark.

Violence loomed as a constant threat to progress—and an unfortunate aspect of political life—during the thirty years of Lincoln's residence in Illinois. Even Senator Stephen Douglas was involved in dustups. Politicians routinely brawled in the streets and challenged each other to duels. Lincoln himself was once called out after he admitted to (or gallantly assumed responsibility for) writing a series of cruel newspaper satires mocking a Democratic officeholder named James Shields. The duel was called off at the last possible moment, when the combatants were already on the field to fight to the death. Lincoln was so embarrassed by the episode that he never again spoke of it and was known to silence people who unwisely attempted to bring up the subject.

Lincoln believed he had a solution, for he knew there could be no progress anywhere without respect for law everywhere—especially when that respect was utterly lacking in many of the nation's political leaders. More ominously, he feared that citizens were likely to turn on a government that "offers them no protection," especially if they conclude "they have nothing to lose." To combat these dangers, Lincoln had proposed in 1838 at the Springfield Lyceum a bold new commitment to order:

Let reverence for the laws, be breathed by every American mother, to the lisping babe, that prattles on her lap—let it be taught in schools, in seminaries, and in colleges;—let it be written in Primmers [sic], spelling books, and in Almanacs;—let it be preached from the pulpit, proclaimed in legislative halls, and enforced in courts of justice. And, in short, let it become the *political religion* of the nation; and let the old and the young, the rich and the poor, the grave and the gay, of all sexes and tongues, and colors and conditions, sacrifice unceasingly upon its altars.

In fact, the case that had really aroused Lincoln he never mentioned by name: the recent assassination of antislavery editor Elijah Lovejoy in the downstate Illinois town of Alton. There, on November 7, 1837, a mob had attacked Lovejoy, sacked his printing press, and shot him to death while he was trying to defend his property. Yet the Lovejoy case seemed almost too controversial to cite with any specificity. Lovejoy had favored the immediate overthrow of slavery by any means, including violence, a radical notion that Lincoln thought truly dangerous. As Lincoln surely knew, there were plenty of citizens in Springfield, not only Democrats but fellow Whigs as well, who had no sympathy for the abolitionist victim and may even have believed he deserved his fate. Yet Lovejoy was also a brave entrepreneur trying to win an audience—and create a thriving business—in a hostile environment. And as such, Lincoln probably believed that he had a right to economic as well as physical security.

Lincoln addressed the issue in general rather than specific language. As he put it at the Lyceum: "Whenever the vicious portion of population shall be permitted to gather in bands of hundreds and thousands, and burn churches, ravage and rob provision stores, throw printing presses into rivers, shoot editors, and hang and burn obnoxious persons at pleasure, and with impunity; depend on it, this Government cannot last." The solution lay not in the "mobocratic spirit" but with "good men, men who love tranquility, who desire to abide by the laws, and enjoy their benefits."

Such was the philosophy of Henry Clay. As a practical politician, Lincoln also knew that Clay paid for his idealistic approach to politics by repeatedly failing to win the highest office in the land. When abolitionist New York Whigs rebelled against Clay's presidential candidacy in 1844, whatever purely emotional sympathy Lincoln may ever have harbored for abolitionism probably ended. These Empire State Whig abolitionist defections helped Democrat James Knox Polk win the state—and cost Lincoln's beloved "beau ideal" the White House.

This was to Lincoln inexcusable, an example of political extremism whose consequences would be felt for years. One costly by-product of that miscalculation by New York Whig Party abolitionists, Lincoln later pointed out, was Polk's controversial war with Mexico, as a result of which the United States acquired vast new southern territory ripe for slavery. Lincoln's experience during the 1844 election taught him that it was time for men of progressive conscience to form alliances to gain political victory.

Lincoln would attempt to put the lessons he had learned from 1844 into practice during the presidential election four years later. As a thirty-nine-year-old congressman in 1848, Lincoln tried to encourage his fellow Whigs to seek abolitionist support for the party's latest presidential nominee, General Zachary Taylor. Lincoln's law colleague Usher Linder challenged him, demanding to know: "Have we, as a party, ever gained any thing, by falling in company with abolitionists?" Lincoln, who had learned that compromise and coalition building were necessary to win elections, was quick to answer in the affirmative: "Yes. We gained our only national victory by falling in company with them in the election of Genl. Harrison [in 1840]. Not that we fell into abolition doctrines; but that we took up a man whose position induced them to join us in his election. But this question is not so significant as a *question,* as it is as a charge of abolitionism against those who have chosen to speak their minds against the President."

To counter this charge, Lincoln took pains to point out that among the thirty-six fellow Whigs then serving alongside him in the House of Representatives in 1849, there were enough who represented slave states to make certain that the Whig Party's synchronized opposition to the Mexican war was based purely on its being "unnecessary and unconstitutional," and not because of latent "abolitionism!" Coordination between Whig Party representatives from free and slave states proved successful in 1848 when Zachary Taylor became only the second Whig candidate ever to win a presidential election. Lincoln, in this instance, had forsaken Henry Clay to support the more electable war hero. Finally, the proeconomic development Whig Party had a president, though not for long (Taylor died sixteen months after his inauguration).

While in Washington, Lincoln fell in with a group that held a more proabolitionist point of view, and it is fair to say that he slowly learned from them. He moved into a boarding establishment that was populated by so many antislavery members of his own Whig Party that it acquired the nickname the "Abolition House" (not meant as a compliment). Here Lincoln met and socialized with a range of new acquaintances that included Joshua Giddings of Ohio, one of the leading abolitionist voices in Congress, a legislator who had been censured a few years earlier merely for defying the prevailing gag rule and attempting to raise the slavery issue on the floor of the House. It was here, too, that Lincoln and his fellow boarders helped their waiter buy his freedom after being unjustly denied it.

By no means did this new environment transform Lincoln into a proponent of immediate abolition everywhere in the United States, but his experiences there surely opened his eyes. So did Washington itself, a city filled with horrific slave pens where African Americans were shamelessly herded, stored, and sold in facilities far worse than the capital's prisons. Lincoln's antislavery views led him in 1849 to propose a bill to ban slavery entirely from the District of Columbia with compensation to owners. The measure went nowhere, but it marked the first time Lincoln made a major legislative move against slavery. Though it marked a personal milestone, it was something of a lost cause, too. The idea of ending slavery in Washington, or anywhere in the South, still lacked enough support to succeed in a Congress focused hungrily on how to divide the huge new territory recently acquired from Mexico. During these floor debates, Lincoln supported the Wilmot Proviso, which sought to ban slavery from all territory acquired from Mexico. That measure failed as well—and repeatedly— though Lincoln later proudly recalled that he had voted for it every time it came before the House. If he could not force freedom on the capital, he would try to ban slavery from the West—and at least bring the American Dream to the new territories.

The abolitionist movement received an unexpected boost from the work of the most widely read antislavery author, Harriet Beecher

Stowe. The daughter of the notable Congregational preacher Lyman Beecher, Harriet Beecher grew up in Cincinnati, Ohio, across the river from slave state Kentucky. As a young woman, she first encountered abolitionist ideas at family gatherings with her father's friends, including such important Cincinnati political figures as Salmon P. Chase, senator from Ohio who later became a member of Lincoln's cabinet. Harriet Beecher married Calvin Stowe in 1836, and the family moved to Massachusetts in 1852. While raising eight children, she found time to build a career writing short stories and articles for popular magazines. After the passage of the Fugitive Slave Act in 1850, Stowe began writing a story about slavery. She used her early experience of visiting plantations in Kentucky and conversations with freed slaves to provide an accurate view of slavery for her novel *Uncle Tom's Cabin*. To expand her knowledge of the evils of the slave system, she asked abolitionist leader Frederick Douglass to put her in touch with former slaves. The weekly publication *National Era* began publishing installments of her novel on June 5, 1851. By using the story form to communicate the pain and suffering of people under slavery, Harriet Beecher Stowe gave her readers an intimate understanding of the substance of her father's preaching that slavery is a sin.

The positive response from readers led to the publication of *Uncle Tom's Cabin* in book form in 1852. The novel sold more than three hundred thousand copies in the United States in its first year and added countless supporters to the abolitionist cause in the years following its publication. Often forgotten in assessments of the morally transformative aspect of the book was the economic success it brought its author. And Lincoln always admired people who worked hard to make themselves successful. So it is not surprising that, as president, Lincoln asked to meet her in 1862 and is reported to have said, "So you are the little woman who wrote the book that started this great war."

Lincoln's nuanced position at the beginning of his campaign to unseat Democratic incumbent senator Stephen Douglas in 1858 seemed to place him closer to the center of Republican political thinking on slavery. In fact, his opposition to the *spread* of slavery pushed him further in the direction of its antislavery wing. This reminds us of an unavoidable fact of life in the midcentury North: though abolitionists had been courageous advocates for change and voices of conscience in American culture for decades, they remained in 1858 well outside the political mainstream. And no mainstream politician outside of New England could hope to win elected office if he supported an immediate end to Southern slavery, which threatened to bring with it, many believed, racial violence and ramped-up competition from free African Americans for jobs. Still, it would be wrong to conclude that Lincoln eschewed abolitionism only because he desired to remain electable. At this point in his career, Lincoln genuinely mistrusted the idea of immediate abolition. He thought it would result in chaos. And he had thought so for decades.

Lincoln never escaped the charge of being a closet abolitionist, especially when he joined the new antislavery Republican Party in 1854 and launched his political comeback five years after his Whig congressional career ended. Lincoln's 1856 speech at Springfield prompted the town's Democratic newspaper, the *Illinois State Register,* to say that Lincoln was "boldly" avowing that "there could be no Union with slavery" and went on to charge that Lincoln had come close to preaching the "ultra abolitionism" of the leaders of the abolitionist movement, "convincing his audience . . . that his niggerism has as dark a hue as that of Garrison or Fred Douglass."

For his part, Senator Stephen A. Douglas routinely attacked Lincoln during their 1858 senatorial debates for harboring a covert plan to make African Americans social equals, voters, and jurors. "In the extreme northern part of Illinois," Douglas railed, "he can proclaim as bold and radical abolitionism as ever Giddings, Lovejoy, or Garrison enunciated, but when he gets down a little further south he claims that he is an old line Whig, a disciple of Henry Clay . . . and declares that he still adheres to the old line Whig creed, and has nothing whatever to do with Abolitionism, or negro equality, or negro citizenship."

Lincoln denied such charges at the Charleston debate with comments that have haunted his reputation since ("I am not, nor ever have been in favor of bringing about in any way the social and political equality of the white and black races"). But at the time, that opinion would have been a common one, especially among listeners in a southern Illinois city like Charleston. Evidence of how extreme the idea of equality remained to the voting public can be found in the transcript of the Charleston debate. Lincoln began his remarks by saying that he had been approached by an "elderly gentleman" who asked "whether I was really in favor of producing a perfect equality between the negroes and white people." The mere suggestion of such a radical position elicited "great laughter," according to a stenographer from the Republican-leaning *Chicago Tribune* transcribing the speech. Mainstream voters and their candidates still did not take abolitionism, or abolitionists, seriously.

That did not prevent Douglas from repeating the attack on Lincoln at their penultimate debate at Quincy, charging that his opponent had said something entirely different "when addressing the Chicago abolitionists," maintaining that "all distinctions of race must be discarded." As Douglas put it, "Did old Giddings, when he came down among you four years ago, preach more radical abolitionism than that? Did Lovejoy, or Lloyd Garrison, or Wendell Phillips, or Fred. Douglass, ever take higher abolition ground than that?"

Events a year later would further fan the fears of Southern—and many Northern—whites about the effects of abolition. In 1859 abolitionist leader John Brown led an ill-fated attempt to incite a slave insurrection in Virginia. Brown's raid on Harpers Ferry created a national sensation and put Republicans, even moderate antislavery Republicans like Lincoln, on the defensive. Democrats now revived the charge that the opposition party, no matter how it tried to hide behind calls for an unthreatening "ultimate extinction" of slavery by attrition, inevitably fomented radical, murderous abolitionists like John Brown merely by failing to allow whites to decide for themselves whether to carry slavery into the new territories.

The charges that Lincoln himself was a supporter of violent abolitionist actions never went away and were made with only greater force and bile in the wake of Brown's failed raid. Lincoln tried to fight back. "He believed the attack of Brown wrong for two reasons," a newspaper reported after Lincoln spoke at Elwood, Kansas, around the time of Brown's execution in December 1859. "It was a violation of law and it was, as all such attacks must be, futile as far as any effect it might have on the extinction of a great evil." In his Cooper Union address in

John Brown—the most famous, feared, and revered abolitionist of the 1850s—whose armed raid into Harpers
Ferry, Virginia, led to his own execution but unleashed
renewed pressure on the Republican Party to support
black freedom, along with renewed resolve by Southern
Democrats to resist it. LIBRARY OF CONGRESS

New York a few months later, Lincoln took pains to respond to critics
who refused to accept Republican insistence that Brown was a radical
with no connection to Republican moderates: "You charge that we stir
up insurrections among your slaves," Lincoln declared in his February 27, 1860, oration. "We deny it; and what is your proof? Harper's
Ferry! John Brown!! John Brown was no Republican; and you have
failed to implicate a single Republican in his Harper's Ferry enterprise."
Of course, several abolitionists partial to the Republicans had, in fact,
supported Brown—including New York's own former congressman
Geritt Smith. But this fact Lincoln conveniently skirted. "John Brown's
effort was peculiar," Lincoln insisted at Cooper Union. "It was not a
slave insurrection. It was an attempt by white men to get up a revolt
among slaves, in which the slaves refused to participate. In fact, it was
so absurd that the slaves, with all their ignorance, saw plainly enough

it could not succeed." To Lincoln, it was equally absurd that opponents now tried to use John Brown to "break up the Republican organization."

Because the Harpers Ferry episode remained a heated and unresolved topic, Lincoln continued to refer to it on the eastern speaking tour that followed Cooper Union. He distanced himself from Brown again at New Haven, Connecticut, calling charges that mainstream Republicans supported Brown's raid "inexcusable." Lincoln distanced himself from Brown yet again in his remarks at Bloomington, Illinois, a month later, in April. Clearly, when they began their quest to capture the White House in 1860, mainstream Republicans regarded John Brown not as a martyr but as an albatross. That Brown's ultra-abolitionist position remained unacceptable to mainstream Republicans even in New England became apparent around the same time as Lincoln was seeking support in New England. Years earlier he had given a pro–Zachary Taylor campaign speech at Boston's famous Tremont Temple, where he was well received as a strange-looking but amusing and effective orator. When African American abolitionist leader Frederick Douglass prepared to visit the same temple to make a speech defending John Brown, an angry crowd refused to let him appear.

Lincoln and other mainstream Republican politicians continued to maintain a clear nonabolitionist position throughout the 1860 campaign. They were focused primarily on overcoming the dominant influence of Southern politicians in Washington. By contrast, William Lloyd Garrison, longtime publisher of the *Liberator,* the leading abolitionist newspaper, and Frederick Douglass, the leading African American abolitionist and publisher of *Douglass' Monthly,* were not deterred by the John Brown debacle from their continuing efforts to persuade public opinion to support the immediate abolition of slavery and equal rights for African Americans. Throughout this period, Lincoln and other mainstream Republican politicians had little, if any, direct contact with the leaders of the abolition movement. Lincoln focused on gaining broad national support for his party and his candidacy and continued to distance himself from the claim that he supported John Brown's violent actions. He did not seek direct support from abolitionist leaders. He believed open abolitionist support would be far from helpful in his campaign for the presidency in 1860.

While abolitionist leaders maintained their efforts to secure freedom and equal rights for all African Americans, the majority of the nation's white voters in the North were still not convinced. They clearly separated slavery, in their minds, into three separate issues: the political issue of preventing the extension of the Southern economic system to the territories, the constitutional issue of abolishing slavery in the Southern states, and the social issue of equality for African Americans. Although many were prepared to address the political issue, they were not prepared to address the constitutional and social issues. Those still seemed extremist ideas.

Lincoln became the choice of the majority of Republican voters in 1860 because he was sworn to eliminate Southern political control of the levers of power in Washington by preventing the extension of slavery to the western territories. Most Northern voters did not expect Lincoln to support the abolitionist efforts of William Lloyd Garrison, Frederick Douglass, and Harriet Beecher Stowe to abolish slavery throughout the United States and provide equal rights for all African Americans. Indeed, in 1860 Lincoln himself did not expect to do so, either.

In the 1860 presidential race, Abraham Lincoln and Stephen Douglas faced each other again. This time they did so without the active participation of Lincoln himself, who, true to the tradition of the day, did no direct campaigning after his nomination. Surrogates took up his cause and, wherever possible, muffled antislavery zealotry. Republican supporters were careful to portray Lincoln almost apolitically, in campaign biographies and newspaper profiles alike, promoting him not as an advocate for freedom for the slaves but as a model American who had admirably risen from poverty and obscurity through hard work, labor that included strenuous jobs like rail splitting and flatboating. Pro-Lincoln political cartoons of the day often showed him wearing a frontiersman's shirt and toting an ax, which in the "Railsplitter's" hands became a symbol of American opportunity. But anti-Lincoln political cartoons just as determinedly portrayed him as an outright abolitionist, depicting him, in one crude example, trying to hide a symbolic African American beneath a pile of log rails of the candidate's own making—the veritable and literal "nigger in the woodpile."

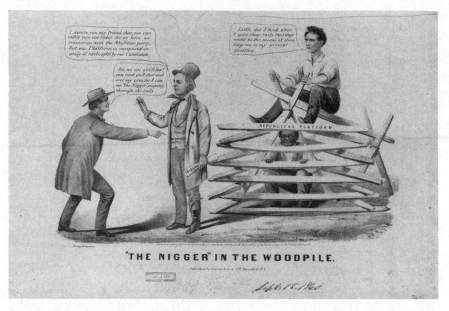

Currier & Ives's 1860 anti-Lincoln print *"The Nigger" in the Woodpile* was cruelly casual about its use of an offensive but all too common racial slur and equally racist in its minstrel-like depiction of the trapped African American. Most of all, however, the cartoon was meant to brand Lincoln a secret antislavery radical attempting to conceal his ardent abolitionism behind a frontiersman's facade of handmade log rails. LIBRARY OF CONGRESS

As viewers of the cartoon surely understood, the metaphor was not only about concealment, but about competition. Who deserved to be part of the American Dream of economic opportunity? That was the question that Abraham Lincoln and all Americans were about to confront; not just in the fury of debate, but in the crucible of war.

Once Lincoln had won the 1860 contest, Frederick Douglass seemed filled with anger. "If Mr. Lincoln were really an Abolitionist President, which he is not," Douglass complained in December 1860, "if he were a friend to the Abolitionist movement, instead of being, as he is, its most powerful enemy, the dissolution of the Union might be the only effective mode of perpetuating slavery in the Southern States." In Douglass's words, "Mr. Lincoln proposes no measure which can bring him into antagonistic collision with the traffickers in human flesh." Lincoln's First Inaugural Address, in which the new president pledged to enforce the Fugitive Slave Act if it kept Southern states in the Union, struck Douglass as "weak," "revolting," and "horrible."

Dissolution of the Union followed Lincoln's election, and Douglass spent the next two years urging Lincoln to abolish slavery in order to win the war. Douglass repeatedly assailed Lincoln in his abolitionist newspaper, *Douglass' Monthly,* criticizing him for failing to understand that slavery was the root cause of secession and rebellion and that its destruction was essential to the country's salvation. But much as Lincoln detested slavery, it took him more than a year in office to find a way to use presidential power to effect abolition. As he later explained it, "I have never understood that the Presidency conferred upon me an unrestricted right to act officially upon this judgment and feeling."

FOREVER FREE

LINCOLN THE EMANCIPATOR

L INCOLN'S DETERMINATION TO GUARANTEE THE FUTURE OF THE American experiment—the "cause" that lay behind his willingness to fight the Civil War—did not significantly change during the course of the conflict. Instead, the war steeled his commitment, even when it seemed that the Confederacy might actually win its "freedom" from the Union.

When the war started, Lincoln assumed that preventing the extension of slavery to the western territories would be enough to ensure the extension of the Northern middle-class society to all the states admitted to the Union in the future. He expected that slavery would continue to exist in the Southern states in the immediate future, even if he hoped it would ultimately disappear. Lincoln remained resistant to the abolitionist cause of granting equal rights to African Americans in the North or the South, but he did hope to move toward eventual freedom for Southern slaves through a policy of compensation for slave owners and voluntary colonization for former slaves. In one proposal aimed at bringing about the ultimate extinction of slavery, he suggested providing cash to slaveholders who would free their slaves. But Lincoln did not expect the freed slaves to move north. He continued to envision Northern society as the home of free white men. Indeed, in 1860, 99 percent of the population of the Northern states was white, and the great majority were firmly opposed to equal rights for Negroes or increasing the African American population in their midst.

The evidence suggests that Lincoln sincerely hoped during the first years of the war that the freed slaves would join with free African Americans from the North to form colonies outside the United States in Central America, the Caribbean, or Africa. But conditions on the ground during the war made Lincoln's compensation and colonization policies increasingly irrelevant. The idea that the war would be over in a short time was shattered by the failure of the Union armies to win decisive victories in 1861 and 1862. In battle after battle, Confederate troops did more than hold their own. If the idea of abolishing slavery did not seem a viable option before the war broke out, it eventually evolved into a potential tool for winning the war and saving the Union.

Lincoln's most aggressive generals and Republican majorities in the Congress eventually became open to new ideas to weaken the Southern war effort when slaves began to free themselves by crossing over to Union army lines.

The first important initiative in this direction was taken early in the fighting. On May 23, 1861, little more than a month into the Civil War, three young black slaves, pressed into service by the Confederate armed forces, rowed across the James River in Virginia and asked for asylum on the Union side. The next morning they were summoned before General Benjamin Butler, who commanded the Union army headquartered in Fort Monroe, Virginia. A savvy attorney in peacetime, Butler had been lately reading up on his military law. While the Compromise of 1850 required returning "fugitive slaves" to their Confederate owners, Butler also knew that a commander had a right to seize "enemy property" that was being used for hostile purposes.

Butler decided not to return the three fugitives to their Confederate owners. They would be regarded, he declared, as "contraband of war"— or, as the thousands of refugees who followed came to be known, "contrabands." Within a week more than forty-five fugitive slaves were in Fort Monroe, with more arriving every day. Many were put to work as laborers in support of the Union army. Butler reported the influx to Lincoln, and within days it became a running story in the Northern press. Weeks after the first fugitives arrived at Fort Monroe, slaves were reported flocking to the Union lines, almost everywhere Union lines existed. When Lincoln and his cabinet met to address Butler's decision, they decided to do and say nothing. At first, the administration gave little guidance to the generals in the field. Without direction from Washington, some followed Butler's example. By contrast, commanding General George B. McClellan—a Democrat—adopted the opposite policy.

The debate was decided soon enough. In August 1861, facing a war that seemed to have no immediate end in sight, Congress passed and Lincoln signed a law authorizing the seizure of all property, including slaves, being used in aid of the rebellion. On July 16, 1862, Congress passed a second Confiscation Act that went further, authorizing the confiscation of all property belonging to rebels and freeing all slaves held by disloyal citizens. Like the first confiscation law, however, the new legislation relied on the courts for enforcement. The federal judicial system in the South was by then all but nonexistent.

Lincoln contemplated vetoing this second Confiscation Act as going too far. But his most aggressive generals weighed in, arguing that freed slaves would provide a positive resource for the Union armies, or, at the very least, a drain on home-front slave labor in the Confederacy. Eventually, Lincoln concluded that he should not only sign but implement the law. Ever the effective politician, he overcame the constitutional protection of slavery by asserting that it was now a matter of military necessity to deploy his power as commander in chief of the Union armies to free the slaves owned by the supporters of the rebellion.

Lincoln's change in political tactics was based on military realities that he could not ignore. At the beginning of the war, there had been little substantial support in the North for the immediate abolition of slavery. Moreover, Lincoln had worried that any action he might take on slavery might cause the border slave states still on the Union side to secede and support the Southern proslavery cause. By the end of 1862, that fear had amounted to nothing, and it had also become clear to most Americans—North and South—that the war would not end quickly. It was also clear that Southern slaves could become a substantial asset in support of the Northern armies. Then and only then did Lincoln decide to emancipate all the slaves "owned" by Southerners in the Confederacy and, following the advice of his generals, encourage them to use the freed slaves to support the Union armies in the field. With one stroke of the pen, President Lincoln used his power as commander in chief of American forces to declare more than 80 percent of all the slaves in the United States "then, thenceforward, and forever free."

Jefferson Davis and the Confederacy faced an entirely different set of challenges. The Confederacy could not ignore the weakening of the Southern economy and its military effort, as an increasing number of slave owners refused to provide slaves to labor in support of the Confederate armies, while an increasing number of slaves continued to emancipate themselves and offer support to the Union armies.

The idea of emancipation entered the Confederate discussion as a military option, too. One farsighted Confederate general, Patrick Cleburne of the Army of Tennessee, went so far as to write to Jefferson Davis in December 1863: "We are waging war with the enemy in the field and an insurrection in the rear." He went on to assert that the Confederate cause could not be sustained without the support of its slaves (who constituted more than 40 percent of the Southern population). He urged Davis to do what he had to do to earn the slaves' loyalty for the Confederacy. This, he argued, could be accomplished only by recognizing the slaves' own political desires and objectives in the war. "We must bind him to our cause by no doubtful bonds and the only bond sufficient is the hope of freedom. . . . It would be preposterous to expect him to fight against it with any degree of enthusiasm. When we make soldiers of them we must make free men of them beyond all questions."

Needless to say, Jefferson Davis was not responsive to Cleburne's advice, at least at that point in the conflict. There was no way that a war waged to preserve a permanent slave society was ready to adopt a Confederate Emancipation Proclamation in 1863.

Facing the beginning of the end of his doomed fight for independence in December 1864, Jefferson Davis did belatedly suggest that slaves should be offered freedom as an incentive to fight in the Confederate army. But by then it was too late—either to act on the suggestion or for such an action to make a difference in the outcome of the war.

Davis may have missed his opportunity to make history, but Abraham Lincoln did not. Nonetheless, Lincoln's leadership in securing emancipation has been viewed through sharply different lenses by different observers at different points in time. That it was immediately viewed as historic and momentous—and to some, outrageous—cannot be denied. The Preliminary Emancipation Proclamation was regarded in its own time with so much trepidation and outright fear that it provoked a Wall Street panic, Union troop desertion, bellicose foreign condemnation, vast racial unease, and severe political rebuke from voters at the polls later in 1862. After the war Lincoln was so celebrated for and closely identified with the achievement of emancipation that many Americans dubbed him "the Great Emancipator." But that term is now considered by some historians as politically incorrect, and Lincoln's reputation as an antislavery leader has been called repeatedly into question. Lincoln's Emancipation Proclamation is viewed by some scholars not as a revolutionary positive step but as delayed, insufficient, and insincere. No wonder revisionists have been debating Lincoln's intentions, with particular emphasis on the fact that African Americans did not achieve their true "emancipation" until the era of the civil rights movement a century after Lincoln's death.

Lincoln's overriding commitment was to establish once and for all that the American government "of the people, by the people, for the people, shall not perish from the earth." He did not waver in the belief that slavery was a moral and economic blight that undermined the essential American promise of government by and for its people. But he did not yet believe that immediate and total abolition of slavery should be presented as a principal object of the war. As Lincoln famously said in a letter to Horace Greeley on August 22, 1862: "My paramount object in this struggle *is* to save the Union, and is *not* either to save or to destroy slavery." He went on to explain, "I intend no modification of my oft-expressed *personal* wish that all men everywhere could be free."

Modern historians who apply twenty-first-century mores to a nineteenth-century man are not the only ones who have made it difficult to see Lincoln's Emancipation Proclamation within the context of its own time. Lincoln himself is responsible for much of the confusion. He so complicated the announcement of his proclamation with continuing public arguments for compensation and colonization that it is little wonder the public had trouble then—and has continued to have problems ever since—in discerning his true motivations.

Interregnum is the archaic word that is most often applied to the four-month secession winter that separated Lincoln's November 1860 election from his March 1861 inauguration, one of the most perilous periods in American history. But the Union endured a second equally dangerous interregnum just a year later, between July 12, 1862, the day Lincoln first revealed to a small circle of intimates his plan to emancipate slaves owned by rebel slaveholders in the South, and his announcement of the plan to the public two months later, on September 22.

To fully understand the emancipation interregnum requires us to examine not only Lincoln's own growing sense of destiny but also his specific public relations strategy.

Lincoln believed that public policy could be successful only if it was in tune with the popular mood. He had emphasized this "central idea" in a speech to fellow Republicans in Chicago in 1856 when he said "our government rests in public opinion. Whoever can change public opinion, can change the government, practically just so much." Lincoln returned to this central idea in the initial Lincoln-Douglas debate in 1858 when he said, "With public sentiment, nothing can fail; without it nothing can succeed."

During the emancipation interregnum in the summer of 1862, the public seemed entirely focused on the war. It is not surprising, then, that Lincoln spent little time reminding the public of his economic ideas, however important they remained to him. Americans were preoccupied by concerns about soldiers and battles and were confronted almost daily by arguments from the proponents and opponents of immediate abolition. Indeed, it is surprising that Lincoln found any time and space, as he did in the Gettysburg Address, to remind the public that the underlying objective of the war was, to his mind, an economic promise: to ensure that the unique American "government of the people, by the people, for the people," with all the promise it held for equal opportunity for all Americans, "shall not perish from the earth."

Even when public sentiment on a specific issue was not definitively on his side, Lincoln was prepared—and certainly able—to do the necessary work to maintain general public support for his leadership. He contributed an abundant arsenal of personal sensitivity, a remarkable sense of political timing, an undiminished gift for great writing, and, when he believed the occasion called for it, a dazzling command of the press in an era in which most of the nation's journals were consistently and openly loyal to one political party or the other. However primitive what we might today call the era's "media platforms," Lincoln certainly knew the terrain and how to dominate it. And while he tended to plan in solitary, when he was ready to act publicly he knew how to rally Republican politicians, loyal editors, and public opinion to his side.

Lincoln's bumpy road to emancipation was paved not only by political guile but also by political weakness—the fear of disappointing both liberals and conservatives, abolitionists and proslavery Unionists, Republicans and Democrats, civilians and soldiers, Northerners and Southerners, the thrones and parliaments of Europe, and the Congress and voters of the United States. To make things more difficult, the drama unfolded during a critical election year for Congress in 1862. When Lincoln read his first emancipation draft to his cabinet in July, his advisers urged him to table the initiative until the army could win a morale-boosting victory on the battlefield. Postmaster General Montgomery Blair left no doubt as to why he counseled delay: as Lincoln remembered it, Blair "deprecated the policy, on the ground that it would cost the Administration the fall elections." Whipsawed by military events and political contingencies, Lincoln believed he had little choice but to send the public mixed messages about his policy, sharing his unannounced plan for emancipation only with those who could help him, even if they did not quite know they had become coconspirators.

Modern critics—indeed, many abolitionists in his own time—condemned Lincoln for waiting as long as he did to act on emancipation. But direct and immediate action was not likely to produce the desired result. Lincoln had good reason to doubt, in the summer of 1862, that he possessed either the public or official support, the military power, or the political opportunity to embark on a new, broad antislavery policy without risking political ruin and, with it, the fall of the Union. Obfuscation became not only a tactic but a life preserver.

That Lincoln believed in the concept of free labor for his entire adult life is beyond dispute. That he acted cautiously on freedom for the slaves once in power is also undeniable. Both predilections were apparent when, on July 12, he had urged border-state senators and congressmen to push for compensated emancipation in the slave states still in the Union. Though Lincoln is known as a master of rhetoric, he frequently chose to present unwelcome policies in a practical and uninspiring lawyerly fashion, to avoid emotional or philosophic arguments that were not likely to be accepted by public opinion. When, for example, one of his most dependable allies in the press, Henry Raymond, editor of the *New York Times,* fretted that paying for compensated emancipation would bankrupt the country, Lincoln used economic logic, not humanitarian zeal, to win over the rather conservative journalist. "Have you noticed the facts," he wrote Raymond on March 9, "that less than one half-day's cost of this war would pay for all [slaves] in Delaware, Maryland, District of Columbia, Kentucky, and Missouri at the same price?" Here was the language of the lawyer proposing compensated emancipation of all the slaves in the border states with the precision of an accountant, not the enthusiasm of a liberator. "Please look at these things," he implored Raymond, "and consider whether there should not be another article in the Times."

Confident that his compensated emancipation policy made economic as well as moral sense, Lincoln summoned the congressional delegations from the slaveholding "border" states still in the Union, plus Tennessee and western Virginia, to the White House on July 12 and read a formal statement pressing the point. "I do not speak of emancipation *at once,*" he pointed out, "but of a *decision* at once to emancipate *gradually.*" Acknowledging—in the form of a warning— the growing power of the forces for freedom, he added, "The pressure, in this direction, is still upon me, and is increasing. By conceding what I now ask, you can relieve me, and much more, can relieve the country, in this important point."

His appeal fell on profoundly deaf ears. Following a "stormy" caucus on July 12, 1862, the delegates of the "border" slave states still in the Union voted twenty to nine to reject Lincoln's proposal for compensated emancipation, dismissing it as economically, socially, and militarily unacceptable. Any form of emancipation, the majority insisted, would not shorten the war, as Lincoln argued, but actually lengthen it, since the military would neither support nor enforce it. Not for five months more would Lincoln attempt again to use eloquence of any kind to sway Congress to support compensated emancipation.

General George McClellan, the commanding general of the Army of the Potomac, represented a particularly formidable impediment to the idea of emancipation. Whenever Massachusetts senator Charles Sumner pressed Lincoln on emancipation, the president confided, "I would do it if I were not afraid that half the officers would fling down their arms and four more states would rise." Now the most prominent of all such officers handed the president, his commander in chief, a peremptory, almost insubordinate letter, proclaiming that "military power should not be allowed to interfere with the relations of servitude" and warning that "a declaration of radical views, especially upon slavery, will rapidly disintegrate our present Armies." The letter clearly contained the threat that McClellan, a Democrat in politics and already rumored a likely candidate for president in 1864, would use his army only to restore federal authority, not to free slaves.

The very next morning, the president made a bold and deft decision that laid bare his feelings on the matter of freeing slaves. He eliminated McClellan as a potential obstacle to emancipation by appointing Henry Halleck as general in chief of all land armies of the United States, with McClellan now his subordinate. A few days later, on July 13, 1862, Lincoln shared a confidence with Secretary of State William H. Seward and Secretary of the Navy Gideon Welles, which even the inscrutable Seward confessed seemed "momentous." Describing himself as "earnest in the conviction that something must be done" to counter "the reverses before Richmond, and the formidable power and dimensions of the insurrection," Lincoln proposed that the time had finally come for "extraordinary measures to preserve the national existence." It was then, Welles remembered, that Lincoln "first mentioned to Mr. Seward and myself," and, he believed, "to any one . . ." "the subject of emancipating the slaves by proclamation." For the record, both Seward and Welles reacted by expressing misgivings, the conservative navy secretary particularly shocked that such a policy could be proposed by a president who "had been prompt and emphatic in denouncing any interference by the General Government" on slavery.

To put this revelation in chronological perspective within a calendar crowded with incident: July 13 was three days after Lincoln's return from his visit to McClellan, one day after he had appealed to the border-state officials to support compensated emancipation, and one day before they would turn him down. Those who saw Lincoln during those tense days understandably found him, as did his old Illinois friend Senator Orville H. Browning, "weary, care-worn and troubled."

McClellan remained bogged down on the Virginia peninsula in his ill-fated campaign to take Richmond, and General John Pope was about to lose the Second Battle of Bull Run. But frustration over military failure was not the only force propelling Lincoln forward. He was also taking advantage of a singular opportunity presented to him by lawmakers. An ever more aggressively antislavery Congress had just passed and sent to him for his approval the sweeping new second Confiscation Act, giving military officers the right to seize slave property as they advanced into the Confederacy. Lincoln hesitated about approving the bill. His friend Orville Browning, for one, ominously advised that "it was a violation of the Constitution and ought to be vetoed," adding that the president's decision "was to determine whether he was to control the abolitionists and radicals, or whether they were to control him." But Lincoln decided to take the first step, moving forward in the direction of the abolitionists and the radical Republicans to emancipate the slaves.

On July 17 the pro-administration *New York Times* advised its readers: "It seems not improbable that the President considers the time near at hand when slavery must go to the wall." But Lincoln remained inscrutable. That day the exhausted president traveled up to Capitol Hill, as was customary for presidents on the last day of congressional sessions. There he infuriated both conservatives and liberals alike (and further confused the public about his own intentions) by signing the landmark confiscation bill while at the same time submitting a lengthy commentary objecting to what he called the "startling" idea "that congress can free a slave within a state." The emancipation power remained a privilege that Lincoln intended to reserve exclusively to himself.

Lincoln was in fact preparing to deflect Congress and to move boldly on his own. He would "not conserve slavery much longer," his secretary John Hay confided to a prominent antislavery activist on July 20. "When next he speaks in relation to this defiant and ungrateful villainy it will be with no uncertain sound." The very next day, Lincoln prepared to unleash that sound with a force he knew would be heard around the world.

On July 22, 1862, with Congress safely in recess, Lincoln decided to act on his own—just as he had after the Sumter attack in 1861. The president convened a cabinet meeting to announce his intention to invoke his power as commander in chief to free slaves in rebel territory as a military measure. As cabinet members Seward, Stanton, Chase, and the others listened, the president read aloud the first draft of the Emancipation Proclamation based almost entirely on the recently signed Confiscation Act. Congress had already laid the groundwork for him, but the next step was entirely Lincoln's. The draft ended with the clear promise that "as a fit and necessary military measure . . . on the first day of January in the year of Our Lord one thousand, eight hundred and sixty[-]three, all persons held as slaves within any state or states, wherein the constitutional authority of the United States shall not then be practically recognized, submitted to, and maintained, shall then thenceforward, and forever, be free." Thus was born the Emancipation Proclamation that would, when implemented, free hundreds of thousands of enslaved people years before the Thirteenth Amendment outlawed slavery permanently and everywhere.

Lincoln did not follow custom that day by asking his ministers' assent. As he remembered it, "I said to the Cabinet that I had resolved upon this step, and had not called them together to ask their advice, but to lay the subject-matter of a proclamation before them."

July 22, 1862, might have been remembered as the epochal day of commitment to emancipation except for what happened next. Not only did the conservative attorney general, Edward Bates of slaveholding

First Reading of the Emancipation Proclamation was A. H. Ritchie's wildly popular 1866 engraving of the 1864 painting by White House artist in residence Francis Bicknell Carpenter. Even though Lincoln actually tabled the proclamation after reading a draft to his cabinet on the day portrayed, July 22, 1862, Carpenter chose this occasion for his picture because he considered it nothing less than the launching of a "new epoch in the history of Liberty." LIBRARY OF CONGRESS

Missouri, object strenuously on legal grounds, but he also brought up the political risk. Even the abolitionist secretary of the treasury, Salmon Chase, objected, declaring that he preferred simply giving generals in the field the power to "organize and arm the slaves" themselves."

Secretary of State William Seward was wary, too. He warned that so radical a step in the wake of recent military reverses would "be viewed as the last measure of an exhausted government, a cry for help . . . our last shriek, on the retreat." It was "an aspect of the case," Lincoln later admitted, that he had "entirely overlooked." In response, as he later told an artist, "I put the draft of the proclamation aside, as you do your sketch for a picture, waiting for a victory." Lincoln, in other words, would issue a proclamation only on the heels of a Union victory, when no one could attribute the move to weakness or desperation.

It proved a longer wait than Lincoln had feared in his worst nightmares, with emancipation now hinged irrevocably to a military triumph that might never come. In the short term, Lincoln instead would endure yet another defeat—the unmitigated Union disaster at the Second Battle of Bull Run at the end of August, a setback that might have tempted a less determined liberator to shelve the emancipation initiative altogether. Instead, it propelled Lincoln to continue what had become an elaborate outpouring of deceptive rhetoric. He sought to embolden emancipation expectations among the antislavery abolitionists in his party without igniting potentially fatal opposition from conservative Northern Democrats and, worse, disunion among proslavery border states. That such a balancing act could have succeeded, without collapsing of its own weight, constitutes perhaps the most amazing backstory of all. What Lincoln allowed the public to know and when helped, however fitfully and imperfectly, to prepare the country's white majority for black freedom, even as it has served since to challenge Lincoln's reputation as a dedicated emancipator.

Lincoln's White House secretaries understood that, however "persistently misconstrued" their boss's words at this time were, they were meant to accomplish but one goal: "to curb and restrain the impatience of zealots from either faction." Lincoln was acting on his long-term understanding that "with public sentiment, nothing can fail; without it nothing can succeed."

The true test, then, was still to come. Lincoln knew he had to take substantial steps to move public sentiment forward without challenging directly the prejudiced view of most white Americans of his time. On August 14, 1862, in one of his first steps to that end, Lincoln invited a "Deputation of Free Negroes" to the White House. All but lost to history now is the fact that no American president had ever before invited a group of African Americans to confer with him officially. As to the substance of the conference, Lincoln launched into a frosty, patronizing lecture to the stunned delegation, conceding that while "your race suffer very greatly . . . many of them by living among us," he added, "ours suffer from your presence." Lincoln's words were harsh and stinging: "In a word we suffer on each side. If this is admitted, it affords a reason at least why we should be separated. . . . The aspiration of men is to enjoy equality with the best when free, but on this broad continent, not a single man of your race is made the equal of a single man of ours. Go where you are treated the best. . . . It is better for us both, therefore, to be separated."

Lincoln suggested that his well-situated African American visitors, all established free residents of the capital, should "sacrifice something of your present comfort for the purpose of being as grand in that respect as the white people."

The president said his preferred solution to the problem was still compensation and emancipation together with voluntary colonization to Liberia or perhaps, in a concession that black people might want to "remain within reach of the country of your nativity," to the Isthmus of Panama. Lincoln persisted that this policy was worth what he called a "try" and offered to "spend some of the money intrusted to me." He said the administration had a budget of six hundred thousand dollars with which to begin evacuation and relocation, though he acknowledged that political affairs in Central America were admittedly chaotic.

Two weeks earlier, abolitionist leader Frederick Douglass had told an Independence Day audience that Lincoln's actions to date had been "calculated in a marked and decided way to shield and protect slavery." Now, Lincoln seemed to be doing just that, and Douglass reacted to the publication of White House lecture with fury. He charged the president with illogically and unfairly using "the language and arguments of an itinerant Colonization lecturer, showing all his inconsistencies, his pride of race and blood, his contempt for Negroes and his canting hypocrisy." Douglass fumed that Lincoln, with his ill-chosen words, had furnished "a weapon to all the ignorant and base, who need only the countenance of men in authority to commit all kinds of violence and outrage upon the colored people of the country." As Douglass pointed out, slavery had caused the war, not slaves: "Mr. President, it is not the innocent horse that makes the horse thief, not the traveler's purse that makes the highway robber, and it is not the presence of the Negro that causes this foul and unnatural war, but the cruel and brutal cupidity of those who wish to possess horses, money and Negroes by means of theft, robbery, and rebellion."

Historian Eric Foner has aptly pointed out that a "heedless" Lincoln failed to appreciate that his words might fuel a wave of violent racism in the country aimed at African Americans. But for better or for worse, at that moment Lincoln had little interest in what the insignificant African American press, or, for that matter, the small number of free African Americans in the North, thought of his words. That was because those words had been aimed at precisely the audience he had not invited to the White House that day: not free and aspiring blacks but the larger constituency of free and fearful voting whites. While some critics have claimed that Lincoln's heartless words revealed his continuing personal interest in colonization and his purported racism, we should remember that his primary goal with this lecture was to sway a public that might otherwise be resistant to emancipation.

Lincoln may have drafted an actual emancipation proclamation and read it to his cabinet, but he sincerely believed that, unless he avoided any appearance of advocating equal rights for the soon to be freed blacks, he would lose so much white support by his action in favor of emancipation that his administration, and with it the Union, would fall.

After Lincoln's cold lecture, Salmon P. Chase spoke for many disappointed abolitionists when he recorded his disillusionment in his diary: "How much better would be a manly protest against prejudice against color!" Excluding profreedom whites—and even long-suffering blacks themselves—from the discussion, Lincoln had directly appealed for support for emancipation to the prejudiced instincts of his larger white constituency in the North.

Lincoln understood that the great majority of his Northern constituency were not willing to live side by side with former slaves and definitely unwilling to grant them equal rights. The free states of the North were not only free of slaves but almost completely free of African Americans. Not only Illinois but a majority of the Northern states had enacted laws that restricted the rights of free Negroes. Differences in social status between whites and blacks were generally considered legitimate—the normal way of life in the North, just as it was in the South.

Lincoln meant for his White House performance at the meeting with the Deputation of Free Negroes to remind Northern whites that he was no friend of black people—that he would not act to secure the potential amalgamation of millions of slaves into white society in the North. Nor did he see the Emancipation Proclamation as an immediate proclamation of equal rights for blacks in the South or in the North. Lincoln tried to persuade the American public that his present and future actions in the days to come would be aimed solely at securing victory in the war and restoration of the Union. The Emancipation Proclamation, after all, had been framed "as a fit and necessary military measure" intended to do just that—and nothing more.

A stain on Lincoln's record as a liberator? Perhaps. But with fall congressional elections looming, Union sentiment in the North fading in the wake of military defeats, border states now on record as hostile to freedom for their slaves, and the press maddeningly divided on all of the above, Lincoln believed he had no choice. The bitter pill of prejudice, along with the impractical and inhumane concept of colonization, was his continuing choice of emetic for a body politic he believed needed purging in preparation for the announcement of the Emancipation Proclamation. That is why, sensing military victory, Lincoln made sure his harsh speech against equal rights for Negroes in the United States did not just leak but poured. There is no question that he wanted this message publicized: he had invited journalists to the White House to record his every word in order to guarantee its wide circulation. He was not disappointed then, even if the episode may disappoint us now.

But victory on the battlefield remained elusive. The following week, with the military situation still murky, Horace Greeley of the *New York Tribune* struck a counterblow for freedom, putting the administration on the defensive and testing Lincoln's public relations skills further. In an editorial entitled "The Prayer of Twenty Millions," Greeley charged that the president had been "strangely and disastrously remiss" on the slavery issue and "unduly influenced" by "fossil politicians" from the border states. Greeley bluntly warned that "all attempts to put down the Rebellion and at the same time uphold its inciting cause," slavery, "were preposterous and futile."

In his famous reply, Lincoln subsumed his long-expressed opposition to slavery to his more urgent goal of reunion—or so he wanted it to appear. As he put it:

My paramount object in this struggle *is* to save the Union, and is *not* either to save or to destroy slavery. If I could save the Union without freeing *any* slave I would do it, and if I could save it by freeing *all* the slaves I would do it; and if I could save it by freeing some and leaving others alone I would also do that. What I do about slavery, and the colored race, I do because I believe it helps to save the Union; and what I forbear, I forbear because I do *not* believe it would help to save the Union.

Lincoln intended to issue the emancipation document exclusively as a military order, to diminish the size of the anticipated backlash from Northern Democrats and border-state loyalists as well as the antifreedom legislators in Congress who had rejected earlier emancipation initiatives. There were reasons for Lincoln to be guardedly hopeful about the success of his public relations strategy. Union general John Pope was in the midst of a major offensive in Virginia, and Lincoln imagined a decisive victory might occur soon so he could finally unsheathe the proclamation.

Union and Confederate armies met at Antietam Creek on Wednesday, September 17, 1862. Federal forces claimed victory when the Confederate army retreated back into Virginia. Lincoln finally had his military victory. Quickly, the president went to work crafting a final proclamation, using the weekend after Antietam to refine his document. On Monday, September 22, he called the cabinet back into session. While Lincoln conceded the continued risk of placing "in greater jeopardy the patriotic element in the border states," he insisted that there was no turning back. As Gideon Welles remembered, "His mind was fixed. . . . [H]e had made a vow, a covenant, that if God gave us the victory in the approaching battle, he would consider it an indication of Divine will." Now, Lincoln concluded, "God had decided this question in favor of the slaves."

In his Annual Message to Congress on December 1, 1862, Lincoln continued his efforts to calm the fears of his Northern white audience by emphasizing his impractical commitment to voluntary colonization. As if speaking beyond Congress to white America, he insisted:

I cannot make it better known than it already is, that I strongly favor colonization. . . . Reduce the supply of black labor, by colonizing the black laborer out of the country, and, by precisely so much, you increase the demand for, and wages of, white labor. . . . But why should emancipation south, send the free people north? People, of any color, seldom run, unless there be something to run from. *Heretofore* colored people, to some extent, have fled north from bondage; and *now*, perhaps, from both bondage and destitution. But if gradual emancipation and deportation be adopted, they will have neither to flee from.

Lincoln issued the final Emancipation Proclamation on January 1, 1863. Continuing his program to treat the proclamation as a necessity of war, the document was couched in his "dry as dust" legal style rather than the commanding emotional rhetoric that we associate with the Gettysburg Address and his other memorable speeches.

For months, Lincoln had waited. By means of a sometimes baffling web of public relations feints, he had made it seem like freedom had finally fallen into the nation's lap thanks to military victory. After a summer-long onslaught of statements that variously confused, dismayed, or heartened Americans of all political persuasions, official silence and selected revelations had emerged as Abraham Lincoln's chief weapons in presenting his decision to issue the Emancipation Proclamation on January 1, 1863.

With the formal issuance of Lincoln's Emancipation Proclamation, Lincoln and his more aggressive generals encouraged the "newly freed slaves" to join the Union armies, first as support personnel and later as actual combatants. With these first steps, Lincoln moved the nation forward to achieve his moral objective of abolishing slavery in the United States and his military objective of obtaining a significant new resource (former African American slaves) to fight for the Union. By the end of the war, there were 166 regiments of black troops enlisted in the Union armies. Records show that they suffered higher casualty rates than their white counterparts.

Throughout the first years of his presidency, Lincoln had maintained distance from the abolitionist wing of the party. During this period, the leaders of the abolitionist movement mounted withering criticisms of his failure to act directly to abolish slavery. In the end, of course, Lincoln made his peace with the abolitionists—and them with him—and ultimately he became the nation's leading abolitionist. But not quickly, and not without much criticism from their leaders.

The rapprochement took time. Frederick Douglass had only reluctantly supported the Republican ticket in 1860. Like Lincoln, however, Douglass was a political realist. If he could not have immediate change, he certainly was not averse to slow change. Legislative abolition of slavery in Washington, DC, which Lincoln signed into law in 1862, followed by announcement of the Preliminary Emancipation Proclamation later that year helped heal the breach between the president and the civil rights advocate. "It is true that the President lays down his propositions with many qualifications, some of which to my thinking, are unnecessary, unjust and wholly unwise," Douglass declared in an 1862 speech in Rochester, but a "blind man can see where the President's heart is."

An overjoyed Frederick Douglass exulted at the end of that historic American summer that this "slow, but we hope sure" president had, "while the loyal heart was near breaking with despair, proclaimed and declared . . . *Thenceforward and forever free.*" "Read the proclamation," he urged his abolitionist subscribers, "for it is the most important of any to which the President of the United States has ever signed his name."

After January 1, 1863, the two men met several times in the White House. At Lincoln's request, Douglass worked on a plan to recruit African Americans for the Union army. Such service, Lincoln believed, would help defeat the Confederacy and ensure that his Emancipation Proclamation would succeed in ending slavery and charting a path for African Americans to join the free labor force in the future. Not quite satisfied, Douglass tried to win equal pay for African American soldiers (a reform Lincoln initially resisted as stubbornly as he had resisted abolition—arguing that the white majority was not ready for such parity).

Later, when Lincoln began to fear that he would lose his quest for a second term and that his Democratic opponent would take office and take action to countermand emancipation, he turned again to Douglass, enlisting him in a plan to spread word of their emancipation to as many newly freed slaves as possible. Here was proof that Lincoln genuinely wanted enslaved people out of bondage and at last part of the free labor force questing for self-improvement. Douglass replied with a detailed memorandum suggesting that the administration set up a mini-army of "twenty or twenty five good men, having the cause at heart." These sessions convinced Douglass that Lincoln was sincere, a genuine antislavery man after all. Their plan, of course, never had to be implemented. Lincoln won a second term in November 1864, and enforcement of the proclamation continued uninterrupted wherever Union soldiers marched in the South.

The success of the Union armies in the last months of 1864 encouraged Lincoln in his new effort to secure passage of the Thirteenth Amendment to the Constitution. The amendment would validate and secure the notable moral achievement of abolishing slavery throughout the United States for all time. Lincoln dedicated himself to the effort, believing this would be an important step to fulfill his dream of an American society released from the moral, political, and economic burden of slavery.

For all his early reluctance, Lincoln was now in the forefront of the struggle to secure the permanent abolition of slavery in the United States. Largely through Lincoln's efforts, public opinion now tilted in favor of the abolition of slavery. But it was clearly not in favor of equal rights for African Americans in the North as well as the South. And Lincoln chose not to add his voice to support abolitionist efforts to provide equal rights to the newly freed slaves. Ever the believer that public opinion was the ultimate driver of political progress, Lincoln did not challenge directly the supremacist views of the majority of white Americans. Rather, he emphasized that "in *giving* freedom to the *slave,* we *assure* freedom to the *free*—honorable alike in what we give, and what we preserve." African Americans were to escape bondage and enter the promised land; their liberation would ensure that a free America would long endure.

A demonstration of how far Lincoln's reputation had evolved within the abolitionist community arrived on the president's desk in July 1864 in the form of a handsome commemorative gift from no less a freedom icon than William Lloyd Garrison, the longtime editor of the leading abolitionist newspaper, the *Liberator*. The gift was, as the presenter proudly described it, "an admirable painting" entitled *Watch Night—or, Waiting for the Hour*. It showed, Garrison wrote, "a group of negro men, women and children waiting . . . for the midnight hour of December 31, 1862 to pass, and the introduction of that new year which was to make them forever free." As Garrison proudly said, "It was my advice that it was presented to you as the most fitting person in the world to receive it."

Lincoln failed to acknowledge the gift with his usual sensitivity. Perhaps Lincoln's reluctance to adopt the mantle of abolitionist helps explain why it took six months for him to offer thanks for the anti-slavery picture Garrison had sent him. Was its subject too toxic for him still? We cannot know for sure, but a few months later Lincoln welcomed to the White House the African American abolitionist crusader and one-woman Underground Railroad, Sojourner Truth. Even then, when the "Moses" of her people tried thanking Lincoln for his help in ending slavery, the president inhospitably replied, "I'm not an abolitionist; I wouldn't free the slaves if I could save the Union in any other way. I'm obliged to do it."

The president finally responded to the painting after Garrison wrote him again to ask if the gift was ever received. Only then did the embarrassed president dispatch the sole letter he ever wrote to the living symbol of a movement he had not embraced until late in his life. "When I received the spirited and admirable painting 'Waiting for the Hour,'" he now apologized, "I directed my Secretary not to acknowledge its arrival at once, preferring to make my personal acknowledgment of the thoughtful kindness of the donors; and waiting for some leisure hour, I have committed the discourtesy of not replying at all. I hope you will believe that my thanks though late, are most cordial, and I request that you will convey them to those associated with you in this flattering and generous gift."

By then Lincoln had in turn extended to his onetime abolitionist adversaries the most important gift of all: a congressional resolution, passed just days before he wrote to Garrison, sending to the states a constitutional amendment abolishing slavery everywhere in the nation. At last, abolition was to be a reality. Demonstrating beyond question that his heart was in the task, Lincoln signed the resolution and marked it "approved"—even though presidential endorsements were not required for constitutional amendments. Lincoln probably did not even mind when the Senate passed another resolution chiding the president for signing the document.

For Lincoln, such minor condemnation was a small price to pay. By then he knew that the abolition of slavery was a transcendent moment that history would remember—and the man who had been so reluctant to embrace the cause for so long wanted his name on it for all to see for all time to come. Lincoln had finally become the abolitionist in chief.

Today, the imposing heroic statues that ring the public gardens alongside Boston Common pay tribute to the abolitionist pioneers who braved scorn and sometimes violence to demand an immediate end to slavery in America. Sculptures of Charles Sumner, William Lloyd Garrison, Wendell Phillips, and William Ellery Channing hold pride of place there. Just a few blocks away, at Park Plaza, Boston placed Thomas Ball's *Emancipation Memorial*, a replica of the statue of Lincoln Frederick Douglass had dedicated a year earlier in Washington. That day, another abolitionist hero, John Greenleaf Whittier, offered a poem to consecrate the unveiling and cement Lincoln's reputation for all time as an abolition hero worthy of celebration in the city that had nurtured the movement for so long:

> O symbol of God's will on earth
> As it is done above!
> Bear witness to the cost and worth
> Of justice and love.

Frederick Douglass wrote that in all his meetings with Lincoln, "I was impressed with his entire freedom from popular prejudice against the colored race. He was the first great man that I talked to in the United States freely, who in no single instance reminded me of

Emancipation, a politically audacious 1865 lithograph by J. L. Magee of Philadelphia, shows Lincoln using his Emancipation Proclamation to usher in "freedom to all, both black and white!"—as well as "education to all classes." Note the background scenes contrasting a slave whipping to school attendance. The print all but illustrated Lincoln's famous 1862 vow that "in *giving* freedom to the *slave,* we *assure* freedom to the *free.*" STERN COLLECTION, LIBRARY OF CONGRESS the difference between himself and myself, of the difference of color, and I thought that all the more remarkable because he came from a State where there were black laws" that restricted the rights of "free" African Americans. Douglass concluded that the Southern-born Lincoln seemed devoid of racial prejudice precisely because he had spent his early days in poverty, yearning for advancement, even as Douglass, born a slave, yearned for liberty and advancement. "I account partially for his kindness to me," Douglass explained, "because of the similarity with which I had fought my way up, we both starting at the lowest round of the ladder."

Well before Lincoln became an abolitionist, he had preached that the common goal of giving Americans the opportunity to work their way up "the ladder" applied to black as well as white men. Douglass said in an 1876 speech, "Viewed from the genuine abolition ground, Mr. Lincoln seemed tardy, cold, dull, and indifferent; but measuring him by the sentiment of his country, a sentiment he was bound as a statesman to consult, he was swift, zealous, radical, and determined."

Lincoln's "new birth of freedom" was to be an economic as well as political liberation for all citizens, both African Americans and white Americans. It was a new essential element in sustaining the exceptionalist middle-class society envisioned by the founding fathers. Lincoln was confident that passage of the Thirteenth Amendment would contribute to the perpetuation of the just, antiaristocratic middle-class society that he expected to emerge from the chaos of the Civil War.

Seven

WHAT WE SAY HERE AND WHAT WE DO HERE

LINCOLN THE WARRIOR

AS HE DID DURING HIS CAMPAIGN TO GARNER SUPPORT FOR THE Emancipation Proclamation, Lincoln regularly used his pen as a major weapon in the fight to preserve democracy and economic opportunity for all Americans. His rare speeches to the public (as president, it should be noted, the famous orator seldom orated), his recorded statements to White House visitors, letters to the press and remarks to troops en route to or returning from battlefields, and his alternatively cajoling and congratulatory dispatches to commanders and politicians constitute a truly remarkable archive of persuasion, morale building, political ingenuity, leadership skill, and, most surprising of all, military sophistication. Abraham Lincoln, it might be said, deployed words as artillery, not merely to establish strategy and issue orders, but to sustain public opinion and stiffen military resolve to engage in the bloody realities of hard fighting.

Lincoln fought the war of words aggressively. He was no match for Jefferson Davis's experience or bearing as a military man, but the president of the United States could turn a phrase far more adroitly than the president of the Confederate states—or just about anyone else of his time. And it was particularly urgent that he win the war of words in an era in which, Lincoln conceded, "he who moulds public sentiment goes deeper than he who enacts statutes or pronounces decisions."

After the Confederacy fired on Fort Sumter in April 1861, Lincoln had rallied the North by crafting appeals to both history and hope in words designed for "plain people" to understand. Today we would call them sound bites. The idea that any state held supremacy over the entire Union, Lincoln termed a "sophism." Secession was patently illegal, its defenders absurd, their arguments "sugar-coated." Its supporters were the enemies not just of the Union, but of the entire concept of popular government.

As Lincoln had explained in his July 4 Message to Congress, the Civil War was more than a fight for national preservation; it was also "a struggle for maintaining in the world, that form, and substance of government, whose leading object is to elevate the conditions of men—to lift artificial weights from all shoulders—to clear the paths of laudable pursuit for all—to afford all, an unfettered start, and a fair chance, in the race of life."

Lincoln himself never uttered a word of his great congressional message. By tradition, he simply sent it to Capitol Hill to be read aloud by clerks; it was then sent to newspapers for wider distribution. In fact, the so-called July 4 message was not actually read until July 5, and even then its first telegraphic transmissions were garbled.

Still, it was an indisputable success, reaching far beyond Congress to the country at large. Lincoln had brilliantly defined the coming struggle in words ordinary Americans could understand, appreciate, and support. Even though border-state legislators chafed, Congress rallied behind him, while friendly Republican newspapers heaped lavish praise. He could now count on public and congressional support for his burgeoning war effort. No president before ever used the power of words more deftly. Had his Independence Day message failed, history—and this nation—might have been far different.

Yet almost immediately, Lincoln found himself presiding over one of the largest, costliest, and deadliest wars in history. "War at the best, is terrible," he conceded to an audience in Philadelphia in 1864, "and this war of ours, in its magnitude and in its duration, is one of the most terrible." Though Lincoln had learned that war was unrelenting, brutal, destructive, and deadly, he did not shrink from it. Nor did he shrink from the task of maintaining support for it.

Most Americans today would be surprised, for they think of Lincoln as the era's least militarized civilian. Lincoln's presented himself both as a man of peace and as a man of war. The fact remains, however, that he was an unrelenting warrior, emotionally and politically dedicated to defeating the rebellion and prepared to commit men and resources in unprecedented numbers to secure the kind of peace worth fighting for—a peace that secured American democracy for all time.

Lincoln had believed in the necessity of war since he first learned about the American Revolution as a child, which he believed was provoked not by hate or revenge, but in pursuit of the "advancement of the noblest of cause." As the man leading a "good war" of his own, Lincoln clearly understood the difference between a just war conducted for a good cause and an unjust war undertaken for a bad cause. He insisted that war, if for a noble purpose, was indeed worth waging.

Even before he was himself compelled to manage the bloody Civil War, Lincoln was animated by the idea of justifiable wars like the American Revolution. Unlike the American commander in chief with whom he is often compared, Franklin D. Roosevelt, Lincoln never said, "I hate war." As it turned out, he was not reluctant to engage in war for a good cause.

A year before he ran for the presidency, Lincoln had told a Wisconsin audience that he yearned for a "world less inclined to wars, and more devoted to the arts of peace, than heretofore." He did not think himself a brave man, yet he never lacked for either personal courage—even under enemy fire—or the resolve, assurance, and talent to compel his army, navy, and civilian constituency to keep fighting.

When Lincoln became commander in chief in March 1861, he knew next to nothing about military matters. As president-elect he had exchanged a handful of letters with veteran general in chief Winfield Scott. Facing a crisis virtually from the moment he took office—compelled immediately to decide whether to reinforce Fort Sumter in Charleston Harbor—he operated largely by instinct and energy, throwing himself into long meetings with advisers and successfully educating himself, just as he had done years earlier with regard to the Bible, Shakespeare, geometry, and the law, simply by reading voraciously. As far as we know, Lincoln never opened Carl von Clausewitz's classic

On War, but he did borrow other military treatises from the Library of Congress, consuming, for example, the essential handbook authored by his own chief administrative general, Henry W. Halleck's *Elements of Military Art and Science.* Searching for officers who were "zealous & efficient," he became more zealous and efficient than any of them. In a way, he proved Clausewitz's argument that knowledge of military affairs was a less important qualification for a commander in chief than "a remarkable, superior mind and strength of character."

A comprehensive examination of Lincoln's speeches, letters, memoranda, orders, telegrams, and remarks on the subject of armed conflict and civilian morale shows a remarkable evolution. He goes from eager young Indian war officer to politically motivated congressional dove and then transforms himself into an astonishingly determined hawk. In this final iteration, he emerges increasingly willing to sacrifice life, to puncture the pride of vainglorious commanders, and even to mislead the public, if such words will help secure the preservation of an unbreakable union of American states.

Firmly committed as he was to the central idea pervading the war, one of his central tasks was to boost Americans' morale and convince them that they were fighting for nothing less than the preservation of America as a permanent example for the world of the value of democratic government working for the people. Lincoln wrote to high officials and ordinary Americans alike, to rouse their spirits, inspire action, give thanks to God for military victories, to "condole," as he once put it, the grieving parents, children, and siblings who had lost loved ones, and to work through, and usually past, constitutional and legal constraints on his authority as commander in chief.

In answer to persistent questions about when the long war would end, he responded: "We accepted this war for an object, a worthy object, and the war will end when that object is attained. Under God, I hope it will never until that time." When Lincoln was asked to explain the struggle and the sacrifice to members of an Ohio regiment who had risked their lives in the war, he said, "This government must be preserved in spite of the acts of any man or set of men. It is worthy of your every effort. Nowhere in the world is presented a government of so much liberty and equality." As he told the working men

Lincoln the orator arrives on the speakers' platform at Gettysburg, Pennsylvania, on November 19, 1863. In a few hours he would deliver his most famous speech—perhaps the most famous in American history. Photographer unknown, possibly one of the Bacharachs. ORIGINAL IN NATIONAL ARCHIVES; PHOTOGRAPH COURTESY LIBRARY OF CONGRESS

of Manchester, England—in a letter widely reprinted at home—the rebellion was above all "a war upon the rights of all working people."

Lincoln reached his oratorical apogee on the sacred ground of Gettysburg, Pennsylvania, on November 19, 1863. He spoke on the site of a new national soldiers cemetery set aside for the Union casualties who fell in what would be deemed the bloodiest battle of the Civil War. Seeking to soothe the pain of a grieving nation and remind them of why they must continue to fight, Lincoln delivered a speech universally remembered as one of the greatest ever written.

Lincoln said:

Four score and seven years ago our fathers brought forth on this continent, a new nation, conceived in Liberty, and dedicated to the proposition that all men are created equal.

Now we are engaged in a great civil war, testing whether that nation, or any nation so conceived and so dedicated, can long endure. We are met on a great battle-field of that war. We have come to dedicate a portion of that field, as a final resting place for those who here gave their lives that that nation might live. It is altogether fitting and proper that we should do this. But, in a larger sense, we cannot dedicate—we cannot consecrate—we cannot hallow—this ground. The brave men, living and dead, who struggled here, have consecrated it, far above our poor power to add or detract. The world will little note, nor long remember what we say here, but it can never forget what they did here. It is for us the living, rather, to be dedicated here to the unfinished work which they who fought here have thus far so nobly advanced. It is rather for us to be here dedicated to the great task remaining before us—that from these honored dead we take increased devotion to that cause for which they gave the last full measure of devotion—that we here highly resolve that these dead shall not have died in vain—that this nation, under God, shall have a new birth of freedom—and that government of the people, by the people, for the people, shall not perish from the earth.

With these extraordinary sentiments, Lincoln reaffirmed what he believed to be America's timeless commitment to build the middle-class society he had experienced in his own adult life—an exceptionalist society with a government that was not only "of the people" and "by the people" but also "for the people."

Generations of historians have struggled to explain what Lincoln meant when he called on the nation in the Gettysburg Address to be "dedicated here to the unfinished work . . . dedicated to the great task remaining before us . . . that this nation, under God, shall have a new birth of freedom—and that government of the people, by the people, for the people, shall not perish from the earth."

Lincoln's lifelong belief that slavery was immoral has led many historians to conclude that Lincoln defined his "unfinished work" as establishing equal rights for African Americans throughout the United

States. The Emancipation Proclamation and his dedicated and successful role in securing passage of the Thirteenth Amendment are cited as evidence of this view. But a closer look at Lincoln's words and deeds indicates that Lincoln viewed his "unfinished work" from a different perspective.

Lincoln's deeply held political view was that slavery was immoral because it violated the just position that one person should not own the fruits of the labor of another person—black or white. He was determined to sustain the unique democratic political and economic society of the free Northern states as the future of America. Lincoln was equally determined to prevent the extension of slavery to the western territories of the United States—to ensure that the slave system would be put "in the course of ultimate extinction." Lincoln believed the western territories had to be free of slavery to fulfill the promise of the exceptional American democratic economic society defined by the founding fathers and implemented in the Northern states. He believed this American system was unique in the world—that it was the "last best hope of mankind."

The Gettysburg Address is sometimes described as the briefest speech Lincoln made as president. But it was also the most complete statement of his commitment to a just and generous nation dedicated to government action to help all its citizens to improve their economic lives. It was the first time he used the phrase "a new birth of freedom" and the words "government . . . for the people, shall not perish from the earth." Looking to the aftermath of the Civil War, he was defining his and the nation's "unfinished work" as the new task of providing all citizens a government committed to helping all its citizens build a middle-class life.

Lincoln knew that he was delivering the Gettysburg Address to two audiences: the relatively small crowd at the cemetery and the millions who would read the text in the press. Lincoln had perfected the art of delivering state papers and political messages through the newspapers, and the Gettysburg Address was in many ways no different—simply better. Lincoln made few formal speeches as president, but he made sure that when he greeted special visitors with important remarks, they were quickly printed in the newspapers. Or, if he wrote an important letter—like the one to Erastus Corning defending his suspension of the writ of habeas corpus—it was aimed as well to thousands of readers who would see the words in newspaper and pamphlet reprints.

Long before American students began committing the Gettysburg Address to memory in the wave of patriotic ardor that swept the country during World War I—years before the words were incised on the marble walls of the Lincoln Memorial in Washington for all visitors to read—the speech lived because Lincoln made certain that it would "long endure": by giving his transcript to the Associated Press, by writing additional copies for souvenir albums and charity auctions, and by basking in the knowledge that it would be reprinted worldwide and praised at least in the newspapers loyal to his own political party.

From the beginning, the Gettysburg Address would be recognized and applauded because the brilliant public relations strategist who agreed to deliver his few remarks (in spite of the fact that he was not invited to be the main speaker of the day) was a consummate literary craftsman. Lincoln enjoyed his finest two minutes at Gettysburg, offering the most famous metaphor for renewal ever articulated by an American president—"a new birth of freedom." There is abundant evidence that Lincoln well understood the positive impact his speech would have on the American public.

But the Gettysburg Address and its call for a recommitment to freedom were not the only way Lincoln sought to convince the nation that this bloody war was necessary. More and more often as the conflict went on, Lincoln invoked God's will, to reassure both Northerners and, perhaps, himself. According to legend, when he was asked during the war whether God was indeed reliably on the Union side, Lincoln wryly commented that it was more important for Northerners to remain on God's side than the other way around.

As the war went on, and hundreds of thousands died in battle, Lincoln's description of God's will changed. He continued to believe that his cause was just. But he was astonished by the toll of death and destruction that accumulated in 1862, 1863, and 1864. He had not anticipated that the North, with its far greater population and resources, would find itself bogged down in such hard fighting year after year after year.

Neither artist nor photographer made a visual record of Lincoln's immortal, but brief, Gettysburg Address. In 1905 an unknown Chicago illustrator credibly imagined the historic scene this way. LIBRARY OF CONGRESS

Lincoln came to believe that God had not yet decided how or when the Civil War "would end." In 1864, after three years of fighting, he wrote Kentucky editor Albert G. Hodges, "The nation's condition is not what either party, or any man, devised, or expected." Then he repeated a phrase he had introduced in his "house divided" speech and added a reference to divine retribution allocated "fairly" to the North and the South, presaging his Second Inaugural the following year: "God alone can claim it. Whither it is tending seems plain. If God now wills the removal of a great wrong, and wills also that we of the North as well as you of the South, shall pay fairly for our complicity in that wrong, impartial history will find therein new cause to attest and revere the justice and goodness of God."

History might be impartial, especially as it evolved, but Lincoln now described God's will as ordained. It was far easier for Lincoln to propose this paradigm than to accept the awful human responsibility that came with three quarters of a million soldiers dead and hundreds of thousands more wounded—even in the name of "a new birth of freedom." Lincoln now insisted that God had ordained war and suffering to rid the nation of its greatest sin and to allocate that sin "fairly" to both sides, but primarily to the Southern slaveholders. He had come to what historian Elton Trueblood called a "prophetic interpretation of American history"—history Lincoln was in the process of reshaping.

There is a lingering debate among historians as to whether or not Lincoln's increasing emphasis on the conflict as God's war reflected the conversion of this rationalist thinker into a devout religious believer. While this debate remains unresolved, it is clear that Lincoln's new description provided a successful basis for maintaining the support of the majority of Americans in the North who were increasingly war weary but had never wavered in their belief in a just God.

Increasingly, and especially in his Second Inaugural Address, Lincoln referred to his own actions as fulfilling God's will. And he found new language to explain why a just God was willing to allow the death and destruction to go on as long as it did. What evil was so monstrous as to justify that outcome? And how could Lincoln explain the justice of the war to the American people?

By inauguration day, March 4, 1865, the voters, civilians and soldiers alike (the latter by a four-to-one margin), had validated their faith in the war by reelecting their president. Ulysses S. Grant was closing in on Robert E. Lee and his starving, depleted army; peace would almost certainly come soon. Here was an opportunity that a lesser orator—a lesser man—might have used for chest-thumping triumphalism. Instead, Lincoln reached out to accept not the laurels of war for the North but to share some of the blame for four score and nine years of the hypocrisy that made slavery acceptable in the South and its products welcome in the North. If not the best speech of Lincoln's life, the Second Inaugural Address was unequivocally the noblest and the most passionate in its distaste for forced labor.

> One-eighth of the whole population were colored slaves, not distributed generally over the Union, but localized in the southern part of it. These slaves constituted a peculiar and powerful interest. All knew that this interest was, somehow,

the cause of the war. To strengthen, perpetuate, and extend this interest was the object for which the insurgents would rend the Union, even by war; while the Government claimed no right to do more than to restrict the territorial enlargement of it. Neither party expected for the war, the magnitude, or the duration, which it has already attained. Neither anticipated that the *cause* of the conflict might cease with, or even before, the conflict itself should cease. Each looked for an easier triumph, and a result less fundamental and astounding. Both read the same Bible, and pray to the same God; and each invokes His aid against the other. It may seem strange that any men should dare to ask a just God's assistance in wringing their bread from the sweat of other men's faces; but let us judge not that we be not judged. The prayers of both could not be answered; that of neither has been answered fully. The Almighty has His own purposes. "Woe unto the world because of offenses! for it must needs be that offenses come; but woe to that man by whom the offense cometh!" If we shall suppose that American slavery is one of those offences which, in the providence of God, must needs come, but which, having continued through His appointed time, He now wills to remove, and that He gives to both North and South, this terrible war, as the woe due to those by whom the offence came, shall we discern therein any departure from those divine attributes which the believers in a living God always ascribe to Him?

When it came to choosing his own favorite among his immortal presidential orations, the best evidence we have—Lincoln's own comments on the matter—indicate that he believed his Second Inaugural Address was the best he ever delivered. It was also his bravest. Lincoln went out of his way to blame all Americans for too long tolerating the sin of slavery, which meant, implicitly, that they had prevented the American nation from fulfilling its promise of a successful democratic middle-class economy and society.

But Lincoln ended his Second Inaugural Address with an almost apocalyptic warning of potential retribution for the greatest American

Lincoln stands on the East Portico of the US Capitol to deliver perhaps his greatest speech, the Second Inaugural Address. Some forty thousand black and white onlookers gathered to hear the brief 703-word address under gray skies that suddenly parted when Lincoln appeared. "It made my heart jump," Lincoln admitted. But a few days later he confided of the speech, "I believe it is not immediately popular." Photograph by Alexander Gardner, March 4, 1865. LIBRARY OF CONGRESS

sin, that of slavery, warning in a breathtakingly long sentence quoting scripture, that Americans North as well as South might now be compelled to pay further for their inhumanity with even greater sacrifice of life to atone for God's displeasure over the wicked institution of slavery.

Listening to the "wonderful address" from the Capitol Plaza on that chilly March afternoon, abolitionist leader Frederick Douglass at first thought it "very short." But when he heard the president invoke that harsh biblical warning out of Matthew, Luke, and Psalm 19, Douglass declared appreciatively, "He answered all the objections raised to his prolonging the war in one sentence . . . a remarkable sentence."

Douglass would not have been alone in recognizing that Lincoln had just provided a stirring new rationale for justifying the long and bloody struggle. Before, Lincoln had argued that "the cause" that justified fighting the Civil War was to sustain the unique and exceptional American middle-class society envisioned by the founders in the Declaration of Independence. But now, Lincoln was using biblical and moral language to make a powerful case that the abolition of slavery was just as important. Indeed, liberty, freedom for slaves, and economic opportunity for all Americans were now inseparable.

Lincoln had originally made this connection a year earlier in a speech at Baltimore. Now, however, he was doing so with less ambivalence, greater urgency, and to a much larger audience. But we can see the roots of the Second Inaugural in his speech at the opening of the Maryland Sanitory Fair on April 20, 1864:

> The world has never had a good definition of the word liberty, and the American people, just now, are much in want of one. We all declare for liberty; but in using the same *word* we do not all mean the same *thing*. With some the word liberty may mean for each man to do as he pleases with himself, and the product of his labor; while with others the same word may mean for some men to do as they please with other men, and the product of other men's labor. Here are two, not only different, but incompatible things, called by the same name—liberty.

Here was Lincoln's final acknowledgment that Southerners had launched their 1861 revolution because they believed the "holy" liberty of states more important than the liberty of slaves and economic opportunity for all Americans—indeed, they saw nothing incompatible in the founding vision of the country, even if it had excluded from that vision millions of people imported specifically to perform unpaid labor for life. By the time he stepped onto the portico of the US Capitol to take the oath of office for a second presidential term, Lincoln was unwilling to extend the benefit of the doubt to Southerners; he had also lost patience with Northerners who for too long believed they could fight for union without freedom for the slaves. The voters had endorsed Lincoln's vision of liberty, and now had come the day of reckoning.

At the onset of the Civil War, Lincoln expected there would be a just result without enormous negative consequences. He thought his limited war aims—preventing the extension of slavery to the western territories and bringing the South back into the Union without the immediate abolition of slavery in the seceding states—were reasonable and could legitimately be described as consistent with God's will.

But the war had continued with no clear end in sight. As early as 1862, Lincoln was aware that his chosen commander of the Union armies, George B. McClellan, was at best a reluctant warrior. Lincoln appointed McClellan after the Union disaster at the First Battle of Bull Run to organize untrained and untested soldiers from state militias into an army capable of fighting a successful Civil War. McClellan was an excellent trainer of soldiers but an unwilling warrior against the South for both personal and political reasons. His continuing emphasis on "strategic advantage" wore thin when he did not pursue tactical opportunities, repeatedly arguing that his opponents outnumbered his troops. While Lincoln was reluctant to replace McClellan because of his success in training and securing the loyalty of the new Union armies, he came to understand McClellan's limitations. In a letter to McClellan on October 13, 1862, Lincoln said: "Are you not over-cautious when you assume that you can not do what the enemy is constantly doing? Should you not claim to be at least his equal in prowess, and act upon the claim?" When McClellan sent a telegram suggesting that his inaction was due in part to horses in his cavalry that were "unable to leave the camp," Lincoln replied on October 25, 1862: "I have just read your dispatch about sore tongued and fatiegued [sic] horses. Will you pardon me for asking what the horses of your army have done since the battle of Antietam that fatigue anything?"

In a memorandum to his generals in November 1862, Lincoln complained about McClellan's tactics: "The Army and the nation has been demoralized by the idea that the war is to be ended, the nation united, and the peace restored by strategy and not by hard, desperate fighting." Some historians have attributed Lincoln's desire to engage in "hard, desperate fighting" to his personal history of wrestling matches that could be won only by such means.

Lincoln became an engaged military commander in chief early in 1862. Encouraged by his intensive study of military strategy and tactics, he developed a clearer sense of direction than his generals, who seemed to be ever unwilling to take the offensive, constantly complaining they were outnumbered by their Confederate opponents. The greatest weakness of the Union armies was their lack of an overall strategy, with four separate armies under four separate generals, operating in four different parts of the country, engaged in intermittent battles against better-managed Confederate forces.

At one point, Lincoln wrote to Generals Henry Halleck and Don Carlos Buell in charge of the Union armies in Kentucky and Tennessee:

> . . . I state my general idea of this war to be that we have the *greater* numbers, and the enemy has the *greater* facility of concentrating forces upon points of collision; that we must fail, unless we can find some way of making *our* advantage an overmatch for *his*; and that this can only be done by menacing him with superior forces at *different* points, at the *same* time; so that we can safely attack, one, or both, if he makes no change; and if he *weakens* one to *strengthen* the other, forbear to attack the strengthened one, but seize, and hold the weakened one, gaining so much.

In the campaign leading up to Gettysburg, Lincoln wired Union army commander General Joseph Hooker: "*Lee's* Army, and not *Richmond,* is your true objective point. . . . Fight him when oppertunity [*sic*] offers." Hooker's unsatisfactory response led Lincoln to replace him with General George G. Meade, who won the victory at Gettysburg but failed to pursue Lee's dispirited army. Lincoln drafted a letter to Meade: "I do not believe you appreciate the magnitude of the misfortune involved in Lee's escape. . . . Your golden opportunity is gone, and I am distressed immeasureably because of it." In the end, Lincoln decided it would serve no purpose to send the letter, but he

Lincoln the impatient but imposing commander in chief confers with his patho-
logically hesitant general, George B. McClellan, at Army of the Potomac head-
quarters, near Antietam, Maryland, October 3, 1862. The conference took place
just a few weeks after McClellan's battlefield victory here enabled the president
to announce the Preliminary Emancipation Proclamation—which McClellan
and most Democrats opposed. With no formal military training, and only brief
military experience, Lincoln became an extraordinarily astute strategist and mo-
tivator. Photograph by Alexander Gardner. LIBRARY OF CONGRESS

continued to remind his generals that the war could be won only by
defeating Lee's army. Outstanding Civil War military historian James
McPherson aptly described Lincoln's contribution as commander in
chief: "A self-taught strategist with no combat experience, Abraham
Lincoln saw the path to victory more clearly than his generals."

Lincoln was not willing to face a continuing stalemate year after
year. He came to realize that the natural advantages of the North
were not being utilized effectively in the war. The Union army's aggressive task required many more troops than the Confederate army's
defensive task—the Union armies had to conquer and occupy thousands of miles of enemy territory. The white population of the North
was four times as great as the white population of the South. Yet in

the first years of the war, the size of the volunteer armies of the North and South did not reflect this advantage.

In 1863 and 1864, Lincoln acted directly by instituting the first involuntary draft in modern times. The new policy was unpopular, producing major public outcries—most notably the 1863 draft riots in New York. But the size of the Union armies increased substantially. Their numbers were increased by young male immigrants from Europe who were encouraged to join the Union armies. At the same time, Lincoln encouraged his generals to make increasing use of freed slaves for the Union armies—first as support troops and later as armed battalions of soldiers. By the end of 1864, the federal armies greatly outnumbered the Southern armies in manpower.

In the early months of 1864, it was also clear that the Union armies were still bogged down in a continuing series of battles with no clear end in sight. Lincoln was uncertain about the outcome of the election of 1864 and fearful that a new president would repudiate the Emancipation Proclamation as unconstitutional. The Northern public was losing patience, and it seemed Lincoln might lose his bid for reelection unless a new rationale for the war and a new battle plan produced a different pattern of military success.

It was in 1864 that Lincoln provided a new rationale for the war that relieved him of personal responsibility for deciding to undertake what seemed to be an almost unending and increasingly bloody war. He found value in the idea that God, rather than the president, could be described as the principal actor in the conflict. Lincoln shifted the burden of guilt to the Southern slaveholders pursuing an immoral economic "interest" and the burden of action in the continuing war to a righteous God when he declared: "[T]he judgments of the Lord are true and righteous altogether" if "God wills that it continue."

Even as he invoked God's will and the immorality of the Southern slave economy to justify continuing the war, Lincoln also used this rhetoric to validate a substantial change in the military strategy of the North. This new strategy was characterized by a scorched-earth approach to the Southern economy.

In March 1864 Lincoln chose his most determined military leader, Ulysses S. Grant, to take command of all the Union armies. With

UNION AND LIBERTY!   AND   UNION AND SLAVERY!

THE OLD BULL DOG ON THE RIGHT TRACK.

(*Top*) This 1864 pro-Lincoln campaign poster favorably compared the pro-freedom, prolabor Republican platform (and candidate) to the procapitulation, proslavery platform of Democratic presidential nominee George McClellan. Republicans put most of their hopes in Union battlefield results, advocating newly promoted commander Ulysses S. Grant (*bottom*) as a "Bull Dog" determined to take Richmond if it took all summer. LIBRARY OF CONGRESS

Lincoln's approval, Grant initiated critical new approaches to winning the war. Instead of pitched battles with few clear results other than enormous loss of life on both sides, Grant mandated that all Union armies should move together to attack their opponents at the same time on all fronts. This forced the Confederate forces, already stretched thin, to fight more than one battle at a time. It also deprived the Southern generals of their previously successful strategy of moving all available troops to the fronts where major battles were about to occur.

Perhaps more importantly, Lincoln encouraged his most aggressive generals, Grant, William T. Sherman, and Philip H. Sheridan, to fight a hard war, supporting a scorched-earth economic strategy that could bring victory to the Northern armies. While Lincoln stressed that the least possible harm should come to civilians, anything that underpinned the economy of the Confederacy—farmlands, factories, roads, and railroads—was fair game. Rather than a continuing frontal assault on Lee's army, Grant laid siege to Petersburg, just south of Richmond, the capital of the Confederacy. Petersburg was the commercial and railroad center that provided food and supplies to the Confederate capital and to General Robert E. Lee's army defending it.

Even with this new strategy, however, not everything went well at first for Union troops. While the Army of the Potomac was focused on the siege of Petersburg, the Confederate Army marched up the Shenandoah Valley of Virginia with little opposition early in July 1864. Confederate forces got as far as six miles from the White House before being turned back. This military setback and public relations disaster increased Lincoln's fear of losing the November presidential election and strengthened his resolve to energize his generals to end the military stalemate. On July 15, General Grant signed an order that the Shenandoah Valley should be made into a "desert" and that "all provisions and stock should be removed, and the people notified to move out."

On August 7, 1864, Grant appointed Sheridan commander of the Army of the Shenandoah, putting him in charge of carrying out the scorched-earth strategy in the region. He directed Sheridan to deny the productive agricultural products of Virginia to Confederate troops.

Grant told Sheridan, "Give the enemy no rest. . . . Do all the damage to railroads and crops you can. Carry off stock of all description, and Negroes, so as to prevent planting. If the war is to last another year, we want the Shenandoah Valley to remain a barren waste."

Sheridan began the punitive economic operations of his mission in late September 1864, sending his cavalry ranging wide over four hundred miles to destroy livestock and provisions and to burn barns, mills, factories, and railroads. Sheridan's cavalry and troops performed their assigned tasks relentlessly and thoroughly—denying the Southern army a base and bringing the war home to the Southern civilian population of the Shenandoah Valley. At the same time, Sheridan remained mindful of Lincoln's mandate to do no bodily harm to the civilian population. Lincoln congratulated Sheridan in a letter on October 22, 1864: "With great pleasure I tender to you and your brave army, the thanks of the nation, and my own personal admiration and gratitude, for the month's operation in the Shenandoah Valley."

Grant appointed Sherman, perhaps the Union's most efficient scorched-earth strategist, to succeed him in command of Union troops stationed in the western theater of the war. Sherman almost immediately proceeded east to invade the state of Georgia, with the objective of a direct frontal assault on Atlanta, its largest city. Sherman captured Atlanta on September 2, 1864. It was a military triumph so important that it reversed simmering anti-Lincoln sentiment and reenergized public support for his reelection in the upcoming presidential contest. At last, Lincoln had generals in the field who not only were winning battles but had a clear plan for winning the war.

Lincoln now sounded more confident in describing God's purpose than ever before in his presidency. This was the moment when he began to say of the war that "God alone can claim it," going on to say that "if God now wills the removal of a great wrong . . . impartial history will find therein new cause to attest and revere the justice and goodness of God." Lincoln was more convinced than ever that he could describe himself as God's agent and say that "great good" would follow all the suffering and sacrifice.

In the weeks and months after Lincoln's reelection, the South faced even more suffering and sacrifice. From November 15 through

December 21, 1864, promising Grant that he would make "Georgia howl," Grant's chief lieutenant pursued the most famous of all the war's scorched-earth campaigns, in what became known as Sherman's March through Georgia. Announcing that "my business is down South," Sherman led sixty-two thousand men from Atlanta to Savannah in five weeks. Sherman was able to move his army forward by living off the land, eliminating the need to wait for food supplies to catch up with his rapidly moving army. The general's strategy was to take what he could use and destroy what he did not take. By his own reckoning, he left in his wake more than $100 million in property damage. Sherman called this new approach "hard war."

Rather than limit himself to fighting pitched battles, Sherman destroyed railroads and private homes and commandeered or destroyed crops and livestock. For the first time in the American Civil War—and perhaps in modern warfare—a general took systematic aim at the infrastructure of the enemy economy. Sherman's strategy was to treat the Southern civilian economy as a critical part of the Southern military infrastructure. The objective was to leave nothing behind that could continue to provide economic support for the Southern armies. The Southern economy and society had become the real enemy and could be treated as a military target. Whereas Lincoln remained committed to a policy that did not treat women and noncombatants as soldiers, he had no qualms about destroying the economic base of the South that supported its armies.

Sherman then persuaded Grant to allow him to march north through the Carolinas. In particular he targeted South Carolina, the first state to secede from the Union. Sherman captured the state capital, Columbia, on February 17, 1865. Fires in the city began that night, and by the next morning most of the central city lay in ruins. Sherman had achieved his three principal objectives: enabling his troops to march quickly by living off the land of his opponents, reducing the economic capability of the South, and striking a direct blow to the morale of the civilian Confederate population.

At the same time, Grant and Sheridan relentlessly pursued Lee's shrinking army, now diminished by a lack of provisions. On April 1, 1865, Sheridan cut off Lee's lines of economic support at Five Forks, forcing Lee to evacuate Petersburg. On April 6 Sheridan captured 20 percent of Lee's men. Fully in support of the results of the scorched-earth policy, Lincoln sent Grant a telegram on April 7: "General Sheridan says 'if the thing is pressed I think that Lee will surrender.' Let the *thing* be pressed." On April 9 Sheridan blocked Lee's escape, and Lee agreed to surrender to Grant, effectively ending the formal military phase of the Civil War.

Lincoln, Grant, Sheridan, and Sherman had successfully implemented the new "hard war" program that, in less than twelve months, fully defeating the Southern rebellion. The Union armies that had taken Richmond and destroyed the economic infrastructure of the Confederacy were, in Lincoln's language, God's army. Lincoln was merely God's agent. Near the conclusion of his Second Inaugural Address, delivered just a month before the fighting finally came to a close, Lincoln reminded his audience (and himself) that God was responsible for continuing the war:

> Fondly do we hope—fervently do we pray—that this mighty scourge of war may speedily pass away. Yet, if God wills that it continue, until all the wealth piled by the bond-man's two hundred and fifty years of unrequited toil shall be sunk, and until every drop of blood drawn with the lash, shall be paid by another drawn with the sword, as was said three thousand years ago, so still it must be said "the judgments of the Lord, are true and righteous altogether."

In a way, Lincoln had long capitalized on the growing anger in the North against the South for perpetuating its unjust war. But he was not alone in giving voice to it. In the last year of the war, more and more Northerners expressed their feelings through the harsh words of "The Battle Hymn of the Republic," sung to the tune of the antislavery anthem "John Brown's Body":

> *Mine eyes have seen the glory of the coming of the Lord;*
> *He is trampling out the vintage where the grapes of wrath*
> *   are stored;*

He hath loosed the fateful lightning of His terrible swift
    sword;
His truth is marching on.

Yet in the end, Lincoln did not give in to this anger, especially re-
alizing (as he must have that March) that the war would soon come to
an end. He knew that anger—"the fateful lightning of [God's] terrible
swift sword"—could not be the basis for peacetime reconstruction,
just as he understood that it served no place in creating the American
society he envisioned for the future. Fondly did he hope, it might be
argued, that the Northern states and the new western states would
continue to build on the nation's middle-class foundation. He may even
have hoped that, after welcoming the South back into the Union, the
abolition of slavery would be accepted by a majority of Southerners
who could then choose to build a new middle-class society of their
own. To encourage this new era of good feelings, Lincoln concluded
his Second Inaugural Address on a positive and welcoming note: "With
malice toward none; with charity for all; with firmness in the right,
as God gives us to see the right, let us strive on to finish the work we
are in; to bind up the nation's wounds; to care for him who shall have
borne the battle, and for his widow, and his orphan—to do all which
may achieve and cherish a just, and a lasting peace, among ourselves,
and with all nations."

Lincoln was at the apogee of his power in April 1865. The fighting
was over. The new "father of the nation" had guided the democratic
country successfully through its greatest trauma since the Revolutionary War. Even at the end of the Civil War, Lincoln did not demand
full equality for the former slaves. But he did expect the states restored
to the Union to move in this direction by acknowledging the right of
former slaves to be paid for the work they would do in the future. Economic fairness, anticipating the twentieth-century idea of "equal pay
for equal work," had always been Lincoln's bedrock idea for America.

Life has its cruel ironies. Listening to Lincoln's reconstruction
speech on April 11, 1865, John Wilkes Booth, an ardent proponent
of slavery, decided to take direct action to punish the leader of the
antislavery cause. At the height of his success, Lincoln was cut down

on April 14 by a bullet fired by Booth. Lincoln did not live to see the fulfillment of his American Dream. But he left a legacy of guidance for subsequent American leaders to work to achieve this goal.

The public outcry over Lincoln's assassination was intense. Lincoln was dead. How could the nation go on without him at the helm?

But first the people of the North needed to say good-bye to their assassinated leader. Americans throughout the Union had not forgotten Lincoln's inaugural journey of 1861. When the announcement was made that Lincoln's final resting place would be in Springfield, Illinois, telegrams poured into Washington from cities and towns throughout the North, asking that the funeral train repeat the path of the 1861 inaugural train, but this time north and west from Washington to Springfield.

Secretary of War Edwin Stanton organized Lincoln's final trip. The funeral train traveled 1,654 miles in twelve days, stopping in 180 cities. Each stopover inspired a major civic event. From April 19 in Washington through May 4 in Springfield, more than a million Americans viewed Lincoln's open coffin. They raised him to the highest level of "American political sainthood," second only to George Washington. They honored his achievements: saving the Union, winning the war, and forever uniting the causes of liberty, freedom, and economic opportunity. They affirmed, in their numbers, that the "cause" was worth fighting for. They bade a glorious farewell to Lincoln himself and to the hundreds of thousands who had perished for his "cause" and their country. For this moment in time, they were united behind his principles and committed to bear the burden of his "unfinished work."

While mourning their leader, Lincoln's cabinet and the new president, Andrew Johnson, brought what remained of the war to a conclusion. Federal cavalry caught up with Lincoln's assassin on April 26, and a rogue sergeant shot him dead. Booth's coconspirators were captured and later tried and convicted. Jefferson Davis, the president of the Confederacy, was captured by Union troops on May 10 and was ironically confined to the same fort where the three runaway slaves had first presented themselves to General Butler four years earlier—to escape the chains in which slavery's last spokesman now found himself locked.

Now, it was time to move on from war to the business of putting the Union back together. But Lincoln was no longer at the helm to guide the reconstruction process. Instead, Congress and President Johnson addressed the task—for ill or good—of managing the aftermath of the Civil War.

PART TWO

Eight

FULL SPEED AHEAD

WITHOUT LINCOLN AT THE HELM

NORTHERN LEADERS WERE DIVIDED THROUGHOUT THE CIVIL WAR about how to deal with the return of the Southern states to the Union. While most generally agreed that the South was to blame for dividing the nation, they were not in agreement when it came to considering alternative ways to end the war and reunite the nation. Their differences were only exacerbated by Lincoln's assassination, which forced them to forge ahead without a transformational leader with a clear vision for the future. It did not take long for Lincoln's dream to be undermined and corrupted.

Three distinct factions emerged, each with a different plan. Democratic members of Congress believed that white citizens of the former Confederate states should simply repledge allegiance to the Union, without committing to economic opportunities such as forty acres and a mule for free blacks. Within the Republican Party, "moderates" once led by President Lincoln believed that the central issue in the war was "restoring" the Union as quickly as possible. The moderates also wanted the former Confederate states to extend the electoral franchise to African American male citizens. But Lincoln and the moderates did not insist that the Southern states take immediate steps to provide equal rights for the now free African American slaves. Like the Democrats in Congress, Lincoln and the moderate Republicans believed the Southern rebel states should be returned to the Union after renewed pledges of allegiance to the Union by 10 percent of the voters of each of the rebellious states. The third faction, the radical Republicans, led by Secretary of the Treasury Salmon Chase, Senator Charles Sumner, and congressional leader Thaddeus Stevens, believed Lincoln did not go far enough in his plans for reconstruction of the rebellious Southern states. The radicals believed that the Southern states should be restored to the Union only after they had provided equal rights to the former slaves.

The great debate in the North over restoration versus reconstruction of the Southern states began in earnest early in 1862, long before the war came to an end. The *Washington National Republican* presented the essence of the radical Republicans' point of view on February 11, 1862: "The revolt of a State against the authority of the General Government destroys its political rights under the Constitution and reduces its territory to the condition of the unorganized public domain. It forfeits all its rights. . . . It is equally clear that the seceded states can never come back into the Union until they have been reorganized. . . . Every vestige of their treason must be repudiated." These proreconstruction Republicans understood "reorganized" to mean loss of voting rights by all secessionists—and punishment for many by excluding them from participating in politics. They also insisted on immediately providing voting rights for the freed slaves and a future open society in which both blacks and whites would have equal access to political and economic opportunities.

Lincoln had expressed a very different point of view. In his First Inaugural Address, Lincoln said that the union of the states was perpetual under the Constitution. No state, on its own initiative, could lawfully secede from the Union. Lincoln's secretaries Nicolay and Hay described Lincoln's view with the following words: "The action of the government in all its departments was based on the idea that the rebellion was the unlawful proceeding of individuals which neither destroyed nor impaired any rights or obligations of Statehood."

Lincoln's Emancipation Proclamation on January 1, 1863, added a new dimension to the anticipated future. Once Lincoln had acted as commander in chief out of so-called military necessity to emancipate the slaves, it was no longer a technical or legal argument over how to parse the Constitution or whether secession was lawful in the first place. It was now a practical question of whether the president or Congress could decide if a seceded state had taken the proper steps to be restored to the Union. Lincoln took the bull by the horns when he delivered his Annual Message to Congress on December 8, 1863. In return for cessation of hostilities, it included a new presidential proclamation of amnesty, offering a full pardon with few exceptions to all those who had participated in the rebellion. The pardon carried with it a restoration of rights to property, excluding former slaves. The critical feature of Lincoln's solution was the requirement that it would become operational in each of the ten seceded states south of Virginia when one-tenth of the total number of voters who had cast votes in the 1860 presidential election took an oath that they would "henceforth faithfully protect and defend the Constitution."

The radical Republicans joined the battle on July 2, 1864, when Congress passed the Wade-Davis Bill. The bill asserted the authority of Congress over the president in managing the reconstruction process. Most critically, the bill specified that 50 percent rather than 10 percent of the voters were required to swear an oath and vote in new elections to qualify a state for return to full status in the Union. Rather than a prospective oath of loyalty, the Wade-Davis Bill required an iron-clad oath that the voters had never voluntarily borne arms against the United States or aided the rebellion.

The bill reflected the continuing opposition of many radical Republicans to Lincoln's leadership on the issues of abolition and equal rights for African Americans. In the short term, however, radical Republicans were forced to follow Lincoln's lead. When the Wade-Davis Bill came before him, Lincoln asserted his authority by waiting for the congressional session to end without acting. His pocket veto infuriated the radicals. The gauntlet had been thrown down by Congress, and Lincoln picked it up. He claimed that Congress did not have the authority to abolish slavery in the reconstructed states, while he, the president, had that authority as commander in chief.

The battle over the Wade-Davis Bill did not resolve the continuing differences between the moderate and radical Republicans. As the war neared its end in the early months of 1865, Lincoln's tireless efforts seemed to be coming to a positive conclusion with the anticipated restoration of the first of the seceding states to the Union on the terms set forth by Lincoln, not Congress. Indeed, at his cabinet meeting on Friday, April 14, 1865, Lincoln said it was providential that he could implement a restoration plan without interference from the "disturbing elements" of the House and Senate. Lincoln told his cabinet, "There were men in Congress, who, if their motives were good, were nevertheless impracticable, and who possessed feelings of hate and vindictiveness in which he did not sympathize and could not participate."

Lincoln's death shifted the balance of power on reconstruction to the radical Republicans in Congress. Without Lincoln's strong executive leadership, the moderate Republicans could not prevail in their efforts to bring the Southern states back into the Union quickly, with few conditions other than an affirmation of loyalty to the Union by 10 percent of the voters of each state. The radical Republicans were determined to reconstruct the Southern states so that former slaves would enjoy equal rights as citizens—including the right to vote. Not incidentally, radical Republicans realized that granting the vote to former slaves, most of whom would probably vote for the party that had liberated them, would help to establish a new Republican presence in the Southern states that would maintain Republican Party dominance of the federal government.

The agent of radical Republican change was the new Freedmen's Bureau, established by Congress with Lincoln's support in March 1865 to extend equal rights and equal treatment to the free African Americans in the Southern states. With little backing from new president Andrew Johnson but much encouragement from the radical Republicans in Congress, the Freedmen's Bureau began encouraging former slaves to become active and equal participants in the political process of the Southern states that were now coming back into the Union.

Passage of the Fourteenth Amendment changed the Constitution from a document that defined the rights of American "white men" to one that expanded those rights to all men, including, most notably, former slaves. Equally significant, it expanded the power of the federal government to protect these rights against violation by the states.

The radical Republican majority in Congress also passed a series of Reconstruction Acts in 1867 over President Johnson's veto that not only empowered African American male citizens to vote but also created barriers to vote for thousands of former Confederate leaders. The Reconstruction Acts together with the passage of the Fifteenth Amendment to the Constitution early in 1870 enabled Republicans from the North who moved to the South to be joined by a newly mobilized African American community to establish Republican majorities in the Southern state legislatures. While white Republicans held most elected offices, for a brief moment in time African Americans held public office at all levels of state government, and a tiny handful were elected to serve in Congress.

But Republicans—radical and moderate alike—had to contend with an extraordinarily resistant white South. After the end of the war, former slaveholders sought to restore their control of Southern economic and political society. Some continued to argue that the Southern slave system had operated not solely for the benefit of white slave owners but also for the slaves. They continued to propagate the myth of benevolence while creating a mirror image of the old slave system.

But a taste of freedom for the former slaves was enough to prevent the restoration of the pre–Civil War South so long as Union troops were on Southern soil. The attitude of one former slave was expressed in a letter dated August 7, 1865, sent from Jourdon Anderson in Dayton, Ohio, to his former master, Confederate Colonel P. H. Anderson in Big Spring, Tennessee.

> Sir: I got your letter, and was glad to find that you had not forgotten Jourdon, and that you wanted me to come back and live with you again. . . .
>
> I want to know particularly what the good chance is you propose to give me. I am doing tolerably well here. I get twenty-five dollars a month, with victuals and clothing; have a comfortable home for Mandy,—the folks call her Mrs. Anderson,—and the children—Milly, Jane, and Grundy—go to school and are learning well. . . .
>
> As to my freedom, which you say I can have, there is nothing to be gained on that score, as I got my free papers in 1864 from the Provost-Marshal-General of the Department of Nashville. . . .

*[W]e have concluded to test your sincerity by asking you to
send us our wages for the time we served you. . . . I served you
faithfully for thirty-two years, and Mandy twenty years. At twenty-
five dollars a month for me, and two dollars a week for Mandy,
our earnings would amount to eleven thousand six hundred and
eighty dollars. . . . We trust the good Maker has opened your
eyes to the wrongs which you and your fathers have done to me
and my fathers, in making us toil for you for generations without
recompense. . . .*

From your old servant,
Jourdon Anderson.

Andrew Johnson played a confused and confusing role in the process of reconstruction. The Republicans had nominated Johnson for
vice president because he was a Unionist Democrat from the seceded
state of Tennessee, sending a message that the Lincoln administration
welcomed the return of the Confederate states to the Union. On the
surface, Johnson's program was consistent with Lincoln's desire for
a quick restoration of the seceded states to the Union. But he failed
to take any steps to provide protection or support for the newly freed
slaves. Furious, the radical Republicans in Congress reacted with a
vote to impeach President Johnson. He avoided conviction by one vote,
but the conflict between the radical Republicans and the president
continued until he left office in 1869. In the confusion caused by the
four-year conflict between Congress and Johnson, the seceded states
attempted to return to the Union on their own terms. Many of the
Southern states returned their old Democratic leaders to Congress and
adopted black codes designed to deprive the freedmen of their newly
declared rights and liberties. In many cases, both sides reacted as
expected: Congress passed legislation refusing to seat the Democrats
from the Southern states, the president vetoed their legislation, and
the large Republican majorities in Congress overrode Johnson's veto.
The conduct in Washington was counterproductive to any long-term
progress consistent with President Lincoln's vision of a peaceful and
productive restoration period. The decade of reconstruction provided
some modest improvements energized by the Freedmen's Bureau for

some former slaves. But by the end of the decade, the leadership of the Southern states had largely returned to their prewar elite population.

While Union troops were watching, most white supporters of the Confederacy in the South nominally accepted the requirement of pledging allegiance to the Union in order to regain their states' voting rights. But for many, this was a hollow pledge.

At one extreme former Confederate soldiers like Jesse and Frank James refused to swear allegiance to the Union and continued to engage in guerrilla warfare. As the war was coming to a close in 1864, a Confederate army no longer existed in his native state of Missouri, so Jesse James joined a small guerrilla group using bushwhacking techniques to harass the dominant federal "occupying" forces. When the war ended in 1865, Jesse and his brother Frank continued to fight. Initially, they robbed banks and railroad trains that arguably represented the interests of Northern "carpetbaggers," but they soon moved on to indiscriminate armed robbery. They claimed they were continuing to fight for the honor of the Southern white man. Thus was launched the legend of Jesse James.

The resentment against the occupying Northerners was so strong in the South that the legend continued to grow. Many Southerners gave little credence to the news of incidents where the James brothers indiscriminately robbed and killed Southerners as well as Northern "carpetbaggers." Recalcitrant Confederate sympathizers continued to support the Jesse James legend because it seemed to mirror their efforts to regain control of the political future of the South.

And regain control they did. Majority white rule reestablished itself in the South. The new South elected white Democrats to the US Senate and House. By 1872 they enjoyed sufficient influence in Washington to secure abolition of the Freedmen's Bureau. The decade-long fight for political and social control of the South finally ended with the Compromise of 1877 in Washington. Republicans agreed to remove all Federal troops from the former Confederate states in return for Democratic acceptance of the election of Republican Rutherford B. Hayes to the US presidency.

Without Federal troops there was no force to overcome the resurgence of a segregated South dominated by white supremacists committed to maintaining their control over Southern political and economic society. Reconstruction died aborning. Northern efforts to establish racial equality in the South were left unfinished. The Southern political elite, frequently the same men who had been slaveholders before the war, regained control over the levers of power in the former Confederate states. They seized the opportunity to restore the separate and unequal structure of the antebellum era. With little to no opposition from Northern Republicans or their president, the leaders of the new South created a new version of their familiar three-level society of wealthy landowners, poor white independent farmers, and black ex-slaves who now typically became "sharecrop" subsistence farmers.

The Southern political elite mobilized quickly and employed new tools to maintain their control over Southern society. Although the new Fourteenth and Fifteenth Amendments to the Constitution, adopted in 1868 and 1870, proclaimed the rights of all citizens to equal treatment, these rights were quickly nullified by state governments or ignored by defiant localities. Throughout the former Confederate states, white supremacists enlisted law enforcement agencies to keep African Americans "in their place" as a subservient class, tied to the land. In some states local officials arbitrarily imprisoned black males for crimes of "vagrancy" or failure to pay nonexistent "debts." By 1890 there were seventeen thousand black males in prison, more than 90 percent of the prison population in the Southern states. The prisoners became a source of revenue: they were rented out to landowners or mine owners. Thus was born "peonage"—a latter-day form of slavery. In Alabama alone, revenue from "convict leasing" reached $164,000 in 1890. Later, at the end of the nineteenth and into the twentieth centuries, prisoners were organized into "chain gangs" and used as "slave" labor to build and rebuild local and state roads.

The indiscriminate incarceration of such a large number of black males served to intimidate former slaves to accept their status as an underclass. In addition, the Ku Klux Klan, a white terrorist organization operating primarily in the Southern states, used the threat and reality of lynching to keep "uppity blacks" in line. The poor whites in the South were reassured that whatever their economic conditions, they would continue to be considered superior to blacks. Finally, the

Supreme Court weighed in to support the new Southern segregation system. The Court's *Plessy v. Ferguson* decision of 1896 asserted that racial segregation was lawful and could be enforced by state and local police power. By the end of the nineteenth century, the former Confederate states had reemerged as a new version of the antebellum South.

Perhaps the clearest evidence of the restoration of antebellum governance in the Southern states can be seen in voting statistics. With Union troops on the ground and black voting guaranteed by the Fourteenth and Fifteenth Amendments to the Constitution, between 1868 and 1876 the turnout of potential white and black voters rose to 67 percent. After Union troops left the South, efforts to prevent black citizens from voting went into high gear, buttressed by a network of local and state election-law changes designed to exclude blacks from the suffrage. The poll tax was only one of many "legal" devices to prevent black citizens from voting. The Supreme Court had a hand in restoring pre-1861 control of elections to each state in *United States v. Reese* in 1876. Chief Justice Morrison Waite opined in his eight-to-one decision that "the Fifteenth Amendment did not positively confer the right of suffrage on anyone." Voting requirements became so restrictive that they began to reduce participation among poor white as well as black voters in the increasingly one-party South. By 1900 the almost exclusively white voter turnout in the Southern states represented only 39 percent of the total potential white and black voters. By contrast, the turnout in the North and West in 1900 was in excess of 75 percent of the potential voters. Turnout declined to only 16 percent in the period from 1932 to 1970. It was only in the 1990s that restrictions became less effective and white and black turnout in the South increased to 40 percent (only 7 percent lower than the level in the North and West).

In spite of Lincoln's hopes for extending the middle-class economy to the South, the Southern economy did not change radically in the decades immediately following the Civil War. The former slaves remained tethered to the land with little opportunity to break away from their subjugated position as sharecroppers. It was only when factory job opportunities opened up in the North during World Wars I and II that substantial black migration from the South occurred. But even then, segregation continued in the North as well as the South until the Supreme Court ruled against segregation in its landmark *Brown v. Board of Education* decision in 1954 and the civil rights crusade took hold in the 1960s.

While the South restored many of the elements of its pre–Civil War political and social structure, including black codes to restrict black civil and voting rights, new radical and unexpected changes came to the economic, political, and social structure of the Northern and western states in the decades following the Civil War. Before long, these seismic shifts would undermine the middle-class society Lincoln had championed as a model for the nation. Lincoln was right that the economy of the North would dominate the nation after the Civil War, but he did not and could not anticipate how that economy would change.

Literally within the span of a generation, America grew from a dominantly agrarian nation into the world's leading industrial power. The transformation of the American landscape proved epochal. From 1870 to 1900, railroad mileage more than tripled, while steel production increased by more than a hundredfold. In the same period, overall manufacturing output quadrupled, while agriculture's share of the economy declined. An abundance of new products became available, and a national system of commerce emerged, linking farmers and manufacturers alike to markets North, South, East, and West. Overall, between 1870 and 1900, the US gross national product more than tripled in real terms, with manufacturing accounting for an ever-increasing share of output.

The old middle-class system of independent artisans and home-based manufacturing was increasingly shifting to large mills and factories, driven by water- and steam power. There, scores and sometimes hundreds of workers labored long hours in harsh conditions, churning out a growing flood of textiles, shoes, and other consumer and durable goods. A major source of labor for the growing industries was the swelling numbers of immigrants—some 13.5 million between 1865 and 1900—who poured into tenement neighborhoods in New York and other cities of the North.

Economic life also began to be organized in larger and larger units. Between 1850 and 1880, the corporation became the standard business entity. And many corporations were in turn absorbed into larger "trusts," as ambitious industrial magnates sought to achieve monopoly power over specific markets. John D. Rockefeller organized the Standard Oil Trust, which by 1879 controlled 90 percent of the nation's oil-refining industry. By 1904 there were more than three hundred such powerful industrial combinations holding dominant positions in a variety of industries.

Enormous amounts of money were being made, but it was increasingly concentrated in very few hands. By 1890 the richest 1 percent of the population was absorbing half of the entire national income and controlled more than half the nation's wealth. This was not at all what Lincoln had envisioned when he described a society in which labor was superior to capital. Within three decades after Lincoln's death, his American Dream of a middle-class society was no longer available to most Americans.

As industrial life came to be organized on a larger scale, the size of the federal government also expanded. In 1860, on the eve of the Civil War, federal spending totaled just over $63 million. In 1870, in peacetime, the federal government was spending five times that amount, some $310 million a year. Lincoln and the Republicans had won the argument in favor of internal improvements funded largely by protective tariffs. In the post–Civil War economy, these improvements were also financed by millions of dollars in government land grants and millions more in generous federal loans. But the new millions in government funds formed a seemingly irresistible temptation to corruption. Many of these millions were finding their way, via government grants, loans, and other subsidies, into the hands of railroad magnates and other businessmen who secured special favors from the federal government. President Ulysses S. Grant's two terms in office from 1869 through 1876 were marred by an endless string of major scandals, in which executive branch officials and various members of Congress were found to be colluding to enrich themselves by accepting bribes to grant government favors to industrialists.

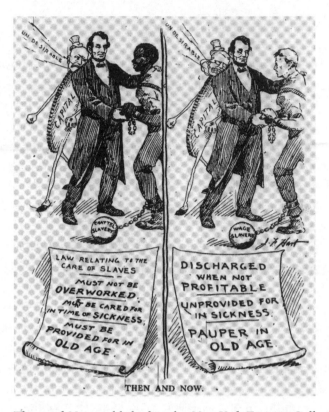

Then and Now, published in the *New York Evening Call*
on Lincoln's hundredth birthday, February 12, 1909,
used Lincoln's enduring image to assail what the anony-
mous cartoonist viewed as the Gilded Age abandonment
of the poor. The great Lincoln, the cartoonist suggests,
would have opposed "Capital's" rejection of "undesirable"
worker-paupers as surely as he opposed slavery. COUR-
TESY OF PROFESSOR BARRY SCHWARTZ

It was a time when those who could do so grabbed for the "fast
buck" and when those who could not generally settled for their meager
lot in life. It was an era when the middle-class ideal gave way to what
Mark Twain and Charles Dudley Warner dubbed the Gilded Age.

The rationale for the new "winner take all" economy was the new
science of political economy, imported from Great Britain. From Adam
Smith to David Ricardo, two generations of British thinkers had sought
to place the study of economics on a systematic, scientific footing.

Adam Smith contributed the insight that free trade between nations could increase the overall gross income (the aggregate wealth) of the nations engaged in free trade. This insight focused on encouraging governments to engage in free trade among nations was converted without any evidence into an argument against government action to enhance economic growth or regulate economic behavior within each nation. The new economic "science" had as its central tenet the nonintervention of government in any aspect of economic life. The term of art at the time for nonintervention was the French phrase *laissez-faire,* meaning, essentially, "leave it be" or "leave it alone." Today it is called "free-market economics."

Under the influence of the new economic doctrine, the notion of "free labor" came to be understood in the 1880s and 1890s in terms quite different from those embraced by Lincoln. It meant, essentially, that the laborer was on his own. Even as factories multiplied, destroying the old artisan system of manufacturing and driving millions of workers into increasingly desperate circumstances, with long hours, dangerous and unhealthy working conditions, and pay below subsistence levels, the advocates of the new economy adamantly resisted government intervention. They opposed legislation on the eight-hour day and disparaged proposals for child labor laws. They wrote diatribes against unions and labor leaders.

At one level, this peculiarly reactionary response to the plight of labor was simply a failure to accept the new industrial realities. The "free-market" advocates of the new economy continued to present the image of the independent "free-labor" craftsmen who dominated the pre–Civil War American economy. They saw the laborer as freely negotiating the sale of his labor, as if he were an independent agent, unhampered by the hard new economic realities of a factory-based economy. "The right of each man to labor as much or as little as he chooses and to enjoy his own earnings, is the very foundation stone of . . . freedom," wrote Horace White, editor of the *Chicago Tribune.* The relationship between employer and employee, White and other advocates insisted, was simply a "contract," and a society based on freely negotiated contracts represented, in their view, the pinnacle of freedom, a great advance over feudalism. It was perhaps no coincidence that White had come of age as a journalist covering—and supporting—Abraham Lincoln during his 1858 debates with Stephen Douglas.

Their arguments failed to address the fact that the whole structure of the economy was undergoing radical change. Whereas the early American Republic had been characterized by a continuing labor shortage that kept wages relatively high, the influx of millions of immigrants in the post–Civil War era created a labor surplus. The notion that the laborer had significant negotiating power was simply a convenient upperclass myth. Workers everywhere were being forced to compete and settle for below-subsistence wages. While on average the US economy saw a gradual rise in living standards between the end of the Civil War and the beginning of World War I, nearly half the workforce survived on below-poverty wages. "By the end of the 1880s," wrote David Montgomery in *The U.S. Department of Labor History of the American Worker,* "an income of roughly $500 a year would have been necessary for a family of five in a middle-sized industrial town to enjoy any of life's amenities (newspapers, beer, lodge membership, outings, tobacco) without literally depriving themselves of basic necessities. About forty percent of working-class families earned less than that." Long periods of unemployment were common, workweeks in excess of fifty hours were routine, child labor was rampant, and health and safety conditions in many workplaces were appalling. From 1880 to 1900, an average of thirty-five thousand American workers died each year from work-related injuries, and another half million were injured.

The extreme laissez-faire versions of the new economic doctrine portrayed government intervention in economic life as nothing less than a violation of "natural law." While the American economy was growing by leaps and bounds, government regulation of economic life was not growing at all. Lincoln had argued that government should actively assist all Americans in their quest for economic advancement. It should help to promote equality of opportunity, to "clear the path for all." By contrast, the new economic doctrine insisted that the government should have absolutely no role. The new argument was that any action by the government—especially taxation—would be counterproductive. It would allocate money inefficiently and take the money from private businessmen who would rationally and efficiently act to increase their own income and the total income of the nation.

The notion that one's economic fortunes were connected with one's character—one's hard work, thrift, persistence, and dependability—ran strong in the American bloodstream throughout the late nineteenth century. The theme had its origins partly in the old Calvinist idea that good economic fortunes were a sign of God's favor, a visible symbol of belonging to the elect. It was also an outgrowth of individual experience, since many, like Lincoln, found that hard work did enable them to get ahead. But with the dawn of the Gilded Age, this belief was transmuted from Lincoln's message of hope into a verdict of condemnation. It became a rationale for blaming laborers for their desperation and condemning the working poor for their very poverty. Meanwhile, any government effort to intervene on workers' behalf was to be fiercely resisted as a violation of natural law. Proposals for legislation to mandate an eight-hour workday "threatened the very foundation of civilization." Even laws forbidding child labor were anathema. One of the leading proponents of laissez-faire economics, E. L. Godkin, argued in the *Nation* against a proposal for a New York state constitutional amendment that would forbid employment in factories of children under ten. The government, wrote Godkin, might as well "tell us what to eat, drink, avoid, hope, fear, and believe."

The harsh version of laissez-faire thinking was made harsher by the claim of scientific authority based on Charles Darwin's new theory of evolution. "Social Darwinism" saw human economic life as analogous to the process of evolution: economic outcomes reflected the "survival of the fittest." Those who prospered economically were the "fit"; those who labored long hours in factories for below-subsistence wages were demonstrably the "unfit." The growing inequality that America witnessed between a tiny group of superrich industrialists and a mass of increasingly degraded and impoverished workers was actually seen as a sign of social progress; its proponents claimed it was good not only for maximum economic growth but also for the advancement of the "race," a necessary price of progress toward ever greater national wealth and prosperity. Social Darwinism integrated the ideas of evolution and laissez-faire economics into a new doctrine that not only forbade government intervention in the economy, but also provided a moral justification for harsh working conditions and growing economic inequality.

White working-class Northerners were not the only group targeted under this new theory. Increasingly, the freed slaves and all other African Americans were thought of as "unfit." The supposedly scientific concept of social Darwinism provided a basis for supporting segregation in the North as well as the South as the new dominant pattern of separating white Americans from "unfit" African Americans.

Any interference in the natural human competition for survival—particularly by government—was utterly counterproductive in the view of the social Darwinists. The role of the state was solely the "defense" of "individuality," a scrupulous protection of individual rights and rigid noninterference in economic activity. Those societies that most perfectly did not interfere with the individual's absolute rights to "life, liberty, and property" would survive and progress; those societies that interfered with these rights would eventually die out.

It followed that any attempt by the state to relieve the unemployed, to guarantee rights of employment, or even to provide charity for impoverished widows and orphans or newly freed African Americans posed a threat to progress. The laborer struggling with wages below subsistence, the sick and infirm, in short society's millions of "losers"—all were "unfit," and the most "unfit" among them deserved to die, so that the "race" as a whole would prosper. To its advocates, the obvious cruelty of this new modern economic system was actually kindness in disguise.

What is remarkable is how, under the influence of social Darwinism, the definition of democracy was gradually turning into something approaching its opposite. Repelled by the huddling masses of underpaid laborers, some self-styled "reformers" even raised questions about the merits of universal suffrage, advocating a return to the old system of voting rights on the basis of property ownership. Such obvious antidemocratic proposals never gained much traction. But they signified a sharp departure from Lincoln's understanding of democracy. Lincoln had regarded the equality posited by the Declaration of Independence as a core democratic value. Increasingly, the social Darwinists saw *inequality* as a sign of a healthy democracy, albeit one that now exhibited sharp divisions between the rich and the wretched.

Social Darwinists produced an ideology tailor-made for business interests. Industrial magnates and the business community enthusiastically took up the slogans of laissez-faire—an irony, since at the same time big business lobbied the federal government increasingly energetically for what amounted to millions of dollars in preferential treatment. Lincoln's program of government action to clear the path for the poor and disadvantaged was translated into government action to support wealthy Americans. Federal land grants and loans for the railroad magnates in the tens of millions, high tariffs to protect selected industries, and banking and financial regulations that enabled investors to line their pockets at the expense of the unwitting—such were the policies of the federal government in the Gilded Age. Far from maintaining a scrupulous laissez-faire or "hands-off" attitude, the government had its thumb on the scale on behalf of its richest citizens. Railroad magnates received federal lands at minimal cost. State government troops were provided by local and state governments to prevent strikes and reduce labor unrest. Still, despite its contradictions—even its hypocrisy—laissez-faire came to reign as a kind of official ideology of the era.

American politics in the years before and during the Civil War had been marked by high idealism—elevated debates about the meaning of democracy, the nature of labor, and the future of the nation. By the end of the war, with three quarters of a million dead on the two sides, Americans were understandably exhausted at the prospect of further ideological struggles between the political parties. In the period from 1870 to 1900, Republican and Democratic policies were often indistinguishable. James Bryce, an English aristocrat who wrote a book about his own Tocqueville-like tour of the United States in the late 1880s, noted that "neither party has any principles, any distinctive tenets." "All has been lost," he wrote, "except office or the hope of it." Both parties claimed to champion the interests of the common citizen, but both parties were most responsive to business interests.

President Grant, the Civil War general who was intimately familiar with Lincoln's reasons for waging war and his hopes for the nation's future, seemed to have quickly forgotten his predecessor's legacy. He openly hobnobbed with James Fisk, the financier who controlled the Erie Railroad, and other business leaders who were described by contemporary journalists as "robber barons." The Republican program of "internal improvements," most notably land grants to support railroad construction, cemented a new and often corrupt alliance between the party and business interests, the latter eager to gain access to the government's millions. The Republican Party in turn increasingly tapped its rich business friends for the growing sums of money needed to run political campaigns.

The Democrats may have attacked Republicans as the party of business, but they increasingly interpreted their own Jacksonian heritage in light of the newfangled laissez-faire doctrines. While ostentatiously championing the cause of the common people, they were prepared to do little for them. After defeating the Republican candidate in 1884, Democratic president Grover Cleveland filled his cabinet with businessmen and corporate attorneys and, in a wholehearted embrace of laissez-faire views, stood steadfast against government intervention in the economy to support the disadvantaged. In words that formed a striking contrast to Lincoln's famous closing lines of the Gettysburg Address, Cleveland affirmed, "Though the people support the Government, the Government should not support the people." So much for government "for the people."

Moreover, the laissez-faire doctrines not only influenced the executive branch and Congress, but had an even more profound influence on the federal judiciary. As the century wound to a close, even as the states and the federal government slowly began to take action to control the excesses of the railroad magnates and the trusts, the Supreme Court consistently ruled that government-chartered corporations were entitled to the same privileges as individual American citizens. Regulation of corporations was rejected as an unjust attempt to deprive them of "life, liberty, or property without due process of law." In 1895 the US Supreme Court ruled in *United States v. E. C. Knight* that the Sherman Antitrust Act—explicitly designed to prevent unfair restraint of trade and monopolies—could not outlaw monopolies in manufacturing. The effect was essentially to gut the act. In *Lochner v. New York,* in 1905, the Court in a similar spirit struck down a New York state law designed to limit the workweek of bakers to no more than ten hours per day or sixty hours per week.

In the course of a generation, American social Darwinists had in effect rewritten the nation's social contract and reinterpreted the country's founding documents as laissez-faire charters enshrining economic freedom as an absolute right of individuals and corporations, empowering the "fit" to prosper while consigning the "unfit" to "deserved" suffering and presumably eventual extinction. In the process, Lincoln's dream of a middle-class society had all but disappeared. In its place was a new vision eulogized by industrialist Andrew Carnegie.

Carnegie's *Gospel of Wealth* turned Lincoln's dream on its head. In Lincoln's America, the underlying principle of economic life was widely shared "equality" of opportunity, based on the ideals set forth in the Declaration of Independence. In Carnegie's America, the watchword was *inequality* and the concentration of wealth and resources in the hands of the few. Whereas in Lincoln's America government was to take an active role in "clearing the path" for ordinary people to get ahead, in Carnegie's America the government was to step aside and let the "laws of economics" run their course. Whereas in Lincoln's America the laborer had a right to the "fruits of his labor," in Carnegie's America the fruits went disproportionately to the business owner and investor as the "fittest." Whereas in Lincoln's America the desire was to help all Americans fulfill the dream of the "self-made man," in Carnegie's America it was the rare exception, the man of unusual talent, that was to be supported. Whereas in Lincoln's America the engine of progress was the laboring of all Americans, in Carnegie's America the true engine of progress was the industrial magnate. Whereas in Lincoln's America government was to be on the side of the laborer, in Carnegie's America government was to be on the side of corporate America.

Not everyone accepted every detail of Carnegie's *Gospel of Wealth*. But in its broad themes, it reflected ideas that enjoyed wide social and political acceptance in late-nineteenth-century America and would enjoy a revival in the twentieth and the twenty-first centuries. For decades to come, the struggle over the government's economic policy would essentially boil down to the question: which was the true vision of America, Carnegie's *Gospel of Wealth* or Lincoln's dream of a middle-class society?

Nine

POSITIVE GOVERNMENT

THE LINCOLN LEGACY

A T THE TURN OF THE TWENTIETH CENTURY, THEODORE ROOSEVELT became the first president, and arguably the first national politician, to give voice to a rising new national consciousness of the injustices, corruption, and abominable conditions of life for the working class under the new American industrial economy. Roosevelt, scion of a wealthy New York family, former governor of New York, and the youngest man to assume the nation's highest office, spoke in a language that the citizens of America's urban North could understand.

Roosevelt, who as a little boy had viewed Lincoln's 1865 funeral procession from his family's home in New York City, proudly told reporters that he kept a portrait of Lincoln behind his presidential desk. "When I am confronted with a great problem," he explained, "I look up to that picture, and I do as I believe Lincoln would have done." He also kept a lock of Lincoln's hair in his ring—a relic he got from his secretary of state John Hay, who had once been assistant private secretary to Lincoln himself.

Roosevelt felt comfortable pursuing what he called a "Jackson-Lincoln theory of the presidency," meaning that he would be an active executive prepared to do even what Congress was reluctant to approve. Because, he insisted, Lincoln and Jackson had done the same. Although Lincoln and Jackson had different beliefs about slavery and economic policy, they both believed that the president should use his power directly to promote the general welfare. Jackson used this power

President Theodore Roosevelt speaks at the Lincoln log cabin in Hodgenville, Kentucky, on February·12, 1909, the Lincoln centennial and the day the outgoing president (and devoted Lincoln admirer) pledged the sacred birthplace site to the federal government. NATIONAL PARK SERVICE

to destroy the national banking system. Lincoln used this power to restore the national bank and to manage the conduct of the Civil War. Roosevelt said Lincoln practiced what he called "tempered radicalism," and so would he.

Roosevelt self-consciously presented himself as the legitimate heir to Lincoln's political philosophy. He declared himself committed to government "for the people" rather than for the corporations or the wealthiest Americans. Roosevelt painted in bold public strokes. He famously called the presidency a "bully pulpit" (the word *bully* being his particular slang for "great" or "wonderful"), and he used it in this fashion just as Lincoln, in a more reticent day, used so-called public letters to speak directly to the general public. In his first State of the Union message, Roosevelt said, "The tremendous and highly complex industrial development . . . brings us face to face . . . with very serious social problems." The "old laws, and the old customs . . . once quite sufficient to regulate the accumulation and distribution of wealth" were "no longer sufficient."

Roosevelt's commitment to use the federal government to tackle the nation's "serious social problems" was put to the test when 140,000 coal miners went on strike in May and June 1902. The whole country suffered under the absence of coal, which was then the principal source of heat for American homes, businesses, and public facilities. What began as a tolerable absence in the summer months would become dire in the fall. Roosevelt faced a difficult national problem, as long as the strike continued with little promise of a settlement. By October one journalist described the strike as "the most formidable industrial deadlock in the history of the United States."

The owners of the coal mines were adamantly opposed to negotiating with the union and expected to be supported by a Republican probusiness administration in Washington. But Roosevelt was a new kind of Republican president. He interjected himself into the conflict on October 3, 1902, by inviting both the owners and the union leaders to come to Washington to discuss their differences with him. The union leaders were eager to meet, and the owners reluctantly agreed. The president greeted the two parties with the statement that there are "three parties affected by the situation in the anthracite trade—the operators, the miners and the general public." Roosevelt said he spoke "for neither the operators nor the miners, but for the general public."

Despite Roosevelt's efforts to broker a deal, the mine operators rejected all suggestions for government intervention, and the strike went on. As winter weather arrived, the public was still without heat, and, not surprisingly, public opinion turned against the mine owners. With public sentiment supporting him, Roosevelt enlisted business leader J. P. Morgan to persuade the owners to settle the dispute by agreeing to accept a decision of a Federal Government Arbitration Commission. The owners reluctantly agreed. The Arbitration Commission ultimately awarded the miners a retroactive wage increase of 10 percent as well as a reduction in daily work hours from ten to nine. For Roosevelt and his supporters, this was a confirmation that Lincoln's idea of taking positive government action for the people was possible in twentieth-century America.

Roosevelt set forth a new agenda, bold in both principle and detail. He called for the federal government to "assume power of supervision and regulation over all corporations doing interstate business" and asked for amendments to strengthen the Interstate Commerce Act to achieve this goal. In doing so, he hoped to use the federal government's power to regulate interstate commerce to limit the power of corporations using monopolistic methods. He proposed the creation of a new cabinet secretary of commerce and industry with jurisdiction over commerce and labor matters. He called for reform of the government's labor policies, including legislation to limit women and child labor hours and a factory law for the District of Columbia. He praised the labor movement and suggested that government action would be necessary to protect unions.

Like Lincoln before him, Roosevelt well understood the power of his presidential statements: the "sermons" he delivered from his "bully pulpit." His rhetoric would prove as important as his policies. His new tone and vision had a galvanizing effect on the nation. His statements echoed the feelings of an increasingly worried and conscience-stricken middle class and unleashed the pent-up energies of a whole generation of idealists and crusaders.

In the process, Roosevelt radically redefined the role and vastly expanded the prerogatives of the federal government. Taking advantage of the long-dormant provisions of the Sherman Anti-Trust Act, his administration pursued a series of highly visible prosecutions against the trusts, beginning with a case against the Northern Securities Company in 1902. Federal prosecutors were successful in breaking up the Standard Oil of New Jersey Trust and the American Tobacco Company Trust. In 1906 and 1908—following the publication of Upton Sinclair's novel *The Jungle*, exposing in gruesome detail the abusive and unsanitary practices in Chicago's meatpacking industry—Roosevelt signed the Pure Food and Drug Act and the Meat Inspection Act, the first real consumer protection legislation. He also sponsored a series of laws aimed at conservation of the natural environment.

Roosevelt described the philosophic roots of his progressive beliefs in a speech in 1910 outside Osawatomie, Kansas, where John Brown had fought the Missouri Riders in 1856. Addressing himself to the Civil War veterans in his audience, Roosevelt said, "There have been

The cartoon *Led by Lincoln's Principles* suggested that the sixteenth president had all but encouraged the twenty-sixth to make another run for the White House as a third-party Progressive candidate in 1912. TR would have agreed. LINCOLN MEMORIAL UNIVERSITY, HARROGATE, TN

two great crises in our country's history: first when it was formed, and then again when it was perpetuated" by Lincoln. Now, he said, there was a looming third crisis that could be met only by the wisdom of Abraham Lincoln. He explained that Lincoln had rallied the public behind a commitment to support laborers in the battles between those who produce and those who profit. Roosevelt quoted Lincoln's economic belief that "Labor is the superior of Capital." He insisted property rights were secondary to the rights of the common welfare.

Roosevelt went on to contend that he was applying Lincoln's vision to America as it existed in 1910: "The essence of any struggle for healthy liberty has always been . . . to take from some one man or class of men the right to enjoy power, or wealth, or position, or immunity, which has not been earned by service to his or their fellows."

Roosevelt asserted that corporate owners were buying favors from local political bosses and national members of Congress. He added:

"The Constitution guarantees protections to property and we must make that promise good. But it does not give the right of suffrage to any corporation. . . . The citizens of the United States must effectively control the mighty commercial forces which they have themselves called into being."

Executives and "especially" the board members of such corporations, he insisted, should be held responsible for breaches of antitrust law. Roosevelt cited one of the proudest creations of his own administration, the Federal Bureau of Corporations, and said that it and the Interstate Commerce Commission should be handed greater powers. He further advocated a judiciary accountable to changing social and economic conditions; comprehensive workmen's compensation acts; higher safety and sanitary standards in the workplace; public scrutiny of all political campaign spending, both before and after elections; and graduated income and inheritance taxes on big fortunes.

Lincoln had made the initial commitment to government for the people in 1863. Roosevelt took Lincoln's commitment a long step forward in 1910. He called his approach a "New Nationalism." One of its principal features would be a judiciary, responding to changing social and economic conditions by favoring people's rights over property rights. In effect, Roosevelt was trying to undo some of the damage the Supreme Court had done in the 1880s and 1890s to protect big businesses from government regulation of their political influence. Roosevelt concluded his speech in 1910 with the following words: "If our political institutions were perfect, they would absolutely prevent the political domination of money in any part of our affairs. We need to make our political representatives more quickly and sensitively responsive to the people whose servants they are. . . . It is particularly important that all moneys received or expended for campaign purposes should be publicly accounted for, not only after election, but before election as well."

Three weeks before the end of his second term in 1909, Roosevelt went off to visit Lincoln's log-cabin birthplace in Kentucky. Even in retirement, Roosevelt was not going to abandon the Lincoln centennial to anyone else, including his chosen Republican successor, William Howard Taft.

By the time the 1912 election rolled around, TR was ready to take back the presidency from Taft, a man he felt had failed in living up to his—and to Lincoln's—vision. He attempted a comeback as the presidential candidate of the new Progressive Party, but by then he was not alone in linking himself to Lincoln. The competition to claim Lincoln had embraced all political faiths and candidates, Republican, Progressive, and Democrat alike. Taft went off to Vermont, there to receive the endorsement of Lincoln's son Robert. To seal the blessing, they played golf together! Roosevelt fought back by declaring that his "progressive platform of today is but an application of Lincoln's" and dismissing Lincoln's rich son as incapable of understanding such things. Democratic candidate Woodrow Wilson created an association of his own with the great man. Explaining that he was in search of the unique inspiration only Lincoln could provide, the Democratic presidential nominee made his own pilgrimage to the sacred and hitherto exclusively Republican mecca of Springfield, Illinois, Lincoln's hometown.

Running mates? A Teddy Roosevelt for President pin dating to his 1904 campaign for a full White House term (and the golden anniversary of the Republican Party) makes an explicit link to Lincoln. FROM THE LINCOLN FINANCIAL FOUNDATION COLLECTION, COURTESY OF THE ALLEN COUNTY PUBLIC LIBRARY AND INDIANA STATE MUSEUM AND HISTORIC SITES

Comparisons between Roosevelt and Lincoln reached a new level when a gun-toting assassin attacked TR during the campaign. Roosevelt survived because he had folded his long speech inside his breast pocket. The bullet stuck within the thick manuscript, saving his life. One only wonders what might have happened had TR been prone to making brief speeches like Lincoln's Gettysburg Address.

Still, Roosevelt finished second that year, although the total Republican vote far exceeded the Democrats. But Wilson prevailed—benefiting from the split opposition—just as Lincoln had in 1860 against a divided Democratic opposition.

Woodrow Wilson became president of the United States in 1913. He was a Southerner by birth and inclination and retained the dominant Southern racial prejudices. In his first year as president, Wilson presided over the fiftieth anniversary of the Battle of Gettysburg—giving a Gettysburg Address of his own that suggested that Union and Confederate veterans both deserved tribute and honor. On racial matters, Wilson could not shake his Southern heritage. He made no mention of the relevance of Lincoln's "new birth of freedom" to the condition of African Americans in 1914. Nor did he mention the importance of the Union's victory in the Civil War.

Wilson was not at all inclined to look to Lincoln for guidance in addressing the increasing pattern of segregation of the African American population. Indeed, he insisted that segregation be practiced in all departments of the federal government. Wilson held the basic Southern prosegregationist view that African Americans were an inferior race. He was sympathetic to the Southern view that the Confederate states had engaged not in a rebellion but rather in a "lost cause" to maintain a superior society. In the South, lost-cause proponents had conducted a sentimental campaign for a half century to overcome the memory of defeat in the Civil War. Their message was clear: the war had nothing to do with slavery. The Southerners had fought against tyranny and more particularly against the tyranny of the federal government to violate the constitutional rights of the Southern states. They presented themselves as valiant underdogs fighting to overcome unwarranted aggression.

The lost-cause proponents in the South were aided in their efforts by movie producers and book publishers in the North. D. W. Griffith's

Lincoln Steadying Wilson's Hand suggests that the nineteenth-century president continued to influence his twentieth-century successors regardless of party, in this case Democrat Woodrow Wilson, a late-blooming Lincoln enthusiast who simultaneously embraced the racist film *Birth of a Nation*. Here Lincoln steels Wilson to restrain a craven politician. LINCOLN MEMORIAL UNIVERSITY, HARROGATE, TN

highly successful 1915 film, *Birth of a Nation*, portrayed the resurgent, repressive, and lynch-prone Ku Klux Klan as a heroic force protecting Southern women from sexually aggressive African American males. President Woodrow Wilson was so enamored of the film that he hosted a private screening of it in the White House.

Despite Wilson's Southern proclivities, it is remarkable that his campaign speeches in 1912 amounted to a self-conscious effort to revive Lincoln's vision of a middle-class society. Theodore Roosevelt had spoken candidly about social evils and had used federal action and new laws to address many of them. But Roosevelt's perspective on the issues during his presidency was always a top-down vision, the view of a patrician, of an aristocrat who felt a responsibility for his society out of a sense of noblesse oblige. His progressive agenda was fully elaborated only after he left office when he was engaged in his unsuccessful campaign for the presidency between 1910 and 1912. By contrast, Wilson looked to Lincoln from the beginning of his presidency when he initiated a series of programs guided by Lincoln's commitment to a middle-class economy and society. Like Lincoln, Wilson reenvisioned the nation's problems, as it were, from the bottom up. He adopted the perspective of the ordinary citizen, the common worker struggling to manage under the existing conditions of the economy and the political system. Citing Lincoln as a model, Wilson explicitly linked his progressive agenda to the cause of reviving America's commitment to social mobility and restoring equality of economic opportunity. For Wilson, it was precisely Lincoln's understanding of the meaning of America as an antiaristocratic middle-class society that needed to be restored. Lincoln, he said, was "a man who rose out of the ranks and interpreted America better than any man had interpreted it who had risen out of the privileged classes or the educated classes of America."

According to Wilson, what had been lost in the Gilded Age—and in the Republican Party—was precisely Lincoln's profound sense that America was all about the fate of the average person, about opportunities for the ordinary worker to get ahead. Wilson chided the Republicans for their elitism. "It is amazing," he said, "how quickly the political party which had Lincoln for its first leader, Lincoln, who not only denied, but in his own person so completely disproved the aristocratic theory,—it is amazing how quickly that party, founded on faith in the people, forgot the precepts of Lincoln and fell under the delusion that the 'masses' needed the guardianship of 'men of affairs.'"

Wilson rejected outright the Gospel of Wealth notion that the industrial magnate was to be revered as the engine of the nation's prosperity, "[F]or indeed, if you stop to think about it, nothing could be a greater departure from original Americanism, from faith in the ability of a confident, resourceful, and independent people, than the discouraging doctrine that somebody has got to provide prosperity for the rest of us."

Lincoln had spoken of the "prudent, penniless beginner." Wilson spoke similarly of the "beginner," the man "with only a little capital." But industrial America was no longer Lincoln's America. "American industry is not free, as once it was free," Wilson said. "American enterprise is not free; the man with only a little capital is finding it harder to get into the field, more and more impossible to compete with the big fellow. Why? Because the laws of this country do not prevent the strong from crushing the weak." Like Lincoln, Wilson believed that America needed to be a middle-class nation, a nation that assimilated beginners to the middle class. There needed to be "the constant renewal of society from the bottom." The "middle class is being more and more squeezed out by the processes which we have been taught to call processes of prosperity," he said. The whole point of American democracy was to provide the humble with access to the American Dream, and government should act to ensure this access. "Anything that depresses, anything that makes the organization greater than the man, anything that blocks, discourages, dismays the humble man, is against the principles of progress." This was vintage Lincoln.

Wilson sought to keep his connection to Lincoln alive. He formally accepted Lincoln's log-cabin birthplace as a donation to the US government in 1916, declaring Lincoln a "typical" American yet a singularly "great" leader. As a historian, the young Wilson had complained that Lincoln had "made the presidency his government." But once he assumed the presidency himself, Wilson suddenly felt "the closest kinship" to Lincoln "in principle and political" lineage.

During World War I, Wilson encouraged the use of Lincoln's image on war-bond and recruitment posters, quoting him to justify American involvement in a new conflict. What seems to have eluded Wilson was the irony of his quoting the Great Emancipator while resegregating the federal bureaucracy. It is no surprise that he never mentioned freedom or equality for African Americans in any of his tributes to his suddenly useful predecessor.

But Wilson's commitment to using the federal government to support a society for the people was indeed vintage Lincoln. And his specific policies went far beyond both Lincoln and Roosevelt in proposing government action to improve the economic condition of underadvantaged Americans. The legislative record of Wilson's first term was unparalleled. The list of his domestic achievements was stunning and amounted to a comprehensive new set of government economic policies.

First came tariff reform. Increasingly, progressives had come to see tariff laws as, in effect, a regressive tax on consumers. Notoriously shaped by the efforts of lobbyists, the tariffs protected the trusts from foreign competition and kept prices high. Consumers footed the bill. Legislation during Wilson's first year as president essentially overturned the tariff regime of the nineteenth century, radically reducing rates on hundreds of items (while raising rates on certain luxury goods) and, following Lincoln's lead, reinstituting a graduated income tax to provide a new revenue base for the government. In effect, the law shifted the source of federal revenues from a regressive consumption tax in the form of tariffs to a progressive tax on income. In 1916 the tax was significantly raised to cover war preparedness (after US entry into World War I income taxes were raised again), and, for the first time, a federal estate tax on large inheritances was established (the latter was a long-standing item on the progressive agenda, advocated by Roosevelt as early as 1906). This was both a new technical approach to and a new philosophy of taxation, an effort to gain lower prices for most Americans through tariff reductions and simultaneously shift the burden of taxation away from lower- and middle-income Americans to upper-income Americans.

During Wilson's first term, he was fortunate to enjoy Democratic majorities in both houses of Congress. This gave him the opportunity to follow Lincoln's approach and use the power of the federal government for the people. With the support of Congress he established worker's compensation and child labor laws, created the Federal Trade Commission and the Federal Reserve Board, and secured passage of the "trust-busting" Clayton Anti-Trust Act.

It is tempting to conclude that Lincoln's vision of America as a middle-class society had made a permanent comeback. Conditions were clearly improving. Once unleashed, the impetus for genuine reform had proved unstoppable. Ironically, Lincoln's torch had been passed to Wilson and the Democrats, who now boasted a comprehensive progressive agenda to support their long-standing claim to the mantle of "champion of the common people." Through his policies, Wilson had restored the essence of Lincoln's economic vision, and he was vocal about doing so. In speech after speech, he made it clear to his fellow citizens that Lincoln was his model.

The *True Sons of Liberty* as depicted in this 1918 Charles Gustrine print are black soldiers fighting in World War I. They are inspired into battle, the print suggests, by the image of a benevolent Lincoln and a paraphrased promise of equality from the Gettysburg Address. The Great Emancipator had introduced African American military service in 1863. COURTESY OF GILDER LEHRMAN INSTITUTE OF AMERICAN HISTORY, GLC09121

But World War I became the last great cause of Woodrow Wilson's progressive movement, and it proved to be the movement's undoing. By 1919, when the president returned from Paris with the Treaty of Versailles and his elaborate plan for the League of Nations, the public was sick to death of war and equally weary of Wilson's seemingly inexhaustible store of idealistic rhetoric. As long as Wilson's vision remained focused on improving the lives of ordinary Americans, the public stood behind him. War in the name of an abstract idea of human progress, however, left a bitter taste.

A prototypical African American veteran returns from the Great War to the embrace of his family—under the gaze of a Lincoln icon gracing the parlor wall. In truth the doughboy will receive a less enthusiastic reintroduction to segregated civilian life than promised in the title to this print: *Welcome Home*. FROM THE LINCOLN FINANCIAL FOUNDATION COLLECTION, COURTESY OF THE ALLEN COUNTY PUBLIC LIBRARY AND INDIANA STATE MUSEUM AND HISTORIC SITES

Republicans correctly gauged the public mood and hit on an apt theme for the 1920 election: "Not heroism, but healing," declared Republican candidate Warren G. Harding, "not nostrums, but normalcy." The swipe at Wilson's rhetorical grandiosity (dismissing it as so many "nostrums") struck a powerful chord. The Republican ticket (Warren Harding and Calvin Coolidge) trounced the Democratic slate (James M. Cox and Franklin D. Roosevelt), winning 16 million votes to the Democrats' 9 million.

In one respect, Harding's postwar administration harked back to President Ulysses S. Grant's administration following the Civil War. It would be remembered for a string of spectacular scandals. Mercifully, perhaps, the president died of a sudden stroke in August 1923 before the malfeasance had come to light. But scandals were not the most important consequence of Harding's presidential leadership. The real significance of the Harding administration was that it ushered in twelve years of unabashed probusiness Republican rule—a revival of laissez-faire economic doctrine and a return to the Gospel of Wealth.

This time the public embraced the Republican probusiness approach with unparalleled fervor. The reason was simple: it seemed to work. The 1920s were a decade of dramatic economic growth and unprecedented rise in the living standards of most Americans. From 1921 through 1929, the gross national product expanded at an estimated real rate of 4.5 percent per year—well above the average annual growth rates of 3 percent per year in the post–World War II decades.

The prosperity of the 1920s was not produced by laissez-faire magic. It was based on increasing consumer demand heavily financed by consumer borrowing. This was all well and good, as long as prosperity continued on the upswing. But amid the exuberance of the era, it was easy to forget an elementary truth: that borrowing carried risk.

"The chief business of the American people is business," affirmed President Calvin Coolidge in January 1925. The Republican administrations of the 1920s saw their economic mission as one of enabling business to do its job. For government, this meant mainly getting out of the way: lower taxes, less regulation, indeed virtually no regulation. Business should be helped or otherwise left alone. As business prospered, so would America. From their probusiness perspective, the 1920s Republicans claimed that prosperity was coming from the producer, from the top down. "Give tax breaks to large corporations," Treasury Secretary Andrew Mellon famously said, "so that money can trickle down to the general public, in the form of extra jobs."

Americans for the most part were initially buoyed by the ride up the 1920s roller coaster, but the ride down was too terrible to forget. Following the stock market crash in October 1929, the American economy descended into a rapid tailspin. By 1932 12 million Americans were out of work—nearly a quarter of the labor force. Tens of thousands of men were riding railroad boxcars from town to town in a vain search of employment, and tens of thousands more were living in makeshift tent camps on vacant lots in major cities (derisively named

The Wanderer Finds Liberty in America was the title of this "Americanization" pageant staged for Jewish immigrant children in 1919 Milwaukee. The man in the Lincoln regalia is unidentified, but the costumed "Statue of Liberty" is believed to be Goldie Mabovitch Meyerson—who later migrated to Palestine and eventually became Israeli prime minister Golda Meir. COURTESY OF STATE HISTORICAL SOCIETY OF WISCONSIN, MADISON, WHI X3 22831

Hoovervilles after Republican president Herbert Hoover). Countless families across the nation lacked shelter, heat, food, or even shoes and clothing for their children. The risk had simply become unacceptable. Business had taken the risks; now ordinary Americans were paying the terrible price. Overnight, the 1920s land of milk and honey had turned into a biblical land of famine.

For almost two decades, Theodore Roosevelt and Woodrow Wilson had done what they could to resurrect Lincoln's vision and overturn the Gospel of Wealth. Now, however, it seemed as if the Gospel of Wealth, back with a vengeance, had utterly destroyed Lincoln's vision of a middle-class society.

Ten

FOR A VAST FUTURE

EXPANDING LINCOLN'S AMERICAN DREAM

WHEN FRANKLIN D. ROOSEVELT ENTERED THE NATIONAL STAGE as the Democratic presidential nominee in 1932, he appeared to be no less a captive of the generally accepted economic orthodoxy than the Republicans. During the campaign, Roosevelt attacked Herbert Hoover as a spendthrift and called for a balanced budget and a reduction in federal spending. In other words, Roosevelt assailed Hoover for just about the only thing that Hoover was doing right. "Given later developments, the campaign speeches often read like a giant misprint, in which Roosevelt and Hoover speak each other's lines," a New Dealer later observed. Still, however similar they sounded, Roosevelt succeeded in characterizing Hoover as a do-nothing president in a time of crisis. Roosevelt handily defeated Hoover in the election.

Although he shared some of the orthodox beliefs of the time—in particular, favoring balanced budgets and sound money in 1932—Roosevelt departed from the orthodoxy in one critical respect. He believed strongly in Lincoln's idea of constructive government action. Roosevelt was an heir to the twentieth-century progressive tradition on two different sides: he had served in Woodrow Wilson's progressive administration (as assistant secretary of the navy), and he had married Theodore Roosevelt's indomitable niece Eleanor. Watching Wilson, and for that matter Teddy, FDR internalized Lincoln's belief that government could be an active instrument of change: it could be used to reshape economic life; it could establish a new and better set of rules for economic activity; it could be a tool for solving problems. It was a tool Roosevelt was fully prepared to use.

When his first term began in March 1933, Roosevelt inherited a shattered economy from his Republican predecessors. The nation's economic institutions were crumbling, the banking system was not functioning, and business confidence had collapsed. As distinguished journalist Walter Lippman observed, "Financial and industrial leaders had fallen from one of the highest positions of influence and power that they had ever occupied in our history to one of the lowest." The public was in despair. President Hoover and his friends in the business community seemed to have no answers. The public had lost faith in the Republican leaders of the nation.

Against the relative passivity of the Republicans—a legacy of their long-standing laissez-faire economic credo—Roosevelt proposed a bold course of government action. The byword of his approach was *experimentation*. "It is common sense to take a method and try it," he said. "If it fails, admit it frankly and try another. But above all, try something."

"Try something." The words spoke directly to the dark public mood caused by pervasive unemployment, hunger, and homelessness. Do something, anything, to halt the slide into economic apocalypse. At the Democratic National Convention, Roosevelt pledged "a new deal for the American people." "New Deal" became the slogan of his administration and the synonym for a revolution in federal government policy.

Roosevelt's New Deal was a modern version of Lincoln's commitment to government action to support a prosperous middle-class society. FDR self-consciously defined his progressive policies in Lincoln's language. In a fireside chat on September 30, 1934, Roosevelt said: "I believe with Abraham Lincoln, that 'The legitimate object of Government is to do for a community of people whatever they need to have done but cannot do at all or cannot do so well for themselves in their separate and individual capacities.'"

A month later, Roosevelt insisted again that his cause was the same as Lincoln's, quoting his 1864 speech at Baltimore:

I can better describe the kind of liberty which our Administration has sought and continues to seek by reading to you the simple words of a great President who believed in the kind of liberty that we believe in—the great President who preserved the American Union. . . .

"The world has never had a good definition of the word liberty, and the American people, just now, are much in want of one. We all declare for liberty; but in using the same word we do not all mean the same thing. With some the word liberty may mean for each man to do as he pleases with himself, and the product of his labor; while with others the same word may mean for some men to do as they please with other men, and the product of other men's labor."

Roosevelt found in Lincoln's commitment to government "for the people" the basis for positive government action to restrain business managers from exercising unlimited power over their employees. He was fully prepared to take positive action to improve the economy. And so he did.

Roosevelt's commitment to the well-being of all citizens was manifested by his New Deal government stimulus programs to provide jobs for all able-bodied workers. Roosevelt treated the government as a direct employer not only of last resort but of first resort. He created the Civilian Conservation Corps, the Civil Works Administration, the Public Works Administration, and later the Works Progress Administration. His intention to take direct action was further signaled by the National Recovery Act, which brought together business leaders, labor leaders, and government officials under the same roof to undertake, industry by industry, national planning to manage economic growth.

When Roosevelt took office in 1933, unemployment stood at an almost unbelievable 24 percent. The unemployment rate declined to 21.7 percent in 1934 and continued to drop to 14 percent by 1937. Roosevelt's stimulus programs were viewed favorably by a substantial majority of American voters.

By 1934 the country was on its way to recovery. With the economy on somewhat more stable ground and public antipathy toward the wealthy cooling slightly, members of the business community quickly tried to reclaim what they viewed as their "rightful" position of power and influence in society. Many wealthy Americans began to turn against Roosevelt, attacking his New Deal's activist government as a threat to their economic power and their social position. They viewed Roosevelt as a "traitor to his class." In their version of "class warfare," wealthy Americans took the first steps in August 1934 to defend their upper-class status and economic profits by establishing the Liberty League. Their objective was not only to protect their incomes from taxation but also to promote their belief that economically successful Americans were superior people whose wealth and talent gave them the unique ability to manage public policy for the nation and the world.

The Liberty League was funded by wealthy American families, including the DuPonts of Delaware, who felt threatened by Roosevelt and the New Deal. The objective of the Liberty League was to "teach the necessity of respect for the rights of persons and property." The Liberty League claimed that the primary duty of government is to foster enterprise and initiative, and the government should in no way hinder one's right to earn and retain profits and to acquire and retain property. The Liberty League undertook to achieve this goal by funding anti–New Deal candidates to regain power to ensure that probusiness policies would be supported by Congress and a new president.

The battle between the Liberty League and Roosevelt's New Deal came to a head at the beginning of election year 1936. Speaking to and for the Liberty League, former New York governor Al Smith accused Roosevelt's New Deal of encouraging class warfare, squandering the taxpayers' money, subverting the Constitution, violating states' rights, and supporting socialistic and communistic policies. His criticisms were cheered by wealthy businessmen, men such as the head of General Motors, Alfred P. Sloan, Sewall Avery of Montgomery Ward, and Nathan Miller of U.S. Steel, who rallied behind the Liberty League in the hope that it would succeed in electing politicians who could defeat New Deal policies.

Nothing energized Roosevelt more than strident opposition. Roosevelt decided to respond to the Liberty League with a point of view derived from Lincoln, who in his Annual Message to Congress on December 3, 1861, had rejected "the effort to place *capital* on an equal footing with, if not above, *labor* in the structure of government."

"Labor," Lincoln had insisted, "is prior to, and independent of, capital. Capital is only the fruit of labor, and could never have existed if labor had not first existed. Labor is the superior of capital, and deserves much the higher consideration."

In accepting the Democratic nomination for a second term in 1936, Roosevelt was similarly forceful in attacking those who, like the Liberty League, would claim that capitalists were superior to laborers. As FDR put it: "The royalists of the economic order have conceded that political freedom was the business of the government, but they have maintained that economic slavery was nobody's business. They granted that the government could protect the citizen in his right to vote, but they denied that the government could do anything to protect the citizen in his right to work and his right to live." Just as Lincoln had argued seventy-five years earlier, Roosevelt was adamant that, "in the structure of government," the citizen's right to work and therefore live was more important than the businessman's opportunity to maximize profits.

Recognizing that "class conflict" was at the center of the 1936 campaign, Roosevelt described his upper-class opponents as "privileged princes" of new "economic dynasties"—not that different, perhaps, from the privileged slave owners Lincoln had criticized. Roosevelt argued that what they really feared was loss of their power. He weighed in "against dictatorship by mob rule and the over privileged alike" and went on to say, "Government can err, presidents do make mistakes, but . . . Divine justice weighs the sins of the cold-blooded and the sins of the warm-hearted on different scales. Better the occasional faults of a government that lives in a spirit of charity than the consistent omissions of a Government frozen in the ice of its own indifference." In this first major battle between Roosevelt and the Liberty League, Roosevelt won. He was reelected in a landslide that November.

Roosevelt summarized the basic elements of his ongoing economic policy in his State of the Union address on January 3, 1938. While he was proud of his actions in correcting the financial excesses that led to the banking crisis, Roosevelt now said his primary objective was to increase average family income and purchasing power. "Again I revert to the increase of national purchasing power as an underlying necessity of the day. If you increase that purchasing power for the farmers and for the industrial workers—especially those in both groups who have the least of it today—you will therefore increase the purchasing power of the final third of those professions which serve these groups, and therefore those of those professions who serve all groups." Here Roosevelt was stressing that the economic fate of the country depended on adequate income for all segments of society: farmers and city workers, low-income workers, middle-income workers, and upper-income workers. He looked forward to a future with an increasing number of families with middle incomes—fulfilling Lincoln's vision of a middle-class society.

Roosevelt described his prolabor and prounion policies as motivated by the necessity of increasing "the purchasing power of the nation as a whole." He said: "I have spoken of labor as another essential in the three great groups of the population in raising the Nation's income. . . . [D]efinite strides in collective bargaining have been made, the right of labor to organize has been nationally recognized. . . . [O]ur principal interest for the near future . . . [is] the immediate desirability of increasing the wages of the lowest paid groups in all industry."

Roosevelt was clear about his reaction to the competing claims of those who advocated balancing the federal budget. "We have heard much about a balanced budget. . . . But I lay down certain conditions which seem reasonable and which I believe all should accept. The first condition is that we continue the policy of not permitting any needy American who can and is willing to work to starve because the Federal Government does not provide work. Government has a final responsibility for the well-being of its citizenship."

Roosevelt's commitment to the well-being of all citizens was manifested by his New Deal government stimulus programs to provide jobs for all able-bodied American workers. When Roosevelt took office in 1933, unemployment was at an almost unbelievable 24 percent. By the time of Roosevelt's second inauguration in 1937, the country was on the mend—national income was improving and unemployment had declined to 14 percent. Roosevelt felt that he could now return to a balanced-budget approach. It had been the dominant economic orthodoxy when Roosevelt first took office in 1933 and remained so four years later. Roosevelt's misguided effort to balance the budget by reducing government expenditures in 1938 and 1939 resulted in a temporary increase in unemployment to 19 percent in 1938 and 17 percent in 1939. Recognizing the negative consequences of his effort to balance the government budget, Roosevelt firmly returned to a policy of increasing government expenditures, and unemployment declined to 15 percent in 1940.

The government's stimulus expenditures increased even further when Roosevelt focused on expanding the military capacity of the nation before and during World War II. Unemployment declined to 10 percent in 1941 and 5 percent in 1942 and less than 2 percent in 1943, 1944, and 1945. The continuation of New Deal domestic stimulus programs supported the American economy for three decades after the end of the war. The postwar unemployment rate remained between 3 percent and 6 percent until 1974 (with only two exceptions, between 6 percent and 7 percent). Before the New Deal, the budget of the federal government was typically less than 4 percent of the nation's gross domestic product. During the thirty-two-year post–World War II period from 1950 to 1981 when New Deal domestic stimulus policies dominated the economy, federal government expenditures rose to a new high level, at close to 20 percent of an expanding GDP. Growth in GDP rose to an average of 3.8 percent, more than 30 percent higher than the period from 1900 to 1950. The evidence is clear. The Roosevelt New Deal programs inspired by Lincoln's commitment to government for the people clearly worked to build a high-employment, high-growth, modern middle-class society.

The increasing demand for able-bodied workers during World War II produced a great migration of rural African American laborers to military-product manufacturing jobs in northern cities like Chicago, Detroit, and New York. While segregation continued in both the North and the South, there was the beginning of an increase in African American middle-class families. At the same time, women began to enter the labor force in greater numbers—forming the initial stage of the change in the working status of women that reached its apex in the five decades after the end of the war.

The New Deal legacy included programs designed to ensure that risk in the American economy was distributed more equitably among all segments of the population. Its major tools were regulation and insurance. Roosevelt sought to use regulation to prevent business from taking undue risks and engaging in corrupt practices of the kind that had brought on the 1929 stock market crash. At the same time, he put in place social insurance programs—such as unemployment insurance and Social Security—to protect ordinary Americans from the worst perils of modern economic life. The two measures—regulation and insurance—were mutually reinforcing. The combination instilled consumer confidence, especially in banks and financial institutions, in a sense gradually giving business back the customers who had fled when the roof came crashing down in 1929. By reducing or eliminating irresponsible business risk taking and by providing ordinary Americans with an insurance policy against the worst economic misfortunes, FDR rewrote the American social contract in a way that preserved the free-market economy and opened the way to continued prosperity. It was a new effort to apply Lincoln's vision of positive government action to fulfill the promise of a government "for the people"—a government now reborn with programs that worked directly to build a modern middle-class society. Lincoln's American Dream was once again front and center, as Roosevelt and his New Deal created the modern American middle-class economy and society.

One major consequence of the New Deal was a rehabilitation of organized labor and the extension of unions from skilled crafts to the nation's major industries—a shift that expanded the promises of Lincoln's, and now Roosevelt's, American Dream to an even broader segment of the American population. The 1930s were a period of extensive labor unrest, characterized by multiple strikes and intermittent violence. But the pain of unemployment had become so widely shared that public opinion, once hostile to unions, grew more sympathetic. Roosevelt supported legislation sponsored by Senator Robert Wagner of New York to strengthen the bargaining power of unions. Ultimately, the New Deal was responsible for two key pieces of legislation that revolutionized the American workplace. The 1935 National Labor Relations Act created a three-member government National Labor Relations Board (NLRB) with the power to protect workers' right to organize, to conduct union elections, and to bargain collectively. As a consequence, by 1940 labor union membership rose to 8.7 million, compared to 3.0 million in 1932. The NLRB was also empowered to intervene to stop unfair labor practices. The 1938 Fair Labor Standards Act established the first mechanism for determining minimum wages, mandated a forty-hour workweek with overtime paid at time and a half, and ended child labor by forbidding the employment of children under sixteen.

Together these elements—government economic regulation, unemployment insurance, Social Security, and protection of workers and their right to organize—would eventually help bring forth a fundamentally new kind of industrial economy in the post–World War II era, one in which ordinary industrial workers could aspire to and attain a middle-class standard of living, in which they enjoyed decent wages, relative job security, savings protected from financial mismanagement and malfeasance, the benefits of home ownership, and a measure of security in retirement. It helped put Lincoln's American Dream within reach once again of the "prudent, penniless beginner" who started from the low rungs of the economic ladder.

The most important New Deal initiatives—the commitments to full employment, to unemployment insurance, to Social Security, and to government regulation of financial markets—became an integral part of American economic life. They became so much a piece of the fabric of American economic activity that Americans took them for granted and failed to appreciate how critical they were to reducing the risks inherent in a modern economy. For more than four decades, Roosevelt's New Deal programs made the world safe for capitalism and in turn made capitalism safe for the ordinary worker and consumer.

Roosevelt tried to codify the gains that had been made in the New Deal and set forth the terms of the nation's new social contract in his 1941 Inaugural Address. As he put it:

The basic things expected by our people of their political and economic systems are simple. They are:

Equality of opportunity for youth and for others.
Jobs for those who can work.
Security for those who need it.

The ending of special privilege for the few.
The preservation of civil liberties for all.
The enjoyment of the fruits of scientific progress in a
wider and constantly rising standard of living.

Not only did Roosevelt define what Americans could expect from their government; he also defined four basic freedoms that all people were due. The world was in the midst of a war that the United States would soon enter, and at stake were these freedoms:

Freedom of speech and expression;
Freedom of every person to worship God in his own way;
Freedom from want;
Freedom from fear.

In his 1944 State of the Union message, Roosevelt reiterated his commitment to a "second Bill of Rights"—essentially a replacement of the laissez-faire belief in an inactive government economic policy. Roosevelt's vision constituted a renewal of Lincoln's commitment to use the power of the federal government to support the dream of a successful middle-class society.

One way Roosevelt sought to implement this vision was by passage of the Servicemen's Readjustment Act of 1944, better known as the GI Bill. Lincoln had encouraged the establishment of land-grant colleges under the 1862 Morrill Act, and now Roosevelt was taking similar steps to encourage American veterans of the war to better their lots in life through education. For the first time, there was a unanimous vote in support of a massive federal program to provide returning veterans with the opportunity to secure the education and training to prosper in the newly developing postwar middle-class economy. The extraordinary bill passed the Senate by a vote of 50 to 0 and the House by 387 to 0. The positive role of government was, for a brief moment, not a partisan issue.

The GI Bill provided unemployment compensation, mortgage loan guarantees, educational stipends, and business start-up loans for returning World War II veterans. Returning GIs received some

$2.5 billion in unemployment payments in 1946 and 1947. From 1945 through 1950, the government provided veterans with more than $10 billion for college and vocational training.

Total spending for veterans (nearly $35 billion from 1945 through 1950) stimulated the economy. It also created a massive new college-educated middle class, whose skills would add to the growth and productivity of the economy for a generation. The federal government had been generous to veterans following previous wars. But after World War II, the money for veterans came in a form largely shaped by the social vision that Roosevelt had set forth in his 1944 State of the Union message. Veterans were given immediate cash to tide them over through unemployment. But they were also given specific assistance, in gaining a college education and purchasing a home. Americans were perhaps especially prepared to extend these "rights" of education and home ownership to individuals who had risked their lives in defense of the nation. But the long-term effect of the GI Bill was that it had used government aid to build an entire new generation of middle-class Americans.

The GI Bill also played a major role in improving and extending access to higher education in the United States. It strengthened higher education by providing billions in indirect subsidies (in the form of the veterans' tuition stipends) to the nation's colleges and universities, allowing them to expand exponentially and meet the needs of tens of thousands of new students. Indeed, Roosevelt's initiative enabled Lincoln's land-grant colleges to flourish anew and become the basis for America's modern public state universities.

Roosevelt had hit upon a nonbureaucratic way of using federal resources to reshape an entire society. Costs of administering GI Bill benefits were relatively minimal. But the program's impact in shaping America's modern middle-class society was probably greater—and more effective—than anything that could have been accomplished through central planning or government command-and-control-style bureaucratic regulation.

Lincoln had anticipated that college education could be a major engine of social mobility in the United States. The children of farmers could gain a foothold on the ladder to economic success through attendance at his land-grant colleges. Roosevelt found a way to give tangible reality to this vision in the twentieth century through the GI Bill. Between 1949 and 2009, enrollment in US colleges rose from 2.4 million to more than 19 million. By 2009 more than 41 percent of young Americans ages eighteen to twenty-four were enrolled in college. And American universities were a beacon to the world, increasingly attracting some of the best and brightest students from other countries. After graduation many of the students from other countries stayed in the United States, which offered them great opportunities to build successful careers and contribute to the economic growth of the American nation.

The GI Bill was only one of the ways FDR and his immediate successors ambitiously redefined the role of government in the economy. In 1945 congressional sponsors of a proposed "Full Employment Act" sought to enshrine in law the "right" to a job, requiring the government to engage in "compensatory spending" in times of recession to ensure "full employment." While the "right" to employment was excised from the bill, as was the requirement for "compensatory spending," the compromise Employment Act of 1946 established government's responsibility to promote "maximum employment." The act also required an annual economic report from the president and established the President's Council of Economic Advisers.

To be sure, the law did not in any way guarantee full employment. But it was a powerful symbolic statement of the federal government's new role. Not only was the government's obligation to intervene in the economy established, but government's role in the economy was now understood to be a responsibility. Like it or not, the unemployment rate had now become the barometer by which presidents and their administrations were to be judged. As perhaps the leading measure of presidential performance, the unemployment rate forged a direct link between the electoral fortunes of the president and his party, on the one hand, and the fate of the ordinary worker, on the other. It stood as a constant reminder that the economy existed to serve American workers and their families, not vice versa.

The American economy that emerged after Roosevelt's presidency differed profoundly from the limited-government, laissez-faire system

Franklin Delano Roosevelt arrives at the Lincoln Memorial for a morale-boosting visit in the midst of World War II—on the Civil War president's 135th birthday, February 12, 1944. FDR embraced Lincoln and became the first Democrat to win the African American presidential vote, so long faithful to the party of Lincoln. FROM THE LINCOLN FOUNDATION COLLECTION, COURTESY OF THE ALLEN COUNTY PUBLIC LIBRARY AND INDIANA STATE MUSEUM AND HISTORIC SITES

of the pre–New Deal era. As the economy slowed in postwar recessions, federal revenues naturally dropped, but federal expenditures continued at a high level. And now the government was large enough for these expenditures to matter. Federal government expenditures had risen from less than 4 percent of gross domestic product before World War II to a continuing postwar level of close to 20 percent. Roosevelt's programs provided a substantial stimulus to the economy during recessionary periods by sustaining aggregate demand with increased federal spending. Unemployment insurance was the most obvious support during economic declines. As unemployment went up, federal disbursements for unemployment payments went up simultaneously. This "automatic" support for aggregate demand kicked in immediately when recessions occurred and employment declined. And the US Federal Reserve Bank was now authorized to encourage economic growth by lowering interest rates under its dual mandate to support maximum employment and support stable prices.

The post–World War II federal budget had become, in short, a kind of counterdepression machine. It automatically produced additional government spending whenever the economy began descending into a slump. The result was a pronounced moderation of downturns. The fiscal stimulus from increased government expenditures was an important hedge against an economic tailspin.

Through each of his initiatives, Roosevelt had taken Lincoln's vision of a government "for the people" a major step forward. Lincoln had fought to preserve America's middle-class economy before industrialization took hold. That vision had foundered in the post–Civil War industrial boom. But now, the Roosevelt administration was creating a modern version of America's middle-class economy, one in which the federal government would protect and support ordinary Americans in an increasingly complex and risky industrial and postindustrial economy.

Like President Lincoln, President Roosevelt was called upon to confront the question of equal opportunity for African Americans who were still predominantly living in the southern states. Franklin and particularly Eleanor Roosevelt certainly did have a desire to improve the condition of African Americans. Franklin Roosevelt was mindful of the need to ensure that African Americans would benefit economically from his New Deal programs. Eleanor was both a private and a public advocate of equal treatment of African Americans. Her unprecedented sponsorship of a concert by the gifted African American singer Marian Anderson at the Lincoln Memorial was widely recognized as a recognition that African Americans should be treated on par with all other American citizens.

Like other presidents before him, Franklin Roosevelt clearly understood the political benefit of embracing the Lincoln tradition. As governor of New York, Roosevelt is reported to have bluntly confided to a journalist that one of his goals was for "us Democrats to claim Lincoln as one of our own." He proceeded to do just that. And this gave him the opportunity to compete successfully for the African American vote, which had remained rock solid for the Republican Party since the end of the Civil War. By 1936 the majority was Roosevelt's—and has been Democratic ever since.

In the first year of his administration, FDR had quoted Lincoln to justify the New Deal domestic policies. When World War II loomed, Roosevelt quoted Lincoln again. He hired Robert E. Sherwood to write his speeches, knowing full well he could rely on the man who had written the play *Abe Lincoln in Illinois* and was intimately familiar with the sixteenth president's writings and speeches. The decision paid off: soon Roosevelt's own remarks echoed with references to what Lincoln would and would not do in the face of the Nazi threat. FDR positioned himself much like the hero of Sherwood's drama—inclined by nature not to fight, but ready to do battle once sufficiently angered.

Like Wilson, FDR stepped back into time and myth by traveling to Lincoln's log-cabin birthplace in Kentucky. Before long, the Democrat Roosevelt had convinced Americans that no politician had more in common with the poor prairie rail splitter than this wealthy New Yorker. By the dawn of World War II, most Americans had come to believe that Roosevelt and Lincoln represented a prominent line of continuity in American leadership.

Roosevelt was not the last president to amplify his connection to Lincoln. Ever since FDR, his real and would-be successors, regardless of party or philosophy, have sought the same brass ring.

Eleven

GOVERNMENT IS
THE PROBLEM

REJECTING LINCOLN'S LEGACY

FRANKLIN ROOSEVELT'S PROGRESSIVE GOVERNMENT POLICIES WERE designed to create a modern economy he believed consistent with Lincoln's dream of a successful middle-class society. Not everyone accepted Roosevelt's ambitious new definition of the role of government in the economy. But FDR succeeded in forging a new economic consensus that would survive mostly intact under both Democratic and Republican presidents for more than three decades after his death.

In the month after the death of her husband on April 12, 1945, Eleanor Roosevelt sealed the link between Presidents Roosevelt and Lincoln by describing her late husband's legacy as a continuation of Abraham Lincoln's "unfinished work."

> Abraham Lincoln was taken away before he had achieved unity within the nation, and the people failed him. This divided us as a nation for many years. . . . Perhaps, in His wisdom, the Almighty is trying to show us that a leader may chart the way, may point out the road to lasting peace, but that many leaders and many peoples must do the building. It cannot be the work of one man, nor can the responsibility be laid upon his shoulders, and so, when the time comes for people to assume the burden more fully, he is given rest. God grant that we may

Abraham Lincoln claimed he knew "little" about art, but the president who presided over the 1959 Lincoln sesquicentennial, Republican Dwight D. Eisenhower, was not only a Lincoln admirer but a skilled amateur artist. This is Eisenhower's undated oil portrait of his White House predecessor. EISENHOWER PRESIDENTIAL LIBRARY & MUSEUM, ABILENE, KS

have the wisdom and courage to build a peaceful world with justice and opportunity for all peoples the world over.

Lincoln's "new birth of freedom" reached worldwide maturity through the work of Franklin and Eleanor Roosevelt. In the United States, the commitment to the four freedoms provides an added pillar to the continuing general public support of the domestic economic policies of the New Deal. The dedication of Eleanor Roosevelt established the vitality of the four freedoms as a continuing beacon of light not only to the United States but also to the rest of the world.

Harry Truman stoutly supported Roosevelt's economic policies and, as president, diligently worked to implement and expand them. Truman

President Eisenhower greets Robert Todd Lincoln Beckwith, the last direct descendant of Lincoln, at a White House visit that most likely took place on the sixteenth president's 150th birthday, February 12, 1959. FROM THE LINCOLN FOUNDATION COLLECTION, COURTESY OF THE ALLEN COUNTY PUBLIC LIBRARY AND INDIANA STATE MUSEUM AND HISTORIC SITES

successfully resisted all Republican efforts to dismantle or reduce New Deal policies and succeeded in securing modest improvements and extensions in some of them. He was a strong advocate of continuing to build on the New Deal with his own Fair Deal initiatives. While most of his proposals were rejected by an increasingly conservative Congress, he was successful in making some progress to improve the treatment of African Americans who had served in the army. He insisted on equality of treatment for African American soldiers during and after their service with an executive order eliminating racial discrimination in the armed services or in government civil service positions.

Eisenhower, the first Republican elected president after Roosevelt, was reluctantly supportive of Roosevelt's version of Lincoln's dream, in part because it was the only politically viable option. As he remarked to his press secretary in 1954, "This party of ours . . . will not appeal to the American people unless the American people believe we have a liberal program." In a letter to his brother, Eisenhower explained, "Should any political party attempt to abolish social security, unemployment insurance, and eliminate labor laws and farm programs, you would not hear of that party again in our political history."

Lyndon Johnson saw himself as an enthusiastic New Dealer. He did more than any president after Roosevelt to ensure that the government would be active in creating a "great society." Committed to Lincoln and Roosevelt's concept of active government working "for the people," Johnson, most notably, added federally funded health insurance to the roster of government supported programs with the enactment of Medicare and Medicaid. The shadow of Roosevelt was so long that it influenced even Republican president Richard M. Nixon and the most notable conservative American economist, Milton Friedman. Working together, they added the earned-income tax credit to the lexicon of generally accepted progressive economic programs. Lincoln's commitment to government action "for the people" had finally, if briefly, united both parties in the task of expanding the American middle-class society.

Roosevelt's economic program had its first substantial post–World War II setback during the administration of Democratic president Jimmy Carter. When Carter assumed office in 1977, he failed to address the weakening economy in an effective way. Instead of introducing direct programs to increase employment and consumer demand, the Carter administration pursued an expansionary monetary policy. Carter relentlessly prodded the US Federal Reserve Bank to expand the money supply, first under Chairman Arthur F. Burns and then under Carter appointee G. William Miller. From 1977 to 1979, the money supply grew at a faster rate than any time in postwar history. The impact on unemployment was minimal, but inflation went through the roof. In 1979 it crested at 13.3 percent. University of Chicago economist Robert Barro devised what he called the "misery index" to measure the combined effect of inflation and unemployment (the index simply added the two percentage figures together). In 1979 the misery index rose to an unbearable 19. The following year it rose to nearly 20. The public was fed up.

"For the public today," wrote astute social observer Daniel Yankelovich in 1979, "inflation has the kind of dominance that no other issue has had since World War II. The closest contenders are the Cold War fears of the early 1950's and perhaps the last years of the Vietnam War. But inflation exceeds those issues in the breadth of concerns it has aroused among Americans. It would be necessary to go back to the 1930's and the Great Depression to find a peacetime issue that has had the country so concerned and so distraught."

Perhaps most important, inflation robbed the economy of much of the stability the New Deal framework had originally introduced: the sense that economic realities were relatively predictable, that there was a cushion against wildly high unemployment, that recessions would end fairly rapidly, and that government had a measure of control over economic life. Maintaining a middle-class standard of life in a highly inflationary economy—providing for one's family and planning for the future—became a much more stressful proposition. Missing was the essential confidence that prosperity would grow steadily year after year—or that the government could do anything to help guarantee it.

The rise of inflation under Carter's Democratic administration had reduced consumer purchasing power with substantial negative effects on economic growth. But its more enduring result was that it paved the way for the return of Gospel of Wealth thinking, focused on tax reductions, support for business enterprise, and a laissez-faire approach to regulation of business.

When Ronald Reagan replaced Jimmy Carter in the White House in 1981, it was clear that he confronted a real economic crisis consisting of economic stagnation and high inflation. The stagflation episode marked the worst economic dislocation since the Great Depression and provided the context for Reagan's economic program. Clearly, inflation had to be gotten under control. There was also strong Republican-inspired public sentiment in favor of tax cuts. Inflation-driven "tax-bracket creep" had in effect meant a steady series of "hidden" tax increases for middle-class as well as upper-class Americans. But the struggle over taxes now took on a powerful new ideological dimension.

Echoing the sentiment of earlier eras, business owners, Republican politicians, and conservative economists and intellectuals argued that the American government, under Democratic stewardship, had become downright business unfriendly. As Reagan famously claimed, "Government is the problem."

In response, Reagan brought a new approach to economic policy, developed and supported by a small cadre of conservative intellectuals, publicists, and economists. Reagan's new strategy was outlined in a "Memo to the President-elect from his Coordination Committee on Economic Policy," dated November 16, 1980, three months before his inauguration. The memo was crafted by a group that included future secretary of state George P. Shultz, future Federal Reserve Board chairman Alan Greenspan, and the leading academic proponent of business-oriented supply-side economics, Milton Friedman.

> Sharp change in present economic policy is an absolute necessity. The problems . . . can be redressed by a change in policy. . . . The essence of good policy is good strategy. . . . *The need for a long-term point of view is essential.* . . . The current regulatory overburden must be removed from the economy. . . . Many of our economic problems today stem from the large and increasing proportion of economic decisions being made through the political process rather than the market process. . . . We urge you to issue a message on regulatory reform. . . . The success of your economic policy will be a direct reflection of your ability to maintain a steady course over your full first term. Rough times will come and crises of one kind or another, some small, some of great moment, will arise. Sustained effort through these testing times means that public understanding and support are essential.

Shultz, Greenspan, and Friedman were calling for a long-term continuing program to persuade American voters to support a new conservative program of low taxes and limited government.

In 1980 the seven-year-old conservative Heritage Foundation produced a 1,093-page public policy blueprint, *Mandate for Leadership:*

Policy Management in a Conservative Administration. This became the policy bible of the newly elected Reagan administration on everything from taxes and regulation to crime and national defense. Reagan gave a copy to each member of his cabinet at their first meeting. The Heritage Foundation claims that nearly two-thirds of the two thousand recommendations in the document were adopted by the Reagan administration.

Reagan and his advisers sought nothing less than to overturn the reigning economic consensus at its foundations—and this meant going after the heart of Roosevelt's legacy. In effect, the conservative Heritage "think tank" orchestrated a revival of the nineteenth-century "political economy"—the laissez-faire doctrine of old—but with a new "explosive growth" twist. The great innovation of the Roosevelt economic revolution was to discover the centrality of consumer demand to the business cycle. Reagan's advisers rejected this approach and returned to antiregulation laissez-faire and antitax doctrines with renewed emphasis on production or "supply." Inflation, they argued, was too much money chasing after not enough goods. The problem, they contended, was not simply that government was artificially inflating demand through deficit spending. The problem was that government policy—and especially tax policy—was inhibiting producers, causing inflation by inhibiting supply. High taxes were inhibiting work, savings, and especially investment. High taxes were discouraging businesspeople from engaging in business. Thus was born "supply-side economics," the modern rebirth of the economic philosophy of the Gilded Age.

The supply-side doctrine was about one-tenth economics and nine-tenths politics. The political problem was how to craft a credible, politically salable Republican alternative to the Democrats' "demand-side" economic policies—policies that had originated with Roosevelt and were supported by the theoretical work of noted economist John Maynard Keynes and that seemed to have worked just fine for three decades.

Before 1980 Republicans' time-honored prescriptions for curing inflation were tight money and fiscal austerity, described by their opponents as "castor-oil economics." Indeed, when in 1976 Reagan challenged President Ford for the Republican presidential nomination, he proposed the typical Republican prescription. Balanced budgets. Fiscal responsibility. Belt tightening. None of it was politically salable, at least not yet. Reagan lost to Ford and Ford lost to Carter.

Reagan and his advisers learned their lesson. They came up with a new idea for the 1980 election—supply-side economics—the idea that tax cuts for everybody, especially for the wealthy, would work to increase production and stave off the inflation that had skyrocketed during Carter's administration. After all, wealthy Americans were the nation's most productive citizens, its job creators. Business owners, he argued, would automatically use their increased income from tax cuts to hire additional workers to increase their supply of products. Reagan rejected the New Deal conviction that an increase in consumer demand was a necessary precondition for business owners to increase production.

Reagan's greatest talent as a politician was an ability to communicate symbolically, to paint his policies in bold strokes that the public could understand. In pursuit of this goal, Reagan presented a new Republican version of the Gospel of Wealth. In order to do so, he turned his back on Lincoln's belief in government action to help "clear the path" for the "prudent, penniless beginner" to rise to the middle class. In its place, Reagan promoted a new vision, proposing to curb the size and influence of the federal government and to sharply reduce government regulation of businessmen and corporations engaged in the pursuit of "wealth." Reagan paid lip service to Lincoln when he said in his First Inaugural Address that "whoever would understand in his heart the meaning of America will find it in the life of Abraham Lincoln." But Reagan immediately proceeded to dismantle the underpinnings of the middle-class economy and society that were the heart and soul of Lincoln's "unfinished work."

As much as Reagan worked to change the political beliefs of the country, he put his real effort into changing the country's mind about economics. Reagan sought to repeal the post–New Deal middle-class economic mind-set. He sought to instill the idea that government should not attempt to manage the economy, that effective government policy should defer to business interests. He sought to replace the idea of government as economic steward and manager with the notion of the free market as king. Low taxes, less government regulation, fewer government programs, economic freedom, and business incentives would rule the day. Economic success, under this model, was based entirely on self-reliance and self-interest. Above all, Reagan encouraged a return to the Gilded Age belief that successful businessmen deserved recognition as the major contributors to American society.

Such ideas had found little resonance among the majority of Americans from 1932 to 1980. Reagan revived them and, over time, persuaded much of the public that they were sound ideas. More than reshaping fiscal policy, Reagan changed the terms of the economic debate. The social contract advocated by Lincoln and revised by Roosevelt—in which government played a constructive role in building a middle-class economy and society—was transformed into the belief that the government had no such responsibility to ordinary Americans.

Reagan set forth this philosophical framework in straightforward language in his First Inaugural Address:

> It is my intention to curb the size and influence of the Federal establishment. . . . It is no coincidence that our present troubles parallel and are proportionate to the intervention and intrusion in our lives that result from unnecessary and excessive growth of government. . . . There are entrepreneurs with faith in themselves and faith in an idea who create new jobs, new wealth and opportunity. They are individuals and families whose taxes support the Government and whose voluntary gifts support church, charity, culture, art, and education. Their patriotism is quiet but deep. Their values sustain our national life.

Reagan shifted the attention from the ordinary worker to the exceptional entrepreneur, what conservative supply-side economists liked to call, in language almost reminiscent of social Darwinist days, our "most productive citizens," who were later described as the only real "job creators." The key to a healthy economy was making sure these "most productive citizens" were free to be productive; it was they who "created wealth" for the rest. Government simply needed to get out of the way.

Perhaps the clearest indication of Reagan's success in changing the nation's perspective on economic matters was the gradual refocusing of attention from employment to overall business profitability and economic growth (growth in GDP) as the primary barometers of economic health and presidential performance. As long as there were business profits, Reagan claimed, wealth would eventually also trickle down into the hands of the "less productive." This new business-oriented economic philosophy, reprising the view of Herbert Hoover's treasury secretary Andrew Mellon, has dominated the political process for more than four decades during the Reagan and post-Reagan years.

Side by side with Reagan's supply-side economic rhetoric was a renewed effort to shift much of the power to regulate the economy from the federal government to the individual states, which would be more responsive to local business interests and less likely to regulate energetically. This effort was originated in 1947 by a coalition of Republicans supported by southern Democrats in Congress who believed that unions would defeat their efforts to maintain the prevailing segregated society in the South. It succeeded with the passage in Congress of the Taft-Hartley Act in 1947. The Taft-Hartley Act authorized individual states to pass "right-to-work" laws to provide private employers with tools to sharply reduce the influence of unions in the private economy. President Truman had denounced the Taft-Hartley bill as a "slave-labor bill," but it became law when Congress overrode his veto. Within a decade ten former Confederate states passed right-to-work laws. Now with the Reagan philosophy in command of public policy and public opinion, the remaining southern states passed right-to-work laws, and a significant number of northern and western states began to join them.

Business leaders used the right-to-work laws as a convenient vehicle for an increasingly successful effort to combat the union movement in the private economy. Today, the once powerful union movement has little power or presence in the private American economy.

Reagan's rhetoric laid the groundwork for a continuing Republican Party effort to convert Lincoln's emphasis on a middle-class society based on government "for the people" into an argument for the individualistic belief that every person was on his own in the ongoing competitive battle for economic success—a battle that they claimed benefited society by producing ever-increasing economic growth. Lincoln had said that the American government had an active role in helping all Americans to secure a middle-class life. Reagan took the opposite position that the government should not interfere with the operations of the economy.

Ronald Reagan won an overwhelming landslide victory—an undeniable public endorsement for both his personality and his politics—when he ran for reelection to a second term in 1984. But not every Democratic voice had been stilled. In his ringing "Tale of Two Cities" keynote speech at the Democratic National Convention in San Francisco, New York Governor Mario M. Cuomo made a case for a different direction. "We believe as Democrats," he said that night, "that a society as blessed as ours, the most affluent democracy in the world's history, one that can spend trillions on instruments of destruction, ought to be able to help the middle class in its struggle, ought to be able to find work for all who can do it, room at the table, shelter for the homeless, care for the elderly and infirm, and hope for the destitute." And then Cuomo paraphrased his personal hero, Abraham Lincoln: "We believe in only the government we need, but we insist on all the government we need." Cuomo's case energized and inspired Democrats pining for a Lincolnian commitment to government for the people, but the majority of Americans remained committed to Reagan's rhetoric and politics.

Reagan could not simply reject Lincoln's approach to a middle-class society based on "government of the people, by the people, for the people." Lincoln remained one of the most admired and iconic presidents, and his legacy endured. Rather than pushing Lincoln aside, Reagan instead adopted Lincoln as one of his own, claiming that his new economic approach came directly from Lincoln.

At the Republican National Convention of 1992, former president Reagan made his most vigorous claim that his economic policies were consistent with Lincoln's teaching. He did so by presenting to the delegates a set of principles Reagan declared had been "eloquently stated" by Lincoln generations earlier. The fortieth president went on to quote what he described as the sixteenth president's most enduring maxims:

Former President Ronald Reagan at the 1988 Republican National Convention that crowned his vice president, George H. W. Bush, as his successor. Bush, a Lincoln admirer in his own right, went on to win the White House that fall.
COURTESY OF RONALD REAGAN LIBRARY

> You cannot strengthen the weak by weakening the strong.
> You cannot help the wage earner by pulling down the wage payer.
> You cannot help the poor man by destroying the rich.
> You cannot help men permanently by doing for them what they could and should do for themselves.

To no one's surprise, the Republican convention floor erupted in delirium. Reagan had brilliantly resurrected a tablet of political commandments better than any of his earlier presidential speeches. No one had ever said it better than the Great Communicator claiming to quote the Great Emancipator.

As it turned out, it was too good to be true. The fact is, Lincoln had never said a word of it. The lines turned out to be written by an obscure German-born minister from Brooklyn in 1916, fifty-one years after Lincoln's death. The minister's pamphlet was called *Lincoln on Private Property.* It featured some words of Lincoln on one page followed by the words Reagan quoted—which were authored by the minister—on the next.

It took Herbert Mitgang, a veteran *New York Times* writer who also happened to be a Lincoln scholar, to burst the balloon the following day. Few of the millions who heard Reagan that summer night ever read the story by Mitgang or the corrections published in newspapers during the days following Reagan's remarks. Yet three full years after Mitgang had discredited Reagan's purported quotations from Lincoln, the most popular newspaper columnist in America, Ann Landers, published the quotes all over again—as Lincoln's.

The words Lincoln had never spoken have been treated time and time again as Lincoln's contribution to conservative gospel. And Republicans continue to gain some mileage with their unwarranted claim that Lincoln was the father of their conservative economic philosophy.

Twelve

THE NEW
ECONOMIC DEBATE

CLINTON, BUSH, AND OBAMA

LINCOLN CONTINUES TO PLAY AN IMPORTANT ROLE IN THE THINKING of our most recent presidents. They are all mindful of the place Lincoln has in the eyes of historians and voters as one of the three most revered presidents—considered the most revered of all by many citizens and historians. The Lincoln legacy is an even stronger touchstone for our most recent Democratic presidents than for Republican presidents.

When the Democrats captured the White House in 1992, President William Jefferson Clinton argued for a middle-ground approach to economic policy. Clinton did not directly challenge Reagan's economic emphasis on the centrality of the market and the importance of investment to the growth of the economy. Nor did he reject Reagan's emphasis on the importance of fiscal responsibility—especially by reducing government spending in an effort to balance the federal budget. At the same time, he supported legislation to eliminate government regulations that he considered to be counterproductive to economic growth. Clinton also supported reduced government regulation of Wall Street and the banking industry by signing the bill repealing the Glass-Steagall Act—the New Deal legislation that prevented commercial banks from risking their depositors' funds by engaging in investment banking and trading directly in stocks and bonds.

Like many of the presidents before him, Clinton made it clear that he was hoping to follow in the footsteps of Abraham Lincoln. He kept a very visible Lincoln bust behind his Oval Office desk, where it was always prominent during televised White House addresses. On a nearby table stood a small statuette of Lincoln and Douglas in debate. A larger Lincoln bust dominated the walkway that leads to the Rose Garden.

The first thing Clinton installed in the Oval Office was a photo of Lincoln. And he said he "felt, as Abraham Lincoln did when he wrote as a young man, 'I will study and get ready, and perhaps my chance will come.'" Clinton continued to express his admiration for Lincoln in speech after speech—long into his postpresidential life.

Clinton loved telling the story of one old lifelong southern Democrat he had invited to spend the night in the White House. Clinton's guest shocked the president by telling him he would not sleep in Lincoln's bed. Clinton told him it wasn't really Lincoln's bed, or even his bedroom, and besides, wasn't Lincoln the greatest president in history? Yes, the old gentleman conceded, he certainly was—for a Republican. But he asked that Clinton put him up somewhere else all the same.

Clinton saw himself in the tradition of Lincoln as a proponent of "communitarian" objectives. He described his approach as a "third way" between the classic conservative and liberal approaches to public policy. He sought to balance the government's commitment to sustain the individual rights of American citizens with the equally important responsibility to promote the general welfare. Clinton's commitment to the "third way" was perhaps his most enduring contribution to America's economic future.

In a clear shift from Reagan's policies, Clinton insisted that government had a "critical" role to play in the economy. He took direct action to restore Lincoln's and Roosevelt's vision of positive government action in support of a middle-class society. Recognizing the new realities of a nation dominated by two-earner families, he initiated legislation spearheaded by the Family and Medical Leave Act of 1993, which "cleared the path" for women to participate more fully in the economy. He supported federal spending for education and training to encourage the growth of "human capital." He strengthened regulations to provide cleaner air and water and safer food.

A pensive Bill Clinton strolls along the Rose Garden, past an 1860 Leonard W. Volk bust of Lincoln. Clinton also kept a smaller Lincoln bust on the table behind his Oval Office desk—as had many of his predecessors, including Richard M. Nixon. WHITE HOUSE PHOTOGRAPH, COURTESY OF HAROLD HOLZER

Clinton also rejected Reagan's claim that lowering taxes on wealthy citizens would increase national economic growth. He acted directly to add two new high marginal income tax rates of 36 percent and 39.6 percent. After the marginal tax rates paid by the highest-income taxpayers were raised, the country experienced a period of rapid economic growth that would be seen as Clinton's greatest achievement as president. Clinton's tax reforms eliminated federal deficits for the first time in decades and generated large federal surpluses to support the government's social welfare programs.

Clinton made the case for his positive government initiatives in the State of the Union address on January 27, 1998.

> These are good times for America. We have more than 14 million new jobs, the lowest unemployment in 24 years, the lowest core inflation in 30 years. Incomes are rising, and we have the highest home ownership in history. . . . We have moved

past the sterile debate between those who say government is the enemy and those who say government is the answer. My fellow Americans, we have found a third way. We have the smallest government in 35 years, but a more progressive one. We have a smaller government, but a stronger nation. . . . Now if we balance the budget for next year, it is projected that we'll then have a sizable surplus in the years that immediately follow. . . . What should we do with this projected surplus? . . . Save Social Security First. . . . Because these times are good, we can afford to . . . raise the minimum wage.

Clinton went on to focus on other communitarian objectives, including education, child care, and funding for medical research.

A month earlier, at a private meeting to discuss his forthcoming State of the Union address, Clinton had explained his successes in terms of Lincoln's efforts on behalf of the nation. He said then, "Today the Republicans want to tear down government to liberate private power and private interest. Democrats . . . believe government can serve justice and remedy inequality. . . . What's happened today is the reflection of a two-hundred-year-old struggle, starting with the Federalists and coursing down through Lincoln's battle for Union. Yes, it's this legacy of Lincoln the modern Republicans have betrayed." Clinton viewed himself as a legitimate successor to Lincoln based on his commitment to positive policies to improve the economic conditions of all the people.

The Clinton presidency was characterized by accelerated economic growth and the eventual generation of substantial federal surpluses in contrast to the annual government deficits that were typical of the Republican and Democratic presidents who immediately preceded and succeeded Clinton. The substantial economic growth in the wake of Clinton's increase in the top marginal tax rates posed a direct challenge to Reagan's claim that tax cuts for wealthy "job providers" were the only way to produce significant economic growth. More than 23 million jobs were added to the American workforce during Clinton's eight years in office, compared to fewer than 6 million during Reagan's eight years and only 1.5 million during George W. Bush's subsequent eight-year administration. Such growth undermined Republican supply siders' claim that the best way to increase growth is to decrease taxes on wealthy Americans. Indeed, the Clinton economy presented new evidence to support Roosevelt's demand-side view that a principal source of economic growth in the United States comes from public and private programs that generate rising middle-class and working-class incomes, which in turn increase American consumer demand for the products made by American companies. Clinton was fully prepared to use the expected government surpluses to support positive government action to fund the Social Security program and increase the minimum wage of American workers.

There is no leap of faith required here. Since the end of World War II, American consumer demand has consistently accounted for close to 70 percent of American gross domestic product. The data for the decades after World War II show clearly that positive changes in American employment and consumer demand are closely correlated with positive changes in total US GDP (see Appendix). Government programs to support employment are clearly consistent with Lincoln's legacy of government action "for the people." By contrast, there is no substantial evidence that low marginal income tax rates or low federal estate tax rates are correlated with high employment or high business investment or high GDP growth. Clearly, there is nothing in the Republican low-tax regime that is consistent with Lincoln's legacy.

The explosive economic growth following the Clinton administration's increase in the top marginal tax rates in 1993 might well have spelled the death knell of Republican supply-side economics focused on lowering taxes on corporations and wealthy individuals. But the economic successes of the Clinton years had a short life in political terms. Entering the White House in 2001, President George W. Bush began to see signs that the economy was edging into recession. Using the recession as a convenient rationale, President Bush aggressively propounded the Reagan Republican economic philosophy and pursued a major restructuring of the tax code based on supply-side ideas.

Bush engineered a cut in marginal income tax rates, as well as tax cuts on dividends and capital gains. Even the estate tax—a centerpiece of Progressive Era legislation—was repudiated as a "death tax." By the beginning of Bush's second term, the tax burden shouldered by the wealthiest households had significantly declined, even as these households absorbed an ever-increasing share of the nation's total yearly income. Yet Bush argued that this was all for the common good. In terms reminiscent of the Gospel of Wealth, President Bush repeatedly cited the entrepreneur as the true engine of economic growth—the key to a vibrant economy. The goal, he argued, was to free this enterprising individual from the burdens of excessive taxes and government regulation and collective bargaining with unions. Indeed, Bush seemed to imagine that America—where the vast majority of citizens still labored for wages and salaries—had transformed itself overnight into a nation of independent entrepreneurs and business owners. He spoke repeatedly of an "ownership society." But in truth the ownership society was one in which government policies increasingly favored wealthy business owners and investors over middle-income and low-income wage earners. This clearly reversed the priorities that Lincoln favored emphasizing government policies supporting the efforts of the "prudent, penniless beginner" to rise.

The increase in income inequality effected by the Bush tax cuts was more profound than it might have seemed at first glance. It was not simply that the rich received a larger tax cut than the middle class, though that was certainly the case. As the population aged, new crises were looming ahead in Social Security and Medicare. The Clinton-era federal surpluses might have gone a long way toward meeting the future liabilities of these programs, certainly of Social Security. But the Bush tax cuts had eliminated these surpluses and replaced them with sizable domestic deficits. Moreover, the enormous military costs of the wars in Afghanistan and Iraq, which were not even counted in the federal budget, multiplied the total federal government deficits exponentially.

The government had been drained of resources; taxes as a percentage of GDP were at their lowest level in a generation. At the beginning of his second term, Bush announced a "crisis" in Social Security. Under the Bush program, the wealthiest households were enjoying a windfall of billions in income and estate tax cuts, while future middle-class retirees could be subject to the prospect of substantial reductions in

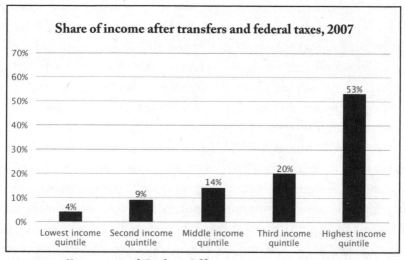

Share of income after transfers and federal taxes, 2007

SOURCE: Congressional Budget Office

Social Security benefits. By 2007 the wealthiest 20 percent of the population had increased its share of the nation's after-tax income to 53 percent at the expense of all other income groups. The lowest-income 20 percent declined in share to a mere 4 percent.

Even more striking, between 1979 and 2007, the wealthiest 1 percent of American taxpayers had more than tripled their share of the nation's after-tax income at the expense of the other 99 percent of Americans. The average after-tax income of the top 1 percent was well over $1,100,000, ten times larger than the average income of the next 19 percent and more than thirty times larger than the average income of all taxpayers.

Lincoln's version of the American Dream had been betrayed. The new Republican conservative ethos under Reagan and Bush completely reversed the policies advocated by Lincoln and Roosevelt to use the government to build and sustain an American middle-class society. The continuing efforts by conservative politicians—supported by lobbyists for the business community—to reduce taxes on the wealthiest Americans was in sharp contrast to Lincoln's Civil War initiative that established the first American income tax, one paid only by the wealthiest Americans.

President Bush's conservative supporters could hardly have been more delighted. In 2003 Grover Norquist, probably the most important behind-the-scenes strategist of the Republican antitax program, candidly stated that the goal of the movement was to turn back the nation's clock not only to the 1920s just before the New Deal, but to the period before the Progressive Era—to the Gospel of Wealth policies dominant during the Gilded Age.

In his First Inaugural Address in 1980, President Ronald Reagan had said, "The taxing power of the government must be used to provide revenues for legitimate government purposes." But the major thrust of Reagan and his successors was to put increasingly sharp limits on the definition of "legitimate government purposes" in order to reduce taxes on the wealthy. Reagan and his successors were strikingly successful in their efforts. As this book goes to press, the highest marginal federal income tax rate is 39.6 percent, down from 70 percent when Reagan took office, and the highest federal estate tax rate is 40 percent, also down from 70 percent.

As Reagan and his Republican successors knew, the emphasis on cutting taxes of the wealthiest Americans was more than an economic policy. It was a political initiative to gain the continuing support of the richest members of American society and ensure a preponderant flow of political campaign funds to Republican political candidates. For the past forty years, Republican candidates and officeholders have emphasized their increasing commitment to low income and estate taxes. Politicians typically argue for reducing government expenditures in a low-tax environment based on the "commonsense" idea that the government budget should be treated like a household budget—it must be balanced. The argument is made that what were once considered normal demand-side counterrecession programs such as Social Security, unemployment insurance, food stamps, public health programs, and government investment in infrastructure need to be cut back in favor of reducing the tax burden on wealthy "job creators." They have claimed that "there is a large body of data" to support their claim that low taxes on the wealthy support economic growth. But, in fact, there is little, if any, data to support this argument. The low-tax regime created and sustained by Republican officeholders has not been shown to increase investment in either physical capital or human capital. Rather, it leads to a government incapable of investing in infrastructure or education for the future.

Post-Reagan presidents—both Republicans and Democrats—have had less and less funds to perform essential government functions. Indeed, federal "government failure" is now built into the system. So long as the low-tax regime is maintained, the government will continue to have insufficient funds to perform its "legitimate government functions." This runs counter to Lincoln's ideas about the role of the federal government. Whereas Lincoln argued that the government should invest in infrastructure and support the poor, penniless beginners to rise, today supporters of the low-tax regime have redefined "legitimate government functions" to little more than military and homeland security activities.

As it turns out, reducing the size of government is not a panacea for full employment or economic stability. In the period from 1890 through 1940, when federal outlays averaged only 5 percent of GNP, average annual unemployment was unhappily 8.7 percent per year. By contrast, in the post–World War II period from 1949 through 1981, when federal outlays averaged 18.2 percent of GDP, average annual unemployment was only 5.3 percent.

The economic record for the most recent sixty-six years from 1949 through 2014 shows no support for the supply-side claim that reducing taxes on high-income individuals results in growth of GDP, business investment, or job creation (see Appendix). During the high-tax post-Roosevelt New Deal period from 1949 through 1981, when top marginal income tax rates averaged 79.7 percent and federal estate tax rates averaged 75.9 percent, the economy grew substantially—real GDP growth was above average at 3.7 percent, business investment growth was above average at 4.9 percent, and US employment growth was above average at 2.2 percent. During the low-tax Reagan and post-Reagan years from 1982 through 2014, when top marginal tax rates were reduced to an average of 38.1 percent and federal estate tax rates were reduced to an average of 51.8 percent, the economy was much weaker, with real GDP growth of only 2.7 percent, business investment growth of only 4.0 percent, and US employment growth of only 1.3 percent.

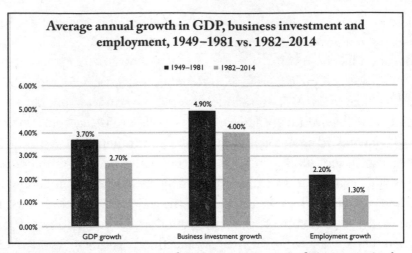

SOURCES: US Department of Commerce, Bureau of Economic Analysis; US Department of Labor, Bureau of Labor Statistics (see Appendix).

During the post–New Deal period, the United States changed from an economy benefiting all the people to an economy narrowly benefiting only the richest families. In the most recent period starting in 1982, the percent of income growth that went to the top 10 percent of earners in the United States increased to 80 percent and continued to increase to 116 percent in 2012.

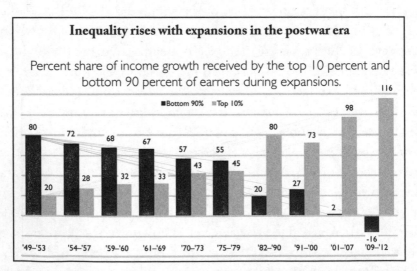

SOURCE: Pavlina R. Tcherneva, based on data from Thomas Piketty and Emmanuel Saez and NBER.

Not content with a low federal tax regime, conservative Republicans throughout the country also pushed successfully for state tax changes that would lower the level of taxation of the wealthiest Americans. They used "trickle-down" arguments supported by "supply-side" probusiness economic arguments to reduce state income, inheritance, and property taxes.

Conservative Republicans succeeded in substantially reducing federal taxes on capital gains and creating special categories of capital gains that deferred taxes on the management fees charged by millionaire and billionaire venture-capital and hedge-fund investment managers, who were suddenly able to pay income taxes at lower rates than the prevailing rates on the earnings of all other American wage earners.

To work toward their stated goal to balance government budgets, conservative Republicans increased sales and other consumption-related taxes, which have a greater percentage impact on the incomes of middle- and lower-income Americans than on the wealthiest Americans.

A study by the Institute on Taxation and Economic Policy issued in January 2015 concluded that in 2015, the poorest fifth of Americans would pay an average of 10.9 percent of their income in taxes, the middle fifth will pay 9.1 percent, and the top 1 percent will average only 5.4 percent. The report concluded, "Virtually every state's tax system is unfair. Unfair tax systems not only exacerbate widening income inequality in the short term, but they also will leave states struggling to raise enough revenue to meet their needs in the long term."

The conservative success in undermining the tax and regulatory policies of the New Deal was followed in the Reagan and post-Reagan years by an unrestrained return of the banks and other financial business organizations to the high-risk policies of the decade that led to the Great Depression. Almost predictably, the conservative antigovernment, low-tax, antiregulation regime under George W. Bush brought on an economic decline and the Great Recession starting in 2007—the worst economic conditions seen in the United States since the Great Depression of 1929–1932.

The most influential proponent of conservative free-market thinking during the Reagan and post-Reagan years was Alan Greenspan, chairman of the US Federal Reserve Board from 1987 until 2006. Greenspan, an acolyte of the libertarian thinker Ayn Rand, provided continued support for conservative economic thinking during the decades following Reagan's administration, even under Democratic president Bill Clinton. It was only in 2008 that Greenspan admitted that he had put too much faith in the self-correcting power of free markets. He acknowledged that he had failed to anticipate the self-destructive power of the excessive risk taken by financial institutions. "Those of us who have looked to the self-interest of lending institutions to protect shareholders' equity, myself included, are in a state of shocked disbelief. . . . This modern risk management paradigm held sway for years. The whole intellectual edifice, however, collapsed in the summer of last year."

The recovery period from 2009 to 2015 under President Obama did not erase the problems of the Great Recession. The only segment of the population that gained substantially from the recovery was the wealthiest 1 percent, who received 95 percent of the total increase in GDP from 2009 to 2012. The other 99 percent saw their real incomes and purchasing power go down. For the 99 percent, the decline in living standards continued for more than five years after the onset of the Great Recession.

The change in the benefits of the American capitalist economy in favor of the wealthiest citizens was recognized by prominent Republicans, Carly Fiorina, former CEO of Hewlett-Packard, and John Huntsman Jr., former Republican governor of Utah, and prominent Democrats, Laura Tyson, former chair of President Clinton's Council of Economic Advisers, and Larry Summers, former chairman of President Obama's National Economic Council. All four were members of the Henry Jackson Initiative for Inclusive Capitalism led by Dominic Barton, global managing director of McKinsey & Company, and Lady Lynn Forester de Rothschild, CEO of E. L. Rothschild. Their analysis, based on data compiled by the US Congressional Budget Office, was published on October 15, 2012:

> In the U.S., between 1979 and 2007, according to an analysis from the Congressional Budget Office, the real after-tax

household income of the top one percent grew 275 percent, and that of the next 19 percent grew 65 percent. The 60 percent in the middle grew just under 40 percent. The after-tax income of the lowest 20 percent grew only 18 percent over this period. In the period 2005–2007, leading up to the financial crisis, the top 20 percent of U.S. income earners made more than the entire 80 percent of wage-earners below them. In 2007 alone, the top 10 percent earned 49.7 percent of total U.S. income, the greatest earning disparity since the 1930s.

The details are even more disturbing. In 2007, 23.5 percent of all American income flowed to the top one percent of earners. Staggeringly, the top 0.1 percent earned 12.2 percent of all income in the United States in 2007, up from an average of 3.5 percent in the 1960s. Sadly, the trend worsened after the Great Recession. From 2009 to 2010, the top one percent of incomes grew by 11.6 percent while the bottom 99 percent grew by only 0.2 percent, meaning that in the first year of the recovery 93 percent of income gains were captured by the top one percent of income earners.

Capitalism was not always like this. From 1943 to 1983, wealth was much more evenly spread. Between 1970 and 1979, CEOs earned approximately 40 times more than the average American worker. Today the average CEO earns 380 times more. The 1950s through the 1980s was the golden age of the American Dream: we all believed that America was a level playing field and if we worked hard and played by the rules, there was no limit to the success we could enjoy in a country of endless possibilities.

The Russell Sage Foundation focused on the same problem in its report on the economy issued in 2014. The *New York Times* summarized the Russell Sage report on July 26, 2014. "It's not merely an issue of the rich getting richer. The typical American household has been getting poorer, too. The inflation-adjusted net worth for the typical household was $87,992 in 2003. Ten years later, it was only $56,335, or a 36 percent decline. . . . When only a few people are winning and more than half the population is losing, surely something is amiss."

This was not the capitalist society envisioned by Adam Smith, the father of modern procapitalist economic theory. Smith understood that market participants should not be guided solely by individual self-interests. He argued that the market works to everyone's advantage when and only when its participants are guided by a generally accepted "moral sympathy" that predisposes all members of society to do well by others, as well as by their individual self-interest.

Public confidence in the state of the nation and its institutions in the years since the onset of the Great Recession has not been encouraging. In March 2010 the Harris national public opinion poll found that fewer than 10 percent of Americans had "a great deal of confidence" in either "Wall Street" or "Congress," while fewer than 30 percent were highly confident about law firms, the press, organized labor, major companies, television news, the public schools, organized religion, the White House, the courts, and the justice system. The "confidence gap" was grounded in the public feeling that the leaders of virtually all American institutions were using artificial, technical, or self-serving rationales for their decisions. A majority of Americans came to believe the leaders of American institutions were no longer being guided by what ordinary citizens viewed as moral and honorable behavior. More and more Americans saw their leaders as believing that anything that was "legal" was "morally legitimate." This new cynicism was reinforced by an increasing awareness that Wall Street firms were being allowed to settle cases of illegal financial practices by paying substantial fines to the Securities and Exchange Commission without admitting that the actions of their leaders were illegal. Rather than feeling a positive connection between themselves and the institutions of their society, most Americans came to feel disappointed, distrustful, and disengaged.

But public concerns did not inspire leaders to embrace the economic philosophy that had inspired Abraham Lincoln and Franklin Roosevelt. The Reagan rhetoric remains the dominant language of American politics. Republican politicians are unified in their support of low taxes, little regulation of business, and little, if any, government

Cartoon by Steve Sack—one of many uncannily similar images that appeared at the time of the Obama inauguration—all imagining the Lincoln of the Lincoln Memorial coming to life to welcome the first African American president in January 2009. BY PERMISSION OF STEVE SACK AND CREATORS SYNDICATE, INC.

investment spending to support employment and economic growth. Their control over one branch of the national government after the midterm elections in 2012 gave Republicans the power to block positive initiatives to use the power of the federal government to rebuild America's middle-class society. Their power increased after the election of 2014, when Republicans captured control of both houses of Congress. Democrats in Congress were divided. Some went along with the low-tax regime imposed by the Republicans. Others campaigned for programs consistent with Lincoln's and Roosevelt's belief in positive government programs to provide opportunity for lower-income people to improve their economic situation.

In his campaign for election as president in 2008, Barack Obama largely ignored partisan economic issues. When he announced his run for the presidency, he said, "In the shadow of the Old State Capitol, where Lincoln once called on a divided house to stand together, where common hopes and common dreams still live, I stand before you today to announce my candidacy for President of the United States." But he did not focus in any particular way on the progressive tradition of government for the people established by Lincoln and Roosevelt. Rather, he presented himself as a postpartisan candidate. He was able to win the presidential election by running against the unpopular war policies of President George W. Bush and promising in particular to end the war in Iraq. He presented himself as a new kind of president who would govern above the fray in a new postpartisan tradition focused primarily on intelligent and efficient government.

But three years of extremely partisan politics in Washington led President Obama to a new focus in his campaign for reelection in 2012. Pointing to his major accomplishment in extending government-sponsored medical care to all US citizens, he also put himself clearly in the Lincoln tradition of government for the people when he self-consciously chose to open his campaign for reelection at Osawatomie, Kansas, on December 11, 2011.

Osawatomie was the site of John Brown's raid in 1856, which many have described as the first battle of the Civil War. It was also the site chosen by Theodore Roosevelt to launch his Progressive Party campaign to regain the presidency in 1910. At Osawatomie Theodore Roosevelt had embraced the legacy of Abraham Lincoln. He said he relied on the wisdom of Abraham Lincoln to guide the nation in addressing the issues of the twentieth century, stressing that Lincoln was the father of the idea that property rights were secondary to the rights of the common welfare. He cited Lincoln as the original advocate of government support not for those who profit, but instead for those who produce.

Barack Obama chose Osawatomie to pursue the same theme in 2011:

> My grandparents believed in an America where hard work paid off, and responsibility was rewarded, and anyone could make it if they tried. . . . And these values gave rise to the largest middle class and the strongest economy that the world has ever known. . . . Today . . . for most Americans, the basic bargain that made this country great has eroded. . . . Fewer

and fewer of the folks who contributed to the success of our economy actually benefitted from that success. Those at the very top grew wealthier. . . . But everybody else struggled with costs that were growing and paychecks that weren't. . . . This is the defining issue of our time. . . . There is a certain crowd in Washington who . . . have said, let's respond to this economic challenge with the same old tune. "The market will take care of everything." . . . We simply cannot return to this brand of "you're on your own" economics if we're serious about rebuilding the middle class in this country.

Obama cited Lincoln in a direct and unqualified way a few months later in a speech on June 14, 2012: "I do share the belief of . . . Abraham Lincoln—that through government, we should do together what we cannot do as well for ourselves. . . . That's how we built this country— together. We constructed railroads and highways. . . . We haven't done these things as Democrats or Republicans. We've done them as Americans. . . . In the last century, this consensus—this shared vision—led to the strongest economic growth and the largest middle class that the world has ever known."

President Obama campaigned for reelection against the Republican trickle-down economic theory with a positive commitment to direct government action to rebuild the modern American middle-class society. For the first time in more than a decade, Lincoln's emphasis on supporting a middle-class society was stated clearly and played a direct role in Obama's success in the election.

In his Second Inaugural Address, on January 21, 2013, President Obama quoted from Lincoln's famous fragment on government: "The legitimate object of government is to do for a community of people whatever they need to have done, but can not do at all, or can not so well do, for themselves—in their separate, and individual capacities."

The reelected President Obama no longer felt the need to nod to his Republican opponents by accepting their claim to Lincoln's heritage. A year earlier in his State of the Union address, Obama had misquoted Lincoln when he said: "I believe what Republican Abraham Lincoln believed: That Government should do for people *only* what

President Barack Obama shows a delegation of elderly African American Washingtonians a signed printed copy of the Emancipation Proclamation that went on loan to the Oval Office on January 8, 2010. The autographed printing—originally created in 1864 for sale at a Philadelphia war-charity fair—has since been moved to the Lincoln Bedroom, the room that once served as Lincoln's office and where he signed the original proclamation on January 1, 1863. WHITE HOUSE PHOTOGRAPH BY PETE SOUZA

they cannot do better by themselves, *and no more.*" Adding "only . . . and no more" to Lincoln's commitment to government action "for the people" was at the time a tacit acceptance by Obama of Ronald Reagan's claim to Lincoln's philosophy. A year later, it was clear to Obama that the long rhetorical shadow of Reagan that had influenced Democratic as well as Republican presidents for thirty years was no longer compelling. This was a new day. The added words *only* and *no more* no longer had a place in Obama's now correct quotation of Lincoln's vision.

Looking back to Lincoln's vision, Obama said: The United States must be a "great nation" that "must care for the vulnerable, and protect its people from life's worst hazards and misfortune . . . that preserving our individual freedoms ultimately requires collective action. . . . Now, more than ever, we must do these things together, as one nation and one people. . . . For we, the people, understand that our country cannot succeed when a shrinking few do very well and a growing many barely make it. We believe that America's prosperity must rest upon the broad shoulders of a rising middle class." A year later President Obama returned to this theme when he said, "The combined trends of increased inequality and decreasing mobility pose a fundamental threat to the American dream, our way of life, and what we stand for around the globe."

President Obama was not optimistic about overcoming the difficulties he faced in making progress toward the goals he believed he shared with Lincoln. In a conversation with the editor of the *New Yorker* at the end of his fifth year in office, Obama said, "I think America was very lucky that Abraham Lincoln was President when he was President. If he hadn't been, the course of history would be very different. But I also think that, despite being the greatest President, in my mind, in our history, it took another hundred and fifty years before African Americans had anything approaching formal equality, much less real equality. I think that doesn't diminish Lincoln's achievements, but it acknowledges that at the end of the day we're part of a long-running story. We just try to get our paragraph right."

Obama had reason to be concerned about his ability to improve economic conditions. Facing a Congress unwilling to act on his proposals, Obama abandoned efforts in 2014 to gain acceptance of the new positive government programs he favored to improve the economic condition of Americans. The public, disheartened yet again, turned against the president in the 2014 midterm elections for what they felt was a lack of presidential leadership.

Voters gave a resounding victory to Republican candidates for the US Senate and House of Representatives in 2014. They also elected more Republican state governors, bringing the total number of Republican governors to thirty-one. The newly invigorated Republicans continue to claim the economy will automatically right itself for the benefit of poor as well as rich Americans if the country reduces individual and corporate taxes and balances the budget. They have proposed little else to improve the economic status of most Americans.

While US gross domestic product improved modestly in 2013 and 2014, the majority of Americans continued to react negatively to the lack of a substantial improvement in their economic conditions. Today politicians in Congress continue to engage in highly specific debates about how to reduce government deficits by reducing government spending. They focus on attempting to prove that government programs are inefficient rather than how to restore the Lincoln and Roosevelt visions of positive government action to reinvigorate America's middle-class economy and society.

There is little opportunity today to gain the support of a majority in Congress for a positive economic program supported by an active federal government. The middle-class and working-class shares of national income continue to decline. Supply-side programs to provide direct financial support to financial and nonfinancial businesses and wealthy individuals continue to dominate government policy.

Corporations have substantial funds available for investment from their increased profits and their ability to borrow funds at low rates, but they have little incentive to increase production or employment because US consumer demand is constrained by the reduced growth in the real income of a majority of Americans.

A recent study by Nobel Prize–winning economist Joseph Stiglitz reminds us that current policies and practices have all been choices. We can choose to do things differently. To fix the economy for average Americans, he says, we need to change the rules and institutions that have generated low investment, sluggish growth, and runaway incomes and wealth for the wealthiest 1 percent. He emphasized that "Corporations have gone from serving all of their stakeholders— workers, shareholders, and management—to serving only top management." Stiglitz's approach to increase economic growth and fair treatment for all Americans centers on increasing private and public investment in our future and ensuring that everyone benefits from an economy that is working at full steam to provide genuine economic security and opportunity for all Americans. He also urges the Federal Reserve to fund a large infrastructure program to increase employment and to restore our roads, airports, and energy and tele-communication systems to a world-class level.

The American middle class—once protected and celebrated by presidents like Lincoln and Roosevelt—has been under threat. The share of middle-income jobs in the United States fell from 52 percent in 1980 to 42 percent in 2010. Middle-income jobs continue to be replaced by low-income jobs, which now make up 41 percent of total employment. The trend is not reversing. Absent a change in economic policy, as we look to the future, lower-wage jobs are predicted to make up 60 percent of the total American workforce. Replacing traditional middle-income jobs with low-wage jobs that lack benefits, stability, and family-sustaining wages is profoundly undermining American communities, contributing to a host of social and political problems, including unemployment, underemployment, poverty, inequality, political apathy, and political polarization.

With the defeat of the Democrats in the 2014 midterm elections, President Obama became "unbound," in the words of one astute *New York Times* journalist. Since he now believed there was little certainty he could achieve his goals through legislation, he decided to use the power of the presidency to take direct action to address major issues—immigration, removing barriers to gender equality, opening the door to rapprochement with Cuba, and addressing the worldwide climate-change issue by an agreement with China to reduce the annual increase in pollution of the atmosphere. Perhaps more important, the president was once again in a position to advocate the economic benefit and economic necessity to rebuild the nation's infrastructure—an economic initiative consistent with Lincoln's insight that infrastructure investment is the most direct and impactful economic program to build the nation's middle-class economy and society.

On January 10, 2015, the US Department of Labor reported that 3.95 million new jobs had been created in 2014, the largest number since the expansive last years of the Clinton administration in the 1990s. The unemployment rate dropped from 6.4 percent to 5.6 percent, the largest one-year decline since 1984.

The economic news was greeted with little enthusiasm by the president's critics. The American Action Forum said, "A strong labor market attracts people to participate and pays them higher wages. It is hard to say the labor market is strong despite the robust top line numbers. The U.S. economy is healing but not yet healthy." Diane Swonk, the chief economist of a Wall Street investment company, pointed out, "This is still a buyer's market, in terms of labor. . . . [E]mployers still have their pick." Jason Furman, the chairman of the President's Council of Economic Advisers agreed: "[T]here is more work to be done to raise wages and address longer standing challenges around family income." Indeed, there was more work to be done. More than 8 million workers were still looking for full-time employment. Many others were working in part-time jobs. The number of people in their prime working years who had officially dropped out of the labor force had more than tripled since the 1960s.

The improving economic data in January 2015 raised President Obama's spirits and led him to take the offensive in the economic debate in Washington. All was not yet well, he said, but it was time to take further steps to improve the economic condition of the underadvantaged segments of the population. "The rising tide of this economic wind at our backs has to lift more boats," Obama's secretary of labor said in a telephone interview on January 9, 2015. "The nation's wage situation is a crucial part of the 'unfinished business' of the nation's economic recovery."

President Obama was finally girding his loins to follow in Lincoln's footsteps and take new steps to use the power of the presidency to improve the status of middle-class and working-class members of the American community. The White House said, "President Obama will not be satisfied until every American who wants work can find a job. That's why he is working to grow our economy, so middle class families feel confident in their futures and their children's futures. . . . Getting back to pre-recession status is not enough; we've got to restore America's middle class."

On January 7, 2015, Obama announced "a major step" to increase home ownership by making mortgages more affordable to "creditworthy families who can afford—and want to purchase—a home."

They "are shut out of homeownership opportunities due to today's tight lending market."

He took another step forward in the continuing debate on raising the minimum wage for American workers. He reminded American business owners that he had required all government contractors to pay a minimum wage of $10.10 starting in 2014 and recommended that all states with a lower rate should increase their minimum wage up to $10.10. He also tackled the nation's tangled immigration problem. "The American immigration system is broken," he said, and he announced a plan "to help build a system that lives up to our heritage as a nation of laws and a nation of immigrants." He said he would take executive action that "offers 4 million undocumented immigrants a path out of the shadows with no fear of deportation."

President Obama surprised both Republicans and Democrats in Congress when he focused directly on taxes and spending in his State of the Union address on January 20, 2015. In a return to Lincoln's vision of a just and generous nation, Obama said his central theme was "middle class economics." He said the nation's economy could not grow effectively if middle-class and working-class Americans' income was declining. He said that government could not play its critical role in increasing jobs if the taxes paid by wealthy Americans were too low to provide adequate funding for rebuilding the nation's roads, bridges, and airports and to provide funding of students' higher education.

The president addressed these issues directly with specific proposals. In particular, he called for a substantial increase in the taxes paid by the wealthiest citizens to provide adequate funds for the nation's infrastructure. At the same time, he proposed a program to use federal funds to pay for two years of community-college tuition to support young people seeking training to qualify for the middle-class jobs available in the nation's new economy. Clearly, the president who had previously despaired of his opportunity to restore Lincoln's ideal of a middle-class society was now actively engaged in an effort to achieve it.

History tells us to suspect the persistent claim that positive government action is inherently inefficient and ineffective. Presidents from Lincoln to Roosevelt have found effective and, in many cases, nonbureaucratic methods of accomplishing major economic and social objectives. Lincoln spearheaded incredibly innovative programs such as the Morrill Land Grant Act to establish colleges, the Homestead Act to provide land inexpensively to Americans migrating west, tariffs to encourage the development of domestic manufacturing, and land grants to provide the funding of the first transcontinental railway in the United States. In the twentieth century, Roosevelt established economic programs such as Social Security, unemployment insurance, and the GI Bill. Both presidents' efforts show that the federal government can accomplish major positive economic and social objectives with a minimum of bureaucratic interference in the economy. And government can undertake nonbureaucratic programs to increase the incomes of lower- and middle-income families to provide the demand-side impetus to support economic growth.

There was no expectation in 2015 that the new Republican majorities in Congress would respond positively to all or any of President Obama's economic policy proposals. They were determined to reject any proposals to increase income or estate taxes. They were even more resistant to providing new funding for the president's new infrastructure and education initiatives. Gridlock was the most likely condition for the immediate future.

What seemed certain was the rhetorical and political battle to rebuild America's middle-class economy and society had entered a new phase. The battle lines were now clearly drawn—to provide a clear framework for the debate on economic policy for the next two years. But there was little expectation of a substantial change in economic policy until after the presidential election two years away in 2016.

There is one bright spot on the horizon. Writing in 2014, John Micklethwait and Adrian Wooldridge, the editors of the *Economist* magazine, argued that the current dysfunction of our economic and political system is not the only way forward. They believe that the economic and political malaise in the United States and Europe can be overcome by a revival of the "third way" approach to government policy, the model championed by Bill Clinton during his presidency.

Micklethwait and Wooldridge suggested that the United States and its European cousins look to the Nordic states, Denmark, Norway, and Sweden, which, they wrote, "continue to pride themselves on the generosity of their welfare states" and continue to build prosperous, well-governed liberal democracies. They believe these countries have found the way to address the three major problems that modern democratic societies face:

- eliminating crony capitalism that has turned "public goods to private gains" by providing "subsidies to the rich and well connected"
- lightening the burden imposed by inefficient and burdensome overregulation of economic life by introducing more consumer choice in government-funded entitlement programs
- restoring the budgeting system "to solvency through implementing a relatively gentle set of taxing and spending reforms"

Micklethwait and Wooldridge reminded readers that Denmark, Norway, and Sweden dealt effectively in the past two decades with seemingly impossible economic conditions. They developed solutions that eliminated crony capitalism and, at the same time, reduced the cost burden of their welfare states by engaging their citizens in making cost-benefit economic choices. Using Sweden as an example of the Nordic solutions the United States might adopt, they wrote:

> Sweden has reduced public spending as a proportion of GDP from 67 percent in 1993 to 49 percent today. It has also cut the top marginal tax rate by 27 percentage points since 1983, to 57%. . . . Its public debt fell from 70 percent of GDP to 37 percent in 2010, and its budget moved from an 11 percent deficit to a surplus of 0.3 percent over the same period. This allowed a country with a small, open economy to recover quickly from the financial storm of 2007–8. . . . [I]ts public debt is still below 40% [of GDP]. . . . Indeed, Sweden has done most of the things that politicians know they ought to do but seldom have the courage to attempt. . . . They continue to

believe in combining open economies with public investment in human capital. . . . The Nordics are important for three reasons. First, they are the part of the West that has hit the future first. . . . Second, they settled one of the central debates about Leviathan: whether it can be brought under control at all. . . . Third, they have only just started to exploit the powers of technology. . . . The Nordics reached the future first. They were forced to change because their old model went bust, and they kept on changing once they discovered that they could produce a better state.

Denmark is particularly notable in providing adequate tax revenue to sustain an efficient modern democratic society. It has the highest level of tax revenue as a percentage of GDP (48.2 percent) and the most income equality of any advanced Western country. By contrast, in the United States tax revenue as a percentage of GDP is only 24.8 percent.

Lincoln's dream of a middle-class society is alive and well in the Nordic countries. But the United States today is not pursuing the Nordic approach, however effective it appears to be to astute observers. Congress is still engaged in efforts to reduce taxes of all kinds on the richest citizens, including estate taxes. In 2002 the tax rate for estates of $1 million or more was 50 percent. Now it is at the historically low rate of 35 percent, with a $10 million exemption for married couples. Even the renowned conservative prime minister of Britain Winston Churchill argued that an effective estate tax provides "a certain corrective against the development of a race of the idle rich." At the turn of the twentieth century, the wealthiest self-made American, Andrew Carnegie, echoed this sentiment: "I say the community fails in its duty and our legislative fail in their duty, if they do not exact a tremendous share" when a wealthy citizen dies. Conservative prime minister of Great Britain David Cameron went even further when he said in January 2012, "Capitalism will never be genuinely popular unless there are genuine opportunities for everyone to participate and benefit."

The majority of Americans are still searching for a return to Lincoln's dream of a successful middle-class economy and society. Can the American political process find its way to a positive Lincolnian approach consistent with the positive "third way" solution pioneered by President Clinton in the United States in the decade before the turn of the new century? Only concerted efforts of concerned citizens can produce the desired future result.

EPILOGUE

GOVERNMENT FOR THE PEOPLE:

LINCOLN'S UNFINISHED WORK

ABRAHAM LINCOLN SHARES WITH GEORGE WASHINGTON AND Franklin D. Roosevelt the status of most respected of American presidents in survey after survey among historians. The American public also celebrates these presidents' leadership in office and their legacy to future generations. Today, at a time when Americans have little faith in their leaders, it is not surprising that we still hark back to Lincoln's presidential leadership as a model for what we expect from current and future presidents.

Abraham Lincoln was a philosophic thinker, a brilliant orator, and a pragmatic politician. Ideological perfection is a rarity among pragmatic politicians. The ability to accomplish great things has become the touchstone of our admiration for our most respected US presidents and other world leaders. The more we learn about great political leaders, the more we respect them as pragmatic politicians. But Lincoln was more than a pragmatist. Not only did he succeed in building the reality of a government "for the people," he also promoted ideas about the American Dream that the nation could support. That combination is the basis for our continuing admiration for his unique legacy.

Lincoln understood that the future of American democracy depends above all on a thriving middle class—a belief we are at risk of losing today when the middle class is faced with little government

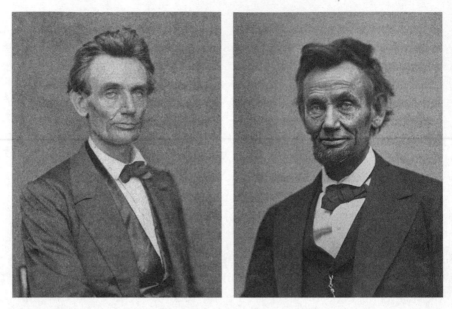

The presidency takes its toll: in less than five years, Lincoln seems to age a lifetime. At left, the newly minted presidential candidate in Springfield, Illinois, on May 20, 1860 (photograph by William Marsh); at right, the exhausted president in Washington on February 5, 1865, a few days after House passage of the Thirteenth Amendment. Photograph by Alexander Gardner. THE METROPOLITAN MUSEUM OF ART; LIBRARY OF CONGRESS

support. Lincoln understood that the nation needs a strong middle class for both economic and political success.

From the standpoint of politics, the existence of a large and vibrant middle class is crucial to stability. The middle class acts as a buffer, softening the age-old struggle between the "haves" and the "have-nots." It is through the middle-class "dream" that Americans come to share common aspirations—aspirations that help to mute the differences in wealth, culture, race, and ethnicity that might otherwise threaten to tear our democracy apart. To survive as a democratic society, America must be a community bound by shared values.

From the standpoint of economics, middle-class and working-class spending remains the primary engine of economic activity and growth in the United States. American consumer spending accounts for 65–72 percent of American gross domestic product. Sustaining the incomes—and therefore the spending—of all Americans is essential to sustaining the growth of the economy as a whole. It is the key to the "virtuous economic cycle," and as the recent past has made all too clear, sustaining the incomes of the wealthiest Americans alone is not a viable substitute.

Lincoln understood that the public needs to believe that America operates on the moral principle of fairness. Americans must view their government as pursuing policies that are fair to all citizens, and not hopelessly skewed to those who, by dint of their wealth, can command greatest control over government policy and the distribution of society's resources. If, under the influence of Gospel of Wealth supply-side economic policies, income inequality continues to grow, and America evolves from a middle-class society into an asymmetrical "hourglass economy"—with a few at the top, many at the bottom, and ever fewer in the middle—it will be increasingly difficult to sustain the belief that Americans share a common destiny. The belief in fairness will wither and, with it, that crucial sense of democratic community.

The challenges Lincoln faced were in many respects very different from the issues that perplex us today. He faced disunity and rebellion. We are dealing with economic inequality and substantial poverty. But Lincoln, as our most clear-eyed president, was the first to fully understand what America is all about and to tell us so in unfailingly clear terms how to use positive government action to build and maintain a successful middle-class society.

Lincoln's genius lay in his ability to see the relationship between the workaday economic realities of American life and the nation's highest moral and political principles. In Lincoln's mind, the opportunity "to improve one's condition" was an essential feature of the Declaration of Independence's assertion that human beings have unalienable rights to "life, liberty, and the pursuit of happiness." More than any other president, Lincoln is the father of the dream that all Americans should have the opportunity through hard work to build a comfortable middle-class life. To Lincoln, the economic, moral, and political elements were inextricably intertwined. Together, they represented what is distinctively American about our economy and democracy.

While these lessons seem clear, they are being obscured today by the ideological debates raging in Washington. There is much confusion in current political discourse over national economic policies. The most contentious arguments center on the relevance and meaning of government "for the people."

One group of citizens believes that government is inherently "inefficient"—that government should be increasingly limited and should do less and less. They argue that individuals and corporations should be left alone to make as much money as they can and pay less and less in taxes, because national economic growth depends on their productive talents. This set of beliefs provides an ideological and political underpinning for a conservative movement supported by a majority of wealthy Americans that gains additional support from people of modest means who are attracted to a set of beliefs that they equate with liberty and freedom.

A second group, which notably includes Bill Gates, Warren Buffett, and Michael Bloomberg, three of America's wealthiest billionaires, believes they should use both their money and their talents to improve the lives of the underadvantaged, poorest, and sickest people in the nation and the world. This is the modern version of what was called, in nineteenth-century France and England, *noblesse oblige*— the idea that with great wealth goes great responsibilities.

A third group, generally called progressives, is favorably predisposed to the concept of positive government action for the people. While the progressives generally accept the validity of the claim that government is sometimes inefficient, they believe that only government can perform the essential functions of a truly democratic society.

The ideological debates are further confused by an ongoing argument over the meaning of equality of opportunity. Some Americans believe that we need a positive government to ensure that all Americans have an equal chance to succeed in life. This belief supports government efforts to provide underadvantaged families with educational, vocational, and financial support to increase their opportunity to be successful participants in the American economic system. Others believe that a free and open society, by definition, provides equality of opportunity. Government action is unnecessary, in their view. Indeed, they believe it is typically counterproductive.

The majority of Americans have little interest in ideological arguments. It is becoming clear that the ongoing contentious debates provide little in the way of conclusive political guidance to the citizens and the leaders of the nation. But one thing is certain—a weak American economy undermines Lincoln's commitment to successful government action "for the people." The evidence is mounting that a strong American economy can be sustained only by positive government policies that support increasing the income and consumer demand of American consumers who account for close to 70 percent of American GDP.

Fortunately, we have a well-defined history of preserving economic opportunity in this country—a history that was established by Lincoln and later brought to our modern society by Franklin Roosevelt. Lincoln and Roosevelt used the resources of the federal government to give reality to the idea of America as an enduring middle-class society. Modern Americans can be grateful for the legacy of Lincoln, Roosevelt, and their positive government successors. We need only chart a path forward using these two leaders as guides. Lincoln's vision of a middle-class society and Roosevelt's positive government economic programs provided the basis for our prosperity in the decades immediately after World War II. They can provide the basis for our prosperity in the twenty-first century.

Those who wish to turn the clock back to a time "before the New Deal" often forget that the same forces that produced the prosperity of the Roaring Twenties also triggered the economic catastrophes of 1929 and 2007. We must not forget that economic policies that maximize business and consumer risk-taking may for a time encourage high rates of growth, but they also incur a much greater chance of economic disaster. The two go hand in hand. This is the primary economic lesson of the Great Depression of the 1930s and the more recent Great Recession starting in 2007.

The battle is not over. Two opposing ideas of American society still compete vigorously today for the support of American citizens. On the one side is the American Dream of a successful middle-class society, inspired by Lincoln and carried forward by Presidents Theodore

Roosevelt, Woodrow Wilson, Franklin Roosevelt, Lyndon Johnson, and more recently William Jefferson Clinton and Barack Obama. On the other is the Gospel of Wealth supply-side economic idea, developed in the second half of the nineteenth century and carried forward by Presidents Warren G. Harding, Calvin Coolidge, Herbert Hoover, and more recently Ronald Reagan and George W. Bush. The success of one or the other of these conflicting ideas will continue to have major economic, moral, and political consequences for the future of American democracy.

The task of rebuilding A Just and Generous Nation will not be easy. In twenty-first-century America, money is a major influence in national, state, and local politics. Politicians of both parties typically spend more time raising money for their political campaigns than working on legislation or governing. Lobbyists for business and other special interests have easy access to, increasing face time with, and substantial ongoing influence over candidates and elected officials both during and after elections.

What seems clear is that fulfilling Lincoln's vision of a successful middle-class society is a continuing work in progress. The nation's political and economic future will increasingly depend on the ability of contemporary political figures to sustain positive public sentiment to support positive government action "for the people." Political leaders seeking to serve the common good can restore the positive path of American history by embracing the Lincoln tradition of using government effectively to address the challenges our society faces.

Americans need to come together to renew our nation's commitment to Lincoln's "unfinished work" to ensure that "government of the people, by the people, for the people, shall not perish from the earth."

Appendix

Percent of marginal income and estate tax rates related to growth in gross domestic product, business investment, and US Employment, 1949–1981

Year	Top marginal income tax rate	Marginal federal estate tax rate	Real GDP growth	Business investment growth	Growth in US employment
1949	82.1	77.0	−0.5	−8.8	−2.5
1950	84.4	77.0	8.7	9.1	3.3
1951	91.0	77.0	8.1	4.2	5.8
1952	92.0	77.0	4.1	−0.1	2.0
1953	92.0	77.0	4.7	10.0	2.9
1954	91.0	77.0	−0.6	−1.4	−2.4
1955	91.0	77.0	7.1	10.7	3.4
1956	91.0	77.0	2.1	6.8	3.4
1957	91.0	77.0	2.1	1.8	0.9
1958	91.0	77.0	−0.7	−9.3	−2.9
1959	91.0	77.0	6.9	8.1	3.8
1960	91.0	77.0	2.6	5.5	1.7
1961	91.0	77.0	2.6	0.8	−0.4
1962	91.0	77.0	6.1	8.1	2.9
1963	91.0	77.0	4.4	5.8	2.0
1964	77.0	77.0	5.8	10.7	2.9
1965	70.0	77.0	6.5	16.7	4.3
1966	70.0	77.0	6.6	12.3	5.2
1967	70.0	77.0	2.7	−0.3	3.0
1968	75.3	77.0	4.9	4.8	3.2
1969	77.0	77.0	3.1	7.0	3.7
1970	71.8	77.0	0.2	−0.9	0.7
1971	70.0	77.0	3.3	0.0	0.5
1972	70.0	77.0	5.2	8.7	3.5
1973	70.0	77.0	5.6	13.2	4.2
1974	70.0	77.0	−0.5	0.8	1.9
1975	70.0	77.0	−0.2	−9.0	−1.7
1976	70.0	77.0	5.4	5.7	3.2
1977	70.0	70.0	4.6	10.8	3.9
1978	70.0	70.0	5.6	13.8	5.1
1979	70.0	70.0	3.2	10.0	3.6
1980	70.0	70.0	−0.2	0.0	0.7
1981	69.1	70.0	2.6	6.1	0.8
Avg for 1949 – 1981 (33 yrs)	**79.7**	**75.9**	**3.7**	**4.9**	**2.2**

SOURCE: http://www.taxpolicycenter.org/taxfacts/displayafact.cfm?Docid=543, http://www.irs.gov /pub/irs-soi/ninetyestate.pdf, http://www.bea.gov/iTable/iTable.cfm?ReqID=9&step=1, http://data .bls.gov/timeseries/CEU0000000001.

Percent of marginal income and estate tax rates related to growth in gross domestic product, business investment, and US Employment, 1982–2014

Year	Top marginal income tax rate	Marginal federal estate tax rate	Real GDP growth	Business investment growth	Growth in US employment
1982	50.0	65.0	−1.9	−3.6	−1.8
1983	50.0	60.0	4.6	−0.4	0.7
1984	50.0	55.0	7.3	16.7	4.7
1985	50.0	55.0	4.2	6.6	3.2
1986	50.0	55.0	3.5	−1.7	2.0
1987	38.5	55.0	3.5	0.1	2.6
1988	28.0	55.0	4.2	5.0	3.2
1989	28.0	55.0	3.7	5.7	2.5
1990	28.0	55.0	1.9	1.1	1.4
1991	31.0	55.0	−0.1	−3.9	−1.0
1992	31.0	55.0	3.6	2.9	0.3
1993	39.6	55.0	2.7	7.5	2.0
1994	39.6	55.0	4.0	7.9	3.1
1995	39.6	55.0	2.7	9.7	2.6
1996	39.6	55.0	3.8	9.1	2.1
1997	39.6	55.0	4.5	10.8	2.6
1998	39.6	55.0	4.5	10.8	2.6
1999	39.6	55.0	4.7	9.7	2.4
2000	39.6	55.0	4.1	9.1	2.2
2001	39.1	55.0	1.0	−2.4	0.0
2002	38.6	50.0	1.8	−6.9	−1.1
2003	35.0	49.0	2.8	1.9	−0.2
2004	35.0	48.0	3.8	5.2	1.1
2005	35.0	47.0	3.3	7.0	1.7
2006	35.0	46.0	2.7	7.1	1.8
2007	35.0	45.0	1.8	5.9	1.1
2008	35.0	45.0	−0.3	−0.7	−0.6
2009	35.0	45.0	−2.8	−15.6	−4.3
2010	35.0	0.0	2.5	2.5	−0.7
2011	35.0	55.0	1.6	7.7	1.2
2012	35.0	55.0	2.3	7.2	1.7
2013	39.6	55.0	2.2	3.0	1.7
2014	39.6	55.0	2.4	6.3	1.9
Avg for 1982 – 2014 (33 yrs)	**38.1**	**51.8**	**2.7**	**4.0**	**1.3**

SOURCE: http://www.taxpolicycenter.org/taxfacts/displayafact.cfm?Docid=543, http://www.irs.gov/pub/irs-soi/ninetyestate.pdf, http://www.bea.gov/iTable/iTable.cfm?ReqID=9&step=1, http://data.bls.gov/timeseries/CEU0000000001.

Acknowledgments

Shivaun McDonagh deserves our gratitude for her unremitting and extraordinary contribution to the editorial and organizational integrity of this book. We also thank Kraig Smith for his great help throughout the publication process.

We are grateful to our agent Frederica Friedman, a consummate publishing professional who worked timelessly on behalf of this work.

We wish to thank Lara Heimert and her excellent editorial and production team at Basic Books for their superb job in presenting the story of this book to interested readers.

Last but not least, for their advice and inspiration, we salute our accomplished, wonderful wives—to whom this book is dedicated.

NOTES

NOTES TO INTRODUCTION

2   **"proposed to give" and allow "the weak to grow":** Roy P. Basler, ed., *The Collected Works of Abraham Lincoln*, 8 vols. (New Brunswick, NJ: Rutgers University Press, 1953–1955), hereafter cited as *CW*, Fragment on Slavery, 2:222.

3   **the uniquely American "right to rise":** Gabor S. Boritt, *Lincoln and the Economics of the American Dream* (Memphis, TN: Memphis State University Press, 1978), 1.

3   **"Whatever is calculated to advance the condition":** Speech to Germans at Cincinnati, Ohio, February 12, 1861, *CW*, 4:203.

4   **"a fair chance, in the race of life":** Message to Special Session of Congress, July 4, 1861, *CW*, 4:438.

4   **Lincoln believed the unique purpose:** Fragment on the Constitution and the Union, ca. January 1863, *CW*, 4:168–169.

4   **He called it the "laudable pursuit":** Message to Special Session of Congress, July 4, 1861, *CW*, 4:438.

6   **"The prudent, penniless beginner":** Annual Message to Congress, December 3, 1861, *CW*, 5:52.

NOTES TO CHAPTER ONE

11   **frequently attributed to the nineteenth-century French writer:** Robert Hendrickson, *The Facts on File Encyclopedia of Word and Phrase Origins* (New York: Checkmark, 2000), 22. In reality, the phrase was first popularized a full century after Tocqueville by historian James Truslow Adams, in a best-selling book called *The Epic of America* (1932).

11   **"Amongst the novel objects":** Alexis de Tocqueville, *Democracy in America* (originally published 1835–1839), translated by Henry Reeve, revised by Frances Bowen, edited by Phillip Bradley, 2 vols. (New York: Vintage, 1945), 1:3.

12   **Tocqueville witnessed a land alive:** Ibid., 2:165–166.

12   **the country was ideally suited:** Ibid., 1:53.

12   **struck by the level of social mobility:** Ibid., 2:36–37.

12   **"I never met in America":** Ibid., 2:137–138.

12   **"Between these two extremes":** Ibid., 2:266.

12   **born . . . to parents from "undistinguished families":** Jesse Fell autobiography, December 20, 1859, Roy P. Basler, ed., *The Collected Works of Abraham Lincoln,* 8 vols. (New Brunswick, NJ: Rutgers University Press, 1953–1955), hereafter cited as *CW,* 3:511.

13   **"picked up from time to time":** Ibid.

14   **Neighbors whispered that he became sterile:** See Charles Friend (a relative) to William H. Herndon (Lincoln's law partner and future biographer), July 31, 1889, Douglas L. Wilson and Rodney O. Davis, *Herndon's Informants: Letters, Interviews, and Statements About Abraham Lincoln* (Urbana: University of Illinois Press, 1998), 674.

15   **"It is a great folly":** John L. Scripps's recollection in ibid., 57.

16   **"gratitude to our fathers":** Address to the Springfield Young Men's Lyceum, January 27, 1838, *CW,* 1:108.

16   **"toil up from poverty":** From Lincoln's Annual Message to Congress, December 3, 1861, *CW,* 5:52–53.

17   **may have converted Abe:** Michael Burlingame, *The Inner World of Abraham Lincoln* (Urbana: University of Illinois Press, 1994), esp. 20–56.

17   **"wild animals still in the woods":** Autobiographical sketch, December 20, 1859, *CW,* 3:511.

17   **"One night," he later reported:** Scripps autobiography, *CW,* 4:62.

18   **"A gentleman had purchased":** Lincoln to Mary Speed, *CW,* 1:260.

18   **"toiling under the weight of poverty":** *Chicago Tribune,* November 27, 1860.

19   **"bunglingly sign his own name":** Autobiography written for John L. Scripps, ca. June 1860, *CW,* 4:61.

20   **The enterprise eventually "winked out":** Scripps autobiography, *CW,* 4:65.

20   **he began jokingly referring to his obligations:** John T. Morse, *Abraham Lincoln,* 2 vols. (Boston: Houghton Mifflin, 1896), 1:40.

21   **he had not "since had any success":** Scripps autobiography, *CW,* 4:64.

22   **Lawyer Lincoln routinely handled:** Two of the best new books on the subject are Allen D. Spiegel, *A. Lincoln, Esquire: A Shrewd, Sophisticated Lawyer in His Time* (Macon, GA: Mercer University Press, 2002); and Mark E. Steiner, *An Honest Calling: The Law Practice of Abraham Lincoln* (DeKalb: Northern Illinois University

Press, 2006). The standard documentary reference work now is Daniel W. Stowell et al., eds., *The Papers of Abraham Lincoln: Legal Documents and Cases,* 4 vols. (Charlottesville: University Press of Virginia, 2008).

24   **"[W]e hope the author of it":** *Scientific American,* December 1, 1860, 356.

24   **Clay's American System featured:** Robert V. Remini, *Henry Clay: Statesman for the Union* (New York: W. W. Norton, 1991), 210–233.

24   **"My politics are short and sweet":** Gabor S. Boritt, *Lincoln and the Economics of the American Dream* (Memphis, TN: Memphis State University Press, 1978), 93.

25   **As Lincoln surely knew:** Ibid., 2.

26   **As Lincoln saw matters, "The true rule":** Speech to House of Representatives, June 20, 1848, *CW,* 1:484.

30   **"Mr. Clay's predominant sentiment":** Eulogy to Henry Clay, July 6, 1852, *CW,* 2:126.

NOTES TO CHAPTER TWO

35   **Lincoln was "full of wit, facts, dates":** Harold Holzer, *Lincoln at Cooper Union: The Speech That Made Abraham Lincoln President* (New York: Simon and Schuster Paperbacks, 2004), 5.

35   **"The whole nation is interested":** Roy P. Basler, ed., *The Collected Works of Abraham Lincoln,* 8 vols. (New Brunswick, NJ: Rutgers University Press, 1953–1955), hereafter cited as *CW,* 2:268.

36   **"When southern people tell us":** Lincoln's Peoria, Illinois, speech, October 16, 1854, *CW,* 2:255–256.

36   **"Let it not be said":** *CW,* 266.

37   **his way to achieve the ultimate goal:** A groundbreaking exploration of this theory can be found in James Oakes, *The Scorpion's Sting: Antislavery and the Coming of the Civil War* (New York: W. W. Norton, 2014).

37   **Lincoln decried "the spread of slavery":** *CW,* 3:14.

38   **"Under the operation of the policy of compromise":** *CW,* 2:461–462. Lincoln took the "house divided" language from the Bible, Mark 3:25: "And if a house be divided against itself, that house cannot stand."

39   **"Have we no tendency to the latter condition?":** *CW,* 2:514.

40   **"greedy chase to make profit of the negro":** *CW,* 2:276.

41   **He reiterated this position:** *CW,* 3:249.

41   **"But in the right to eat the bread":** *CW,* 3:16.

42   **who foresaw "an 'irrepressible conflict'":** *CW,* 4:451.

42   **he described them as equally guilty:** Holzer, *Lincoln at Cooper Union*, 36–37.

42   **"Did you ever hear a Republican that dissented":** Justin G. Turner and Linda Levitt Turner, eds., *Mary Todd Lincoln: Her Life and Letters* (New York: Alfred A. Knopf, 1972), 59; "Speech of Senator Douglas at Cincinnati," *New York Times,* September 12, 1859.

42   **"We want, and must have, a national policy":** *CW,* 3:435.

43   **Ohio had gone Republican in 1859:** *Illinois State Journal,* November 18, 1859.

44   **"I love Mr. Lincoln dearly":** William Herndon to Edward McPherson, clerk of the US House of Representatives, February 4, 1866.

45   **expressed his personal conviction:** George Washington to Robert Morris, April 12, 1786, W. W. Abbott, ed., *The Papers of George Washington,* Confederation Series, 6 vols. (Charlottesville: University Press of Virginia, 1992–1997), 4:15–17.

45   **With no researchers to assist him:** Leonard W. Volk, "The Lincoln Life-Mask and How It Was Made," *Century Magazine,* December 1881, 223–228.

45   **"[B]ut he has no right," Lincoln wrote:** Holzer, *Lincoln at Cooper Union,* 53.

46   **"Such is Abraham Lincoln":** *New York Tribune,* February 24, 1860.

46   **he quoted the words used by Douglas:** *CW,* 3:522.

48   **"Neither let us be slandered":** *CW,* 3:550.

49   **"yielding and accommodating":** Francis Fisher Browne, *The Every-Day Life of Abraham Lincoln* (New York: N. D. Thompson, 1886), 737.

49   **Greeley's *Tribune* agreed:** *New York Tribune,* February 28, 1860.

49   **Bryant's antislavery *New York Evening Post*:** *New York Evening Post,* February 28, 1860.

49   **"Right makes might":** *CW,* 3:541.

50   **The "'equality of man' principle":** Speech at Hartford, Connecticut, March 5, 1860, *CW,* 4:3.

50   **he offered his most direct synthesis:** Speech at New Haven, Connecticut, March 6, 1860, *CW,* 4:24–25.

50   **As the *New York Tribune* reported:** *New York Tribune,* February 28, 1860.

51   **the "wildest enthusiasm" erupted:** J. G. Holland, *The Life of Abraham Lincoln* (Springfield, IL: Gurdon Bill, 1866), 223.

52   **He would not "write, or speak":** *CW,* 4:93.

52   **his "positions were well known":** *CW,* 4:60.

52   **Lincoln was already on record:** Speech at Chicago, March 1, 1859, *CW,* 3:366, 370. Voters could find Lincoln's views on these

questions in the best-selling editions in circulation of both the Lincoln-Douglas debates and the Cooper Union address.

52 **Lincoln remained willing to "tolerate" it:** Lincoln's address at Chicago, July 10, 1858, *CW,* 2:488, 491.

52 **slavery could be destroyed by simply hemming it in:** See Oakes, *Scorpion's Sting,* esp. Chapter 1, "'Like a Scorpion Girt by Fire.'"

53 **slavery would not completely disappear:** See Lincoln's Annual Message to Congress, December 1, 1862, in which he admits that full freedom—extended to border states through a system of gradual compensated emancipation—might require another thirty-seven years, until 1900. *CW,* 5:531.

53 **"This is the same old trick":** John G. Nicolay and John Hay, *Abraham Lincoln: A History,* 10 vols. (New York: Century, 1890), 3:280–281.

53 **As for "those who will not read, or heed":** Lincoln to William S. Speer, October 23, 1860, *CW,* 4:130.

53 **"What is it I could say":** Lincoln to George T. M. Davis, October 27, 1860, *CW,* 4:132–133.

NOTES TO CHAPTER THREE

58 **Lincoln's logic-driven conviction:** As recently as 2007, historian William C. Harris argued in an excellent new study that Lincoln took "a sanguine view of the impact of his election on Southerners." See Harris, *Lincoln's Rise to the Presidency* (Lawrence: University Press of Kansas, 2007), 248. Richard Carwardine similarly wrote of "Lincoln's larger misreading of the southern surge toward secession," though he conceded that "Lincoln's general policy of silence was not unwise." See Carwardine, *Lincoln: A Life of Purpose and Power* (New York: Alfred A. Knopf, 2006), 140–141.

59 **"I could say nothing":** Lincoln to Truman Smith, November 10, 1860, Roy P. Basler, ed., *The Collected Works of Abraham Lincoln,* 8 vols. (New Brunswick, NJ: Rutgers University Press, 1953–1955), hereafter cited as *CW,* 4:138.

59 **"Every newspaper he opened":** Harold G. Villard and Oswald Garrison Villard, *Lincoln on the Eve of '61: A Journalist's Story by Henry Villard* (New York: Alfred A. Knopf, 1941), 23.

59 **"I want the slaveholders":** Philip S. Foner and Yuval Taylor, eds., *Frederick Douglass: Selected Speeches and Writings,* Library of Black America Series (Chicago: Chicago Review Press, 2000); *Douglass' Monthly,* January 1861.

60 **"Mr. Lincoln is not pledged":** Lincoln to Henry J. Raymond, December 18, 1860, *CW,* 4:156.

61   **"I am for no compromise":** Lincoln to William H. Seward, February 1, 1861, *CW,* 4:183.

62   **he made his views clear:** Kenneth M. Stampp, *The Imperiled Union* (Oxford: Oxford University Press, 1981), 167.

62   **"Let there be no compromise":** Lincoln to Lyman Trumbull, December 10, 1860, *CW,* 4:149–150.

62   **Lincoln employed the same emphatic phrase:** William Kellogg to Lincoln, December 6, 1860, Abraham Lincoln Papers, Library of Congress.

62   **"The tug has to come":** Lincoln to Kellogg, December 11, 1860, *CW,* 4:150. Unbeknownst to Lincoln, who did not meet him until after writing these letters, Edward Bates had expressed the same view (privately, to his diary) a few weeks earlier, on November 22: "If we must have civil war, perhaps it is better now than at a future date." It is reasonable to assume the two men discussed the potential for war when they conferred in Springfield. Howard K. Beale, ed., *The Diary of Edward Bates, 1859–1866* (Washington, DC: GPO, 1933), 158.

62   **"Prevent, as far as possible":** *CW,* 4:151.

62   **"My opinion is that no state":** Lincoln to Thurlow Weed, December 17, 1860, *CW,* 4:154.

63   **"resume a separate, equal rank":** *New York Times,* December 22, 1860.

63   **Secession fever had grown incurable:** David M. Potter and Don E. Fehrenbacher, *The Impending Crisis, 1848–1861* (New York: Harper & Row, 1976), 491–496. Based on a study by Michael P. Johnson, "A New Look at the Popular Vote for Delegates to the Georgia Secession Convention," *Georgia Historical Quarterly* 56 (1972): 259–275. Potter and Fehrenbacher estimate that popular support for secession amounted to only 50 to 51 percent.

63   **Lincoln had achieved his objectives:** William H. Seward, *An Autobiography* (New York: Derby and Miller, 1891), 479.

63   **"Compromise has gone up the spout":** *Springfield (MA) Daily Republican,* December 28, 1860, quoted in Carroll C. Arnold, "The Senate Committee of Thirteen, December 6–31, 1860," J. Jeffery Auer, ed., *Antislavery and Disunion, 1858–1861: Studies in the Rhetoric of Compromise and Conflict* (New York: Harper & Row, 1963), 327.

64   **"Without the *Constitution* and the *Union*":** Fragment on the Constitution and the Union, January 1861, *CW,* 4:168–169.

65   **"This middle-class country":** Ralph Waldo Emerson, remarks at the funeral services of the president, Concord, Massachusetts, April 19, 1865, *The Works of Ralph Waldo*

Emerson, Fireside Edition, 12 vols. (Boston and New York, 1909), 11:312, http://oll.libertyfund.org/titles/1961#Emerson _1236-11_328.

65 **"adherence to the Union and the Constitution"**: Speech at Trenton, New Jersey, February 21, 1861, *CW*, 4:26.

66 **"a task before me"**: Farewell address to Springfield, Illinois, "A" version (rewritten by Lincoln on the train), February 11, 1861, *CW*, 4:190.

66 **"[A]way back in my childhood"**: Speech to the New Jersey state senate, February 21, 1861, *CW*, 4:235–236.

67 **Lincoln planned to use this message**: All these and subsequent quotes from the first printed draft of the Inaugural Address, Lincoln Papers, Library of Congress, reprinted in *CW*, 4:249–262.

67 **"Having been so elected"**: Draft for the Inaugural Address, March 4, 1861, *CW*, 4:250.

68 **"One section of our country"**: Lincoln's Inaugural Address, March 4, 1861, *CW*, 4:268–270. President Obama quoted this phrase—perhaps equally in vain, some might say—when he declared victory in Grant Park, Chicago, after his first race for the presidency.

68 **"to shift the ground"**: *CW*, 4:200–201.

68 **"Fellow citizens of the United States"**: Rufus Rockwell Wilson, *Intimate Memories of Lincoln* (Elmira, NY: Primavera Press, 1945), 366.

69 **Lincoln delivered a stern warning**: Wilson, *Lincoln's Sword* (New York: Vintage, 2007), 50.

69 **"In *your* hands, my dissatisfied fellow countrymen"**: *CW*, 4:261.

69 **"We are not enemies"**: First Inaugural Address, *CW*, 4:249–271.

70 **commander in chief responded within hours**: Proclamation 15, 1861, *CW*, 4:332.

70 **denounced Lincoln as a "military dictator"**: *New Orleans Daily Picayune*, April 17, 1861.

70 **likened his threat to "save the Union"**: *New York Evening Day-Book*, April 16, 1861.

71 **"maintain its own existence"**: Special Message to Congress, July 4, 1861, *CW*, 4:426.

71 **In one particularly sublime passage**: Message to Congress, July 4, 1861, *CW*, 4:438.

72 **"the day when slavery can no longer extend itself"**: John Stuart Mill, "The Contest in America," *Fraser's Magazine*, February 1862.

NOTES TO CHAPTER FOUR

75   **"The legitimate object of government":** Fragment on govern-
        ment, July 1, 1854[?], Roy P. Basler, ed., *The Collected Works of
        Abraham Lincoln,* 8 vols. (New Brunswick, NJ: Rutgers University
        Press, 1953–1955), hereafter cited as *CW,* 2:220–221.

77   **"I have never had a feeling politically":** Speech at Indepen-
        dence Hall, Philadelphia, February 22, 1861, *CW,* 4:240.

77   **Republicans assumed large majorities in both houses:** David
        Donald, *Lincoln* (New York: Simon and Schuster, 1955), 304–305.

78   **"a blueprint for modern America":** Leonard P. Curry, *Blueprint
        for Modern America: Nonmilitary Legislation of the First Civil War
        Congress* (Nashville: Vanderbilt University Press, 1968).

79   **"Mr. Lincoln listened with earnest attention":** Frederick Dou-
        glass in Allen Thorndike Rice, ed., *Reminiscences of Abraham Lin-
        coln by Distinguished Men of His Time* (New York: North American
        Reviews, 1886), 187–188.

81   **"It is not needed, nor fitting here"; "Again":** Annual Message
        to Congress, December 3, 1861, *CW,* 5:51–53.

83   **"Fellow-citizens," he declared:** Annual Message to Congress,
        December 1, 1862, *CW,* 5:537.

84   **They were originally scheduled to remain:** New York State,
        Annual Report of the Adjutant General (Albany, January 15, 1862).

85   **"In no other way":** *CW,* 7:522.

85   **By 1864 the gross national product:** *American Railroad Journal*
        37 (October 8, 1864): 486, 989. For a detailed discussion of the
        economic boom in the Northern states during the Civil War, see
        Allan Nevins, *The War for the Union* (New York: Charles Scribner's
        Sons), 3:212–270.

86   **Thanksgiving Day Proclamation of 1863:** *CW,* 6:496.

87   **"It is easy to see":** Annual Message to Congress, December 8,
        1863, *CW,* 7:10.

87   **A year later he reported:** *CW,* 7:40.

87   **"We do not approach exhaustion":** *CW,* 8:146, 150–151.

87   **The total number of new immigrants:** Thomas Brinley, *Mi-
        gration and Economic Growth* (Cambridge: Cambridge University
        Press, 1954), 93.

87   **1 out of 10 immigrants in 1864:** Maldwyn Allen Jones, *Ameri-
        can Immigration* (Chicago: University of Chicago Press, 1961), 173.

87   **wages in the US Northern states:** *American Railroad Journal* 37
        (August 13, 1864): 1478.

88   **"Agriculture," as he lamented in December 1861:** Annual
        Message to Congress, December 3, 1861, *CW,* 5:46.

89   **"peculiarly the people's Department":** Annual Messages to
      Congress, December 1, 1862, December 6, 1864, *CW,* 5:526–527;
      8:147–148. See also Wayne D. Rasmussen, "Lincoln's Agricultural
      Legacy," US Department of Agriculture National Agricultural Li-
      brary, http://www.nal.usda.gov/lincolns-agricultural-legacy.

89   **The Department of Agriculture reported:** Monthly report of
      the US Department of Agriculture, February 1865, 31, https://books
      .google.com/books?id=Y0zOAAAAMAAJ&pg=PA2&dq=%22
      monthly+report%22+department+of+agriculture++February+
      1865&hl=en&sa=X&ei=YykcVbOLDa-ZsQSzxoKQAg&ved=0C
      CUQ6wEwAQ#v=onepage&q=Comparison&f=false.

89   **resulted in raising the national income:** Nevins, *War for the
      Union,* 3:212–270; Annual Message to Congress, December 6,
      1864, *CW,* 8:146.

89   **750,000 Union and Confederate soldiers:** See David Hacker,
      "A Census-Based Count of the Civil War Dead," *Civil War History*
      57 (December 2011).

90   **"Intelligence, patriotism, Christianity":** First Inaugural Ad-
      dress, March 4, 1861, *CW,* 4:271.

90   **"Let us diligently apply the means":** Speech to a Union rally at
      Springfield, Illinois, written as a letter to James C. Conkling, Au-
      gust 26, 1863, *CW,* 6:410.

NOTES TO CHAPTER FIVE

91   **"I am naturally anti-slavery":** Lincoln to Albert G. Hodges, April
      4, 1864, Roy P. Basler, ed., *The Collected Works of Abraham Lin-
      coln,* 8 vols. (New Brunswick, NJ: Rutgers University Press, 1953–
      1955), hereafter cited as *CW,* 7:281.

92   **"Fair play is a jewell":** Lincoln to Simon Cameron, August 10,
      1861, *CW,* 4:480.

92   **"I have always hated slavery":** Speech at Chicago, July 10, 1858,
      CW, 2:492.

92   **used the phrase *ultimate extinction:*** See "house divided" ad-
      dress, June 16, 1858, and speech at Chicago, July 10, 1858, *CW,*
      2:461, 490–493.

93   **"That is the issue that will continue":** Lincoln at Alton, Illinois,
      October 15, 1858, *CW,* 3:315.

93   **there should be "no war, no violence":** *CW,* 3:316.

94   **"founded on both injustice and bad policy":** Protest (with Dan
      Stone) to the Illinois Legislature, March 3, 1837, *CW,* 1:75.

94   **Lincoln's speech reveals the limits:** Lyceum address, January
      27, 1838, *CW,* 1:109.

95   Lincoln chose not "to recount the horrors": *CW*, 1:109–110.

95   the "mobocratic spirit": *CW*, 1:111.

95   Those happening in the State of Mississippi: *CW*, 1:109–110.

96   "that offers them no protection": *CW*, 1:111.

96   "Let reverence for the laws": *CW*, 1:112.

97   "Whenever the vicious portion": *CW*, 1:111.

98   quick to answer in the affirmative: Lincoln to Usher F. Linder, March 22, 1848, *CW*, 1:458.

98   its being "unnecessary and unconstitutional": *CW*, 1:458.

100   "So you are the little woman": Annie Fields, ed., *Life and Letters of Harriet Beecher Stowe* (Boston: Houghton Mifflin, 1897), 268–269.

101   Lincoln was "boldly" avowing: *Illinois State Register* report of Lincoln's Springfield speech of June 10, 1856, *CW*, 2:345.

101   "extreme northern part of Illinois": Stephen A. Douglas, opening speech at Galesburg debate, October 7, 1858, *CW*, 3:213.

101   Lincoln denied such charges: Lincoln's remarks at Charleston, September 18, 1858, *CW*, 3:145.

102   "Did old Giddings": Douglas at Quincy, Illinois, October 13, 1858, *CW*, 3:263.

102   "He believed the attack of Brown wrong": Speech at Elwood, Kansas, December 1 [November 30?], 1859, *CW*, 3:496.

103   "You charge that we stir up insurrections": Speech at Cooper Union, February 27, 1860, *CW*, 3:538.

103   "John Brown's effort was peculiar": *CW*, 3:541.

104   He distanced himself from Brown: Speech at New Haven, Connecticut, March 6, 1860, *CW*, 4:23.

104   Lincoln distanced himself from Brown yet again: Speech at Bloomington, Illinois, April 10, *CW*, 4:23, 42.

105   political cartoons of the day: See, for example, Currier & Ives, *"Uncle Sam" Making New Arrangements* and, conversely, *"The Nigger" in the Woodpile*, both published in 1860, Bernard F. Reilly Jr., *American Political Prints, 1766–1876: A Catalog of the Collections in the Library of Congress* (Boston: G. K. Hall, 1991), 441, 451.

106   "If Mr. Lincoln were really an Abolitionist President": Philip S. Foner and Yuval Taylor, eds., *Frederick Douglass: Selected Speeches and Writings*, Library of Black America Series (Chicago: Chicago Review Press, 2000); *Douglass' Monthly*, December 1860.

107   struck Douglass as "weak," "revolting," and "horrible": *Douglass' Monthly*, April 1861.

107   "I have never understood that the presidency": Lincoln to Hodges, April 4, 1864, *CW*, 7:281.

NOTES TO CHAPTER SIX

111   **the administration gave little guidance:** Adam Goodheart, "How Slavery Really Ended in America," *New York Times,* April 1, 2011.

112   **"then, thenceforward, and forever free":** Preliminary Emancipation Proclamation, September 22, 1862, Roy P. Basler, ed., *The Collected Works of Abraham Lincoln,* 8 vols. (New Brunswick, NJ: Rutgers University Press, 1953–1955), hereafter cited as *CW,* 5:434.

112   **"We are waging war":** Craig L. Symonds, *Stonewall of the West: Patrick Cleburne and the Civil War* (Lawrence: University Press of Kansas, 1997) 181–201.

113   **Lincoln's reputation as an antislavery leader:** See, for example, Lerone Bennett, *Forced into Glory: Abraham Lincoln's White Dream* (Chicago: Johnson, 1999).

113   **revisionists have been debating:** A good recent story that encompasses this phenomenon is John McKee Barr, *Loathing Lincoln: An American Tradition from the Civil War to the Present* (Baton Rouge: Louisiana State University Press, 2014), esp. Chapter 5.

113   **"My paramount object in this struggle":** Lincoln to Greeley, August 22, 1862, *CW,* 5:388–389.

113   **"our government rests in public opinion":** Speech at Chicago, December 10, 1856, *CW,* 2:385.

114   **"[W]ith public sentiment, nothing can fail":** From Lincoln's reply at the first Lincoln-Douglas debate, Ottawa, Illinois, August 21, 1858, *CW,* 3:27.

115   **Blair "deprecated the policy":** F[rancis]. B. Carpenter, *Six Months at the White House with Abraham Lincoln: The Story of a Picture* (New York: Hurd and Houghton, 1867), 21.

116   **fretted that paying for compensated emancipation:** *New York Times,* March 7, 1862.

116   **"Have you noticed the facts":** Lincoln to Henry J. Raymond, March 9, 1862, *CW,* 5:153.

116   **"I do not speak of emancipation":** Appeal to Border State Representatives on Compensated Emancipation, July 12, 1862, *CW,* 5:318.

116   **His appeal fell on profoundly deaf ears:** "Stormy meeting" reported in Allen C. Guelzo, *Lincoln's Emancipation Proclamation* (New York: Simon and Schuster, 2005), 109.

117   **"I would do it if I were not afraid":** Edward L. Pierce, *Memoirs and Letters of Charles Sumner,* 4 vols. (Boston: Roberts Brothers, 1894), 4:185.

117   **peremptory, almost insubordinate letter:** George B. McClellan to Lincoln, July 7, 1862, and to Mary Ellen McClellan, July 10,

1862, Stephen W. Sears, ed., *The Civil War Papers of George B. McClellan: Selected Correspondence, 1860–1865* (New York: Ticknor and Fields, 1889), 344–345, 348.

117 **It was then, Welles remembered:** Gideon Welles, *Diary,* 3 vols. (Boston: Houghton Mifflin, 1911), 1:70–71.

118 **"weary, care-worn and troubled":** Theodore Calvin Pease, ed., *The Diary of Orville Hickman Browning,* 2 vols. (Springfield: Illinois State Historical Library), 1:559.

118 **"it was a violation of the Constitution":** Ibid.

119 **what he called the "startling" idea:** Message to Congress, July 17, 1862, *CW,* 5:328–331.

119 **He would "not conserve slavery much longer":** John Hay to Mary Jay (daughter of John Jay), July 20, 1862, Michael Burlingame, ed., *At Lincoln's Side: John Hay's Civil War Correspondence and Selected Writings* (Carbondale: Southern Illinois University Press, 2000), 23.

119 **The draft ended with the clear promise:** Lincoln later entitled this draft "Emancipation Proclamation as first sketched and shown to the Cabinet in July 1862," *CW,* 5:336–337.

119 **"I said to the Cabinet":** Carpenter, *Six Months at the White House,* 21.

120 **he also brought up the political risk:** Ibid.

120 **"organize and arm the slaves" themselves:** John Niven, ed., *The Salmon P. Chase Papers,* 5 vols. (Kent, OH: Kent State University Press, 1993), 1:351.

120 **"I put the draft of the proclamation aside":** Carpenter, *Six Months at the White House,* 22.

121 **"to curb and restrain the impatience":** John G. Nicolay and John Hay, *Abraham Lincoln: A History,* 10 vols. (New York: Century, 1890), 6:148–149.

121 **"with public sentiment, nothing can fail":** From Lincoln's reply at the first Lincoln-Douglas debate, Ottawa, Illinois, August 21, 1858, *CW,* 3:27.

121 **Lincoln launched into a frosty, patronizing lecture:** For a modern reinterpretation of the meeting, the delegation, and their status, see Kate Masur, "The African American Delegation to Abraham Lincoln: A Reappraisal," *Civil War History* 56 (June 2010): 117–144, esp. 131; *CW,* 5:372.

122 **"sacrifice something of your present comfort":** Address on Colonization to a Deputation of Free African Americans, August 14, 1862, *CW,* 5:373.

122 **Douglass had told an Independence Day audience:** Philip S. Foner and Yuval Taylor, eds., *Frederick Douglass: Selected Speeches*

and Writings, Library of Black America Series (Chicago: Chicago Review Press, 2000); Frederick Douglass, "The Slaveholders' Rebellion," speech at Himrods Corner, New York, July 4, 1862, and "The President and His Speeches," *Douglass' Monthly*, September 1862.

123   **Historian Eric Foner has aptly pointed out:** Eric Foner, *The Fiery Trial: Abraham Lincoln and American Slavery* (New York: W. W. Norton, 2010), 225–226.

123   **"How much better would be a manly protest":** David Donald, ed., *Inside Lincoln's Cabinet: The Civil War Diaries of Salmon P. Chase* (New York: Long, Green, 1954), 112–113.

123   **Differences in social status:** Social psychologist Jonathan Haidt argues that the majority of any group has an intuitive tendency to assume that people should be treated differently according to social role or status. See Haidt, *The Righteous Mind: Why Good People Are Divided by Politics and Religion* (New York: Pantheon Books, 2012).

124   **"all attempts to put down the Rebellion":** Horace Greeley, "Prayer of Twenty Millions," *New York Tribune*, August 20, 1862.

125   **"My paramount object in this struggle":** Lincoln to Greeley, August 22, 1862, *CW*, 5:388.

125   **"His mind was fixed":** Welles, *Diary*, 1:143. For a riveting account of the historic cabinet meeting, see John Hope Franklin, *The Emancipation Proclamation* (1963; reprint, Wheeling, IL: Harlan Davidson, 1995), 42–45.

126   **"I cannot make it better known":** Abraham Lincoln, Annual Message to Congress, December 1, 1862, *CW*, 5:534–535.

126   **Records show that they suffered:** William F. Fox, *Regimental Losses in the American Civil War, 1861–1865* (Albany, NY: Albany Publishing, 1889), cited in the *New York Times*, April 3, 2012.

127   **"It is true that the President":** Douglass speech at Rochester, New York, March 25, 1862, Foner and Taylor, *Frederick Douglass*, 491.

127   **"Read the proclamation," he urged:** Ibid.; *Douglass' Monthly*, October 1862.

128   **Douglass replied with a detailed memorandum:** Douglass to Lincoln, August 29, 1864, Lincoln Papers, Library of Congress.

128   **"In *giving* freedom to the *slave*":** Annual Message to Congress, December 1, 1862, *CW*, 5:537.

129   **"a group of negro men, women and children":** William Lloyd Garrison to Lincoln, January 21, 1865, Lincoln Papers, Library of Congress.

129   **"I'm not an abolitionist":** Lucy N. Coleman recollection quoted in Don E. Fehrenbacher and Virginia Fehrenbacher, *Recollected Words of Lincoln* (Stanford, CA: Stanford University Press, 1996), 116.

129 **"the spirited and admirable painting":** Lincoln to William Lloyd Garrison, February 7, 1865, *CW,* 8:265–266.

130 **"O symbol of God's will on earth":** Reprinted in Harold Holzer, Edna Greene Medford, and Frank J. Williams, *The Emancipation Proclamation: Three Views* (Baton Rouge: Louisiana State University Press, 2006), 83.

132 **"I account partially for his kindness to me":** Frederick Douglass in Allen Thorndike Rice, ed., *Reminiscences of Abraham Lincoln by Distinguished Men of His Time* (New York: Century, 1888), 193.

132 **"Viewed from the genuine abolition ground":** Speech at the dedication of the *Freedom Memorial* statue by Thomas Ball, Washington, DC, April 14, 1876, Philip S. Foner and Yuval Taylor, eds., *Frederick Douglass: Selected Speeches and Writings,* Library of Black America Series (Chicago: Chicago Review Press, 2000), 621.

NOTES TO CHAPTER SEVEN

133 **"he who moulds public sentiment":** From the first Lincoln-Douglas debate at Ottawa, Illinois, August 21, 1858, Roy P. Basler, ed., *The Collected Works of Abraham Lincoln,* 8 vols. (New Brunswick, NJ: Rutgers University Press, 1953–1955), hereafter cited as *CW,* 3:27.

134 **"a struggle for maintaining in the world":** Special Message to Congress, July 4, 1861, *CW,* 4:438.

134 **"War at the best, is terrible":** Remarks at the Great Central Sanitary Fair, Philadelphia, June 16, 1864, *CW,* 7:394.

135 **he was an unrelenting warrior:** Two important, and excellent, 2008 books shed considerable light on Lincoln's military leadership. See James M. McPherson, *Tried by War: Abraham Lincoln as Commander in Chief* (New York: Penguin, 2009); and Craig L. Symonds, *Lincoln and His Admirals: Abraham Lincoln, the U. S. Navy, and the Civil War* (New York: Oxford University Press, 2008).

135 **"advancement of the noblest of cause":** Lyceum address, *CW,* 1:114.

135 **he operated largely by instinct and energy:** For Clausewitz, see McPherson, *Tried by War,* 6. For Lincoln's book borrowing, see Earl Schenk Miers, ed., *Lincoln Day by Day: A Chronology, 1809–1865,* 3 vols. (Washington, DC: Lincoln Sesquicentennial Commission, 1960), 3:88.

136 **officers who were "zealous & efficient":** Lincoln to Secretary of War Simon Cameron, August 7, 1861, *CW,* 4:475.

136   **"a remarkable, superior mind":** *On War,* quoted in T. Harry Williams, *Lincoln and His Generals* (New York: Alfred A. Knopf, 1952), 7.

136   **to "condole," as once put it:** Lincoln actually used the word *condole* to acknowledge the loss of Chief Justice Salmon P. Chase's sister in 1865. See Lincoln to Chase, January 2, 1865, *CW,* 8:195.

136   **"We accepted this war for an object":** Remarks at the Great Central Sanitary Fair, Philadelphia, June 16, 1864, *CW,* 7:395.

136   **"This government must be preserved":** Speech to the 148th Ohio Regiment, August 31, 1864, *CW,* 7:528; letter to the New York Workingmen's Democratic Republican Association, March 21, 1864, *CW,* 7:259.

137   **"Four score and seven years ago":** Gettysburg Address, *CW,* 7:23.

140   **abundant evidence that Lincoln well understood:** Edward Everett copy of the Gettysburg Address, *CW,* 7:21; Bancroft copy, *CW,* 7:22; and revised Bancroft copy (now in the White House), *CW,* 7:23.

141   **"The nation's condition is not what either party":** Lincoln to Hodges, April 14, 1864, *CW,* 7:282.

142   **"prophetic interpretation of American history":** Elton Trueblood, *Abraham Lincoln: Theologian of American Anguish* (New York: Harper & Row, 1973), 118.

142   **"One-eighth of the whole population":** Second Inaugural Address, March 4, 1865, *CW,* 8:332–333.

143   **Lincoln ended his Second Inaugural Address:** Ibid., 333.

144   **"He answered all the objections":** Ibid.; Douglass quoted in Rice, *Recollections of Abraham Lincoln,* 191.

145   **"The world has never had a good definition":** Address at Sanitary Fair, Baltimore, April 18, 1864, *CW,* 7:301–302.

145   **they saw nothing incompatible in the founding vision:** For the conflicting notions of liberty, North and South, during the secession crisis and beyond, see the excellent book by James McPherson, *Battle Cry of Freedom: The Civil War Era* (New York: Oxford University Press, 1988), esp. Chapters 7–8.

146   **"Are you not over-cautious":** Lincoln to General George B. McClellan, October 13, 1862, *CW,* 5:460.

146   **"I have just read your dispatch":** Lincoln to McClellan, October 24 [25], 1862, *CW,* 5:474.

146   **In a memorandum to his generals:** Memorandum on furloughs, November 1862, *CW,* 5:484.

147   **"I state my general idea of this war":** Lincoln to Brigadier General Don C. Buell, January 13, 1862, *CW,* 5:98.

147   **"*Lee's* Army, and not *Richmond*"**: Lincoln to General Joseph Hooker, June 10, 1863, *CW*, 6:257.

147   **"I do not believe you appreciate"**: Lincoln to General George G. Meade, July 14, 1863, *CW*, 6:328.

148   **"A self-taught strategist with no combat experience"**: James McPherson, "Commander in Chief," *Smithsonian Magazine*, January 2009, 38.

149   **"[T]he judgments of the Lord"**: *CW*, 8:333.

151   **"all provisions and stock should be removed"**: Ulysses S. Grant to Halleck, July 15, 1864, http://gathkinsons.net/sesqui/?p=6646.

152   **"Give the enemy no rest"**: Philip Sheridan, *Personal Memoirs of P. H. Sheridan*, 2 vols. (London: Chatto & Windus, 1888), 1:486.

152   **"With great pleasure I tender to you"**: Lincoln to Grant, October 22, 1864, *CW*, 8:73.

152   **"God alone can claim it"**: Lincoln to Hodges, April 14, 1864, *CW*, 7:282.

152   **he could describe himself as God's agent**: Ibid.

154   **"General Sheridan says 'if the thing is pressed'"**: Lincoln to Grant, April 7, 1865, *CW*, 392.

154   **God was responsible for continuing the war**: See Lucas Morel, *Lincoln's Sacred Effort: Defining Religion's Role in American Self-Government* (Lanham, MD: Lexington Books, 2000), esp. Chapter 5, "The Political Limits of Reason and Religion: An Interpretation of the Second Inaugural Address."

154   **"Fondly do we hope"**: Second Inaugural Address, *CW*, 8:333.

154   **"Mine eyes have seen the glory"**: The latest book on Julia Ward Howe's song is John Stauffer and Benjamin Soskis, *The Battle Hymn of the Republic: A Biography of the Song That Marches On* (New York: Oxford University Press, 2013). Howe's meeting with Lincoln is described on page 82.

155   **"With malice toward none"**: Second Inaugural Address, *CW*, 8:333.

156   **The funeral train traveled**: http://www.history.com/topics /president-lincolns-funeral-train.

156   **For this moment in time**: James L. Swanson, *Bloody Crimes* (New York: Harper and Collins, 2011), 293.

NOTES TO CHAPTER EIGHT

162   **"The revolt of a State"**: *Washington National Republican*, February 11, 1862.

162   **"The action of the government"**: John G. Nicolay and John Hay, *Abraham Lincoln: A History*, 10 vols. (New York: Century, 1890), 6:47–48.

163 **"henceforth faithfully protect and defend":** Roy P. Basler, ed., *The Collected Works of Abraham Lincoln,* 8 vols. (New Brunswick, NJ: Rutgers University Press, 1953–1955), hereafter cited as *CW,* 7:53–56.

164 **"There were men in Congress":** Gideon Welles quoted in Edmund G. Ross, *History of the Impeachment of Andrew Johnson, President of the United States* (Project Gutenberg ebook, December 2000), http://www.gutenberg.org/files/2442/2442-h /2442-h.htm, Chapter 1.

165 **an extraordinarily resistant white South:** For a more detailed discussion of the reconstruction period, see Eric Foner, *Reconstruction, America's Unfinished Revelation, 1863–1877* (New York: Harper & Row, 1988); and James M. McPherson, *Battle Cry of Freedom: The Civil War Era,* Oxford History of the United States Series (New York: Oxford University Press, 2003).

165 **"Sir: I got your letter":** The letter appeared in the August 22, 1865, edition of the *New York Daily Tribune.* The newspaper suggests the letter was a collaboration between Jourdon and his friend Valentine Winters. Anderson asked his former master to send his wages to Valentine Winters, a barrister in Dayton, Ohio's Third Ward.

169 **Perhaps the clearest evidence:** Walter Dean Burnham, *Democracy in Peril: The American Turnout Problem and the Path to Plutocracy* (Roosevelt Institute, Working Paper No. 5, December 1, 2010).

170 **Literally within the span of a generation:** US Department of Commerce, Bureau of the Census, *Historical Statistics of the United States: Colonial Times to 1970* (Washington, DC: GPO, 1975), 2:728–731, 693–694, 667, 1:224.

170 **A major source of labor:** Ibid., 1:105–106.

171 **Economic life also began to be organized:** Thomas C. Cochran and William Miller, *The Age of Enterprise: A Social History of Industrial America* (New York: Harper Torchbooks, 1961), 143–144, 190–191.

171 **Enormous amounts of money:** Eric Foner, *The Story of American Freedom,* Norton Paperback Series (New York: W. W. Norton, 1999), 117.

171 **when he described a society:** *CW,* 5:52.

171 **the size of the federal government also expanded:** *Historical Statistics of the United States,* 2:1104.

172 **the middle-class ideal gave way:** Mark Twain and Charles Dudley Warner, *The Gilded Age: A Tale of To-Day* (Hartford: American Publishing, 1874).

172 **"The right of each man":** Foner, *Story of American Freedom,* 120.

174   **"By the end of the 1880s":** David Montgomery, "Labor in the Industrial Era," Richard B. Morris, ed., *A History of the American Worker* (originally published as *The U.S. Department of Labor History of the American Worker* [Princeton, NJ: Princeton University Press, 1983]), 96; Melvyn Dubofsky, *Industrialism and the American Worker, 1865–1920* (New York: Thomas Y. Crowell, 1975), 19.

174   **the new economic doctrine insisted:** John G. Sproat, *Best Men* (Chicago: University of Chicago Press, 1982), 166.

175   **"tell us what to eat, drink, avoid":** Ibid., 210–211.

175   **Darwin's new theory of evolution:** Charles Darwin, *The Origin of Species* (New York and London: Mentor, 1958).

175   **"Social Darwinism" saw human economic life:** Herbert Spencer coined the term in volume 1 of his *Principles of Biology*, published in 1864. See Spencer, *The Principles of Biology* (New York: D. Appleton, 1896), 1:444. On Spencer's influence in America, see Richard Hofstadter, *Social Darwinism in American Thought* (Boston: Beacon Press, 1992), 31–50.

176   **Any interference in the natural human competition:** Herbert Spencer, *The Principles of Sociology* (New York: D. Appleton, 1908), 2:607–608.

176   **some self-styled "reformers":** Foner, *Story of American Freedom*, 119–20.

177   **laissez-faire came to reign:** Sidney Fine, *Laissez Faire and the General-Welfare State* (Ann Arbor: University of Michigan Press, 1956), 3.

177   **"neither party has any principles":** Louis Gould, *Grand Old Party: A History of the Republicans* (New York: Random House, 2004), 79.

178   **"Though the people support the Government":** Sproat, *Best Men,* 166.

178   **In 1895 the US Supreme Court ruled:** Robert G. McCloskey, *The American Supreme Court,* 2nd ed., revised by Sanford Levinson (Chicago: University of Chicago Press, 1994), 84.

178   **In *Lochner v. New York:*** Ibid., 102–107; Richard A. Posner, ed., *The Essential Holmes: Selections from the Letters, Speeches, Judicial Opinions, and Other Writings of Oliver Wendell Holmes, Jr.* (Chicago: University of Chicago Press, 1992), 306.

NOTES TO CHAPTER NINE

182   **"The tremendous and highly complex":** Theodore Roosevelt, First Annual Message to Congress, December 3, 1901, http://teachingamericanhistory.org/library/index.asp?document=940.

183   **"the most formidable industrial deadlock":** Walter Wellman, "The Progress of the World," *American Monthly Review of Reviews* (October 1902).

183   **"three parties affected by the situation":** *New York World,* October 4, 1902.

183   **For Roosevelt and his supporters:** For a detailed discussion of Roosevelt's role, see Doris Kearns Goodwin, *The Bully Pulpit* (New York: Simon and Schuster, 2013), 311–319.

183   **Roosevelt set forth a new agenda:** Theodore Roosevelt, "State of the Union Message," December 3, 1901, http://www.presidency.ucsb.edu/ws/?pid=29542.

184   **Roosevelt radically redefined the role:** Lewis L. Gould, *The Presidency of Theodore Roosevelt* (Oxford: Oxford University Press, 2012), 47–53, 217–219.

186   **"If our political institutions were perfect":** President Theodore Roosevelt speech's at Osawatomie, Kansas, August 31, 1910, http://www.whitehouse.gov/blog/2011/12/06/archives-president-teddy-roosevelts-new-nationalism-speech.

188   **They presented themselves as valiant underdogs:** The story of prewar benevolence and postwar dignity under duress gained new momentum in 1936 with the publication of Margaret Mitchell's book *Gone with the Wind*. The enormous success of the novel, which received the coveted Pulitzer Prize for Fiction in 1937, was due largely to reader sympathy for its Southern belle heroine, Scarlett O'Hara, in her on-again, off-again love affair with the handsome but imperfect blockade runner Rhett Butler. But there was no mistaking the underlying message of Southern grit, determination, and goodwill in the Civil War and reconstruction period—complete with the reinvigoration of the myth of the grateful and loyal slave. Mitchell's story of the positive lifelong relationship between Scarlett O'Hara and her black nanny did more than anything else to support the myth of the benevolent attitude of upper-class Southern society toward the subservient black population.

When *Gone with the Wind* was made into the most successful movie of the twentieth century, the story of Southern grit and benevolence became widely accepted in the largely segregated North as well as the South. Arguably, Margaret Mitchell went a long way to help the South compete successfully in the "war of words" (and images) over the causes and consequences of the Civil War.

Even more important, a number of important historians took up the cudgels to describe the Civil War as an unnecessary war. Writing in 1942, David M. Potter, professor of history at Yale

University, argued that Lincoln erred in wrecking the effort to forge a compromise solution to the major issues dividing the North and South in 1861. Perhaps the strongest academic criticism of Lincoln's policies was offered by Avery Craven, professor of history at the University of Chicago and president of the Organization of American Historians. In his 1947 article entitled "The Civil War and the Democratic Process," Craven argued that the war marked a breakdown of the democratic process of rational discussion of issues and compromise of differences. He argued that both Lincoln and the leaders of secession were responsible for believing that "the totality of right and justice was on their side" and consequently "faced each other with a willingness and determination to use violence for the achievement of their ends." Craven and the new group of revisionist historians blamed Lincoln and his supporters for reducing the business of politics to "abstract" issues of "right and wrong" rather than "practical" tasks of finding compromise solutions. The revisionist historians provided new arguments in the continuing "war of words" over the causes of what they now described as the "War between the States." See Norton Garfinkle, *Lincoln and the Coming of the Civil War* (Boston: D. C. Heath, 1958), 66–69, 77–79.

190 **"a man who rose out of the ranks":** Woodrow Wilson, *The New Freedom: A Call for the Emancipation of the Generous Energies of a People* (Englewood Cliffs, NJ: Prentice Hall, 1961), 60.

190 **"It is amazing," he said:** Ibid., 47.

190 **"[F]or indeed, if you stop to think":** Ibid., 60.

190 **"American industry is not free":** Ibid., 106, 125, 162, 126, 162–163.

192 **First came tariff reform:** Arthur S. Link, *Woodrow Wilson and the Progressive Era* (Charleston, SC: BiblioBazaar, 2012), 36–43, 193–196; Gould, *Presidency of Theodore Roosevelt*, 162.

194 **"Not heroism, but healing":** William E. Leuchtenburg, *The Perils of Prosperity, 1914–1932*, 2nd ed. (Chicago: University of Chicago Press, 1993), 289.

195 **"The chief business of the American people":** Calvin Coolidge, address to the American Society of Newspaper Editors, Washington, DC, January 25, 1925, http://www.presidency.ucsb.edu/ws/?pid=24180.

195 **"Give tax breaks to large corporations":** Andrew Mellon, *Taxation: The People's Business* (New York: Macmillan, 1924).

195 **Americans for the most part:** William E. Leuchtenburg, *Franklin D. Roosevelt and the New Deal* (New York: Harper Torchbooks, 1963), 1–3. For the unemployment estimate, see US Department of

Commerce, Bureau of the Census, *Historical Statistics of the United States: Colonial Times to 1970* (Washington, DC: GPO, 1975), 1:135.

NOTES TO CHAPTER TEN

197 **"Given later developments":** William E. Leuchtenburg, *Franklin Roosevelt and the New Deal* (New York: Harper Torchbooks, 1963), 11.

198 **"Financial and industrial leaders":** Lippman on fall of business leaders, see Mark H. Leff, *The Limits of Symbolic Reform: The New Deal and Taxation, 1933–1939* (Cambridge: Cambridge University Press, 1984), 158.

198 **"It is common sense":** Arthur M. Schlesinger Jr., "The 'Hundred Days' of F.D.R.," *New York Times*, April 10, 1983.

198 **"I believe with Abraham Lincoln":** Franklin Delano Roosevelt, fireside chat, September 30, 1934, http://docs .fdrlibrary.marist.edu/093034.html.

198 **"I can better describe":** Franklin Delano Roosevelt, address at Wilmington, Delaware, October 29, 1936, http://www.pres idency.ucsb.edu/ws/index.php?pid=15215.

200 **"the effort to place *capital*":** Annual Message to Congress, December 3, 1861, Roy P. Basler, ed., *The Collected Works of Abraham Lincoln*, 8 vols. (New Brunswick, NJ: Rutgers University Press, 1953–1955), hereafter cited as *CW*, 5:51–53.

201 **"The royalists of the economic order":** Franklin Delano Roosevelt, speech before the 1936 Democratic National Convention, http://www.austincc.edu/lpatrick/his2341/fdr36 acceptancespeech.htm.

201 **He weighed in "against dictatorship":** Ibid.

201 **"Again I revert to the increase":** Franklin Delano Roosevelt, State of the Union address, January 3, 1938, http://www.let .rug.nl/usa/presidents/franklin-delano-roosevelt/state-of-the -union-1938.php.

202 **Roosevelt described his prolabor and prounion policies:** Ibid.

202 **When Roosevelt took office in 1933:** Bureau of Labor Statistics, "Labor Force, Employment, and Unemployment, 1929–39: Estimating Methods, Technical Note," http:// www.bls.gov/opub/mlr/1948/article/pdf/labor-force-employ ment-and-unemployment-1929-39-estimating-methods.pdf. See also Maurice W. Lee, *Economic Fluctuations* (Homewood, IL: R. D. Irwin, 1955), 236.

203 **Recognizing the negative consequences:** Ibid.

203   **The government's stimulus expenditures:** Ibid.

204   **Roosevelt supported legislation:** Leuchtenburg, *Franklin Roosevelt*, 150–152.

205   **by 1940 labor union membership rose:** Gerald Mayer, "Union Membership Trends in the United States" (Cornell University, August 2004), http://digitalcommons.ilr.cornell.edu/cgi/viewcontent .cgi?article=1176&context=key_workplace, 29.

205   **The 1938 Fair Labor Standards Act:** US Department of Labor, http://www.dol.gov/oasam/programs/history/flsa1938.htm.

205   **Roosevelt tried to codify the gains:** Franklin D. Roosevelt, State of the Union address, January 6, 1941, http://www.pres idency.ucsb.edu/ws/index.php?pid=16092#axzz2fvBBNA6l.

206   **The GI Bill provided:** *Historical Statistics of the United States: Millennial Edition* (New York: Cambridge University Press, 2006), 2:1147.

207   **Total spending for veterans:** Ibid.

208   **Roosevelt found a way to give tangible reality:** Ibid.

208   **the compromise Employment Act of 1946:** G. J. Santoni, "The Employment Act of 1946: Some History Notes," *Federal Reserve Bank of St. Louis Review* (March 1986): 5–16.

210   **bluntly confided to a journalist:** Brett Zongker, "Education Center Explores Lincoln's Life, Death," *Wisconsin State Journal*, April 14, 2012.

NOTES TO CHAPTER ELEVEN

213   **Abraham Lincoln was taken away:** Eleanor Roosevelt, *Yank Magazine*, May 25, 1945.

216   **"This party of ours":** Harvey Kaye, *The Fight for the Four Freedoms* (New York: Simon and Schuster, 2014), 171.

216   **"Should any political party":** Ibid.

216   **He did more than any president:** Norton Garfinkle, *The American Dream vs. the Gospel of Wealth* (New Haven, CT: Yale University Press, 2006), 133–136.

216   **The shadow of Roosevelt was so long:** Ibid., 138–139.

216   **Roosevelt's economic program:** A. M. Okun, "Efficient Disinflationary Policies," *American Economic Review* 68 (1978): 348–352; Herbert Stein, *Presidential Economics* (Washington, DC: American Enterprise Institute for Public Policy Research, 1995), 217–218.

217   **"For the public today":** Daniel Yankelovich, "Taking Account of the Non-economic Features of Inflation," presented to American Council of Life Insurance, February 1979, cited in Robert J. Samuelson, "Unsung Triumph," *Washington Post*, June 9, 2004, A21.

218 **"Government is the problem"**: Ronald Reagan, Inaugural Address, January 20, 1981, http://www.reagan.utexas.edu/archives/speeches/1981/12081a.htm.

218 **Sharp change in present economic policy**: Coordinating Committee on Economic Policy, "Economic Strategy for the Reagan Administration," November 16, 1980, http://www.wsj.com/articles/SB10001424052970204880404577225870253766212.

219 **The Heritage Foundation claims**: The Heritage Foundation, http://www.heritage.org/about/our-history/35th-anniversary.

220 **"whoever would understand in his heart"**: Reagan, Inaugural Address, January 20, 1981.

221 **"It is my intention to curb"**: Ibid.

221 **our "most productive citizens"**: See, for example, Jack F. Kemp, "New York State's (Groan) Taxes," *New York Times,* May 20, 1978, 19.

222 **This new business-oriented economic philosophy**: Andrew Mellon said, "Give tax breaks to large corporations, so that money can trickle down to the general public, in the form of extra jobs." Lewis Gould, *Grand Old Party: A History of the Republicans* (New York: Random House, 2004), 152.

222 **Now with the Reagan philosophy in command**: Ira Katznelson, *Fear Itself* (New York: Liveright, 2013), 394–398.

223 **"We believe as Democrats"**: *New York Times,* July 17, 1984.

223 **The fortieth president went on to quote**: Ronald Reagan, Republican National Convention speech, August 18, 1992, http://www.cnbcfix.com/ronald-reagan-1992-convention.html.

225 **most popular newspaper columnist in America**: Ann Landers column, *Gettysburg Times,* July 26, 1995.

NOTES TO CHAPTER TWELVE

228 **"felt, as Abraham Lincoln did"**: Bill Clinton, *My Life* (New York: Alfred A. Knopf, 2004), 62, 480.

228 **Clinton loved telling the story**: Harold Holzer, *Why Lincoln Matters to American Presidents* (Ontario: Centre for American Studies, University of Ontario, 2011), 12.

228 **Clinton saw himself in the tradition**: Clinton, *My Life,* 458–463, 490–497, 694–696, 719–721, 743–745, 754–755, 795, 842–843, 889–894, 911, 951–955.

228 **Clinton insisted that government**: See, for example, *White House: Economic Report of the President, 1996* (Washington, DC: GPO, 1996), 18–21.

229 **Clinton also rejected Reagan's claim**: Norton Garfinkle, *The American Dream vs. the Gospel of Wealth* (New Haven, CT: Yale

University Press, 2006), 158–159. For a more detailed discussion of the "third way" approach to economic issues, see Norton Garfinkle, "Communitarian Economics," *Journal of Socio-Economics* 26, no. 1 (1997).

229   **"These are good times for America":** William Jefferson Clinton, State of the Union address, January 27, 1998, http://www .washingtonpost.com/wp-srv/politics/special/states/docs/sou98htm.

230   **Clinton had explained his successes:** Sidney Blumenthal, *The Clinton Wars* (New York: Farrar, Straus, and Giroux, 2003), 314–317, 376–378.

230   **The Clinton presidency was characterized:** The great economic growth during the Clinton years came to a considerable extent from the burgeoning computer hardware and software industry built on the foundation of the government-created "Internet." By the end of the Clinton presidency in 2001, half the US population was using the Internet. The number of registered dot-com Internet domain names increased from fewer than 1,000 in 1990 to more than 20 million in 2000.

230   **More than 23 million jobs were added:** US Department of Labor, Bureau of Labor Statistics, latest employment statistics, http:// data.bls.gov/timeseries/CEU0000000001.

231   **Since the end of World War II:** Garfinkle, *American Dream vs. the Gospel of Wealth,* 201–204.

232   **The goal, he argued:** George W. Bush, remarks by the president to women business leaders, March 20, 2001, http:// georgewbush-whitehouse.archives.gov/news/releases/2001/03 /20010320-2.html; president's remarks to the Latino Coalition, February 26, 2003, http://georgewbush-whitehouse.archives.gov/news /releases/2003/02/print/20030226-3.html.

233   **By 2007 the wealthiest 20 percent:** U.S. Congressional Budget Office, "Trends in the Distribution of Household Income Between 1979 and 2007," October 2011, http:/www.cbo.gov /sites/default/files/10-25-HouseholdIncome_0.pdf.

233   **the wealthiest 1 percent of American taxpayers:** Ibid.

234   **candidly stated that the goal of the movement:** Cited in William Greider, "Rolling Back the Twentieth Century," *Nation,* May 12, 2003.

234   **"The taxing power of the government":** Ronald Reagan, First Inaugural Address, January 12, 1981.

235   **not a panacea for full employment or economic stability:** For a more extensive discussion of this subject, see Garfinkle, *American Dream vs. the Gospel of Wealth,* 142–188.

235   **when federal outlays averaged:** Bureau of Labor Statistics, Un-
       employment Rate, http://data.bls.gov/timeseries/LNS14000000;
       White House, Office of Management and Budget, Table 1.2, http://
       www.whitehouse.gov/omb/budget/Historicals/.

235   **The economic record:** See Appendix.

237   **A study by the Institute on Taxation and Economic Policy:**
       New York Times, January 14, 2015, B1, B3.

238   **"Those of us who have looked":** *New York Times,* October 28,
       2008.

238   **The only segment of the population that gained:** Thomas
       Piketty and Emmanuel Saez, "Top Incomes and the Great Reces-
       sion: Recent Evolutions and Policy Implications," paper presented at
       the Thirteenth Jacques Polak Annual Research Conference, Wash-
       ington, DC, November 8–9, 2012. See also Thomas Piketty, *Capital
       in the Twenty-First Century* (Cambridge, MA: Belknap Press/Har-
       vard University Press, 2014).

238   **"The change in the benefits of the American capital-
       ist economy":** Henry Jackson Initiative for Inclusive Capital-
       ism, "Towards a More Inclusive Capitalism" (2012), http://www
       .mckinsey.com/global_locations/europe_and_middleeast/
       united_kingdom/en/latest_thinking/renewing_capitalism.

239   **"It's not merely an issue":** *New York Times,* July 27, 2014.

240   **capitalist society envisioned by Adam Smith:** Adam Smith,
       The Wealth of Nations, Bantam Classics (New York: Random
       House, 2003) and *The Theory of Moral Sentiments* (New York:
       Gutenberg, 2011).

240   **More and more Americans saw their leaders:** Public Agenda
       and Kettering Foundation, "Don't Count Us Out," Report on Ac-
       countability and Democracy, 2011, 16.

241   **"In the shadow of the Old State Capitol":** Illinois senator
       Barack Obama's announcement speech, *Washington Post,* February
       10, 2007.

242   **He said he relied on the wisdom:** President Theodore Roos-
       evelt speech at Osawatomie, Kansas, August 31, 1910, http://www
       .whitehouse.gov/blog/2011/12/06/archives-president-teddy-roo
       sevelts-new-nationalism-speech.

242   **"My grandparents believed in an America":** The White House,
       Office of the Press Secretary, December 6, 2011, http://www.white
       house.gov.

243   **"I do share the belief":** Remarks by the president on the
       economy, June 14, 2012, http://www.whitehouse.gov/the-press
       -office/2012/06/14/remarks-president-economy-cleveland-oh.

243   **"The legitimate object of government":** Lincoln fragment on
       government, July 1, 1854[?], Roy P. Basler, ed., *The Collected Works
       of Abraham Lincoln,* 8 vols. (New Brunswick, NJ: Rutgers Univer-
       sity Press, 1953–1955), hereafter cited as *CW,* 2:220.

243   **"I believe what Republican Abraham Lincoln believed":**
       President Obama, State of the Union address, January 24, 2012.

244   **The United States must be:** President Obama, Second Inaugu-
       ral Address, January 1, 2013, http://www.whitehouse.gov/the-press
       -office/2013/01/21/inaugural-address-president-barack-obama.

245   **"The combined trends":** President Obama, "Making Our Econ-
       omy Work for Every Working American," December 4, 2013,
       https://www.whitehouse.gov/blog/2013/12/04/making-our-economy
       -work-every-working-american.

245   **"I think America was very lucky":** Conversation with David
       Remnick, *New Yorker,* January 27, 2014, 61.

246   **Stiglitz's approach to increase:** Joseph Stiglitz, "Rewriting the
       Rules of the American Economy—An Agenda for Growth and
       Shared Prosperity" (New York, the Roosevelt Institute, May, 2015),
       23–40, 57, 73–76. The *New York Times* provided further details on
       executive compensation in *New York Times,* May 17, 2015, Sunday
       Business, 1, 4–5. Addressing the same question, Eduardo Porter re-
       ported in the *New York Times,* "Evidence suggests that American cor-
       porations, constantly pressured to increase the next quarter's profits
       . . . are walking away from basic science . . . It's time for a different
       paradigm . . . to finance the innovation that will power America's fu-
       ture," (*New York Times,* Innovation Lies on Weak Foundation, May
       20, 2015), Business 1, 5. The *Economist* magazine also took note
       of the fact that "there has been a big change in income inequality,
       driven by the high rewards given to corporate executives who make
       up three-fifths of the top 0.1% of American earners" and "there is
       little correlation between executive compensation and the creation
       of wealth for shareholders," *Economist* (June 20, 2015), 68.

247   **The American middle class:** Bureau of Labor Statistics.
       See also New America Foundation, "The American Middle
       Class Under Stress," April 2011, http://growth.newamerica.net
       /sites/newamerica.net/files/policydocs/26–04–11%20Middle
       %20Class%20Under%20Stress.pdf.

247   **With the defeat of the Democrats:** Timothy Egan, "Obama Un-
       bound," *New York Times,* December 10, 2014, A21.

247   **The economic news was greeted:** *New York Times,* January 10,
       2015, A1, B2, B3.

248   **"This is still a buyer's market":** Ibid.

248   **"[T]here is more work to be done":** Ibid.

248   **"President Obama will not be satisfied":** http://www.white
       house.gov/economy.

248   **President Obama announced "a major step":** http://www.white
       house.gov/the-press-office/2015/01/07/fact-sheet-making-home
       ownership-more-accessible-and-sustainable.

249   **The president addressed these issues:** Barack Obama, State of
       the Union address, January 20, 2015.

249   **At the same time he proposed a program:** Ibid.

250   **They believe that the economic and political malaise:** John
       Micklethwait and Adrian Wooldridge, *The Fourth Revolution: The
       Global Race to Reinvent the State* (New York: Penguin Press, 2014),
       174–178, 237–248.

251   **"Sweden has reduced public spending":** Ibid., 264–275.

252   **By contrast, in the United States:** Organization for Eco-
       nomic Cooperation and Development, "Revenue Statistics—
       Comparative Tables," http://stats.oecd.org/Index.aspx?Data
       SetCode=REV.

252   **an effective estate tax provides "a certain corrective":** Martin
       J. Daunton, *Just Taxes: The Politics of Taxation in Britain* (Cam-
       bridge: Cambridge University Press, 2002), 124.

252   **"I say the community fails":** "Wealth Tax Views in Notable
       Talks," *New York Times,* December 14, 1906.

252   **"Capitalism will never be genuinely popular":** Andrew
       Woodcock, "Cameron Sets Out Vision for 'Popular Capital-
       ism,'" *Independent,* January 19, 2012, http://www.independent
       .co.uk/news/uk/politics/cameron-sets-out-vision-for-popular
       -capitalism-6291768.html.

NOTES TO EPILOGUE

256   **American consumer spending accounts for:** US Department of
       Commerce, Bureau of Economic Analysis, http://www.bea.gov/iTable
       /iTable.cfm?ReqID=9&step=1#reqid=9&step=3&isuri=1&904=201
       4&903=5&906=a&905=1929&910=x&911=0.

259   **The evidence is mounting:** See Appendix.

INDEX

Harold Holzer is one of the country's foremost authorities on Lincoln. His most recent book, *Lincoln and the Power of the Press*, was awarded the 2015 Lincoln Prize. Holzer lives in Rye, New York.

Norton Garfinkle is an economist, chair of The Future of American Democracy Foundation, and author of *The American Dream vs. The Gospel of Wealth*. He lives in New York City.